21st Century Research on Drugs and Ethnicity: Studies Supported by the National Institute on Drug Abuse

21st Century Research on Drugs and Ethnicity: Studies Supported by the National Institute on Drug Abuse has been co-published simultaneously as *Journal of Ethnicity in Substance Abuse*, Volume 6, Number 2 2007.

21st Century Research on Drugs and Ethnicity: Studies Supported by the National Institute on Drug Abuse

Peter L. Myers, PhD
Editor

21st Century Research on Drugs and Ethnicity: Studies Supported by the National Institute on Drug Abuse has been co-published simultaneously as *Journal of Ethnicity in Substance Abuse*, Volume 6, Number 2 2007.

Routledge
Taylor & Francis Group
New York London

First published by The Haworth Press, Inc.

This edition published 2013 by Routledge

Routledge
Taylor & Francis Group
711 Third Avenue
New York, NY 10017

Routledge
Taylor & Francis Group
2 Park Square, Milton Park
Abingdon, Oxon OX14 4RN

Routledge is an imprint of the Taylor & Francis Group, an informa business

21st Century Research on Drugs and Ethnicity: Studies Supported by the National Institute on Drug Abuse has been co-published simultaneously as *Journal of Ethnicity in Substance Abuse*™, Volume 6, Number 2 2007.

Library of Congress Cataloging-in-Publication Data

21st century research on drugs and ethnicity : studies supported by the National Institute on Drug Abuse / Peter L. Myers, editor.

p. cm.

"Co-published simultaneously as Journal of Ethnicity in Substance Abuse, volume 6, number 2, 2007."

Includes bibliographical references and index.

ISBN-13: 978-0-7890-3753-4 (hard cover : alk. paper)

ISBN-13: 978-0-7890-3754-1 (soft cover : alk. paper)

1. Minorities--Drug use--United States--Statistics. 2. Drug abuse--United States--Statistics. I. Myers, Peter L. II. Journal of ethnicity in substance abuse. III. Title: Twenty-first century research on drugs and ethnicity.

HV5824.E85 2007

362.29089'00973--dc22

2007047080

21st Century Research on Drugs and Ethnicity: Studies Supported by the National Institute on Drug Abuse

CONTENTS

ABOUT THE EDITOR

Peter L. Myers, PhD, is an anthropologist and addiction studies specialist. He is the founding editor of the *Journal of Ethnicity in Substance Abuse*, co-author of *Becoming an Addictions Counselor: A Comprehensive Text* (2nd Edition, 2007, Jones and Bartlett), Editor of the forthcoming *Tobacco and Ethnicity* (Haworth), and a contributor to many academic journals on interdisciplinary social science concerns. He serves on the Addiction Professionals Certification Board of New Jersey and on the Editorial Board of the *Journal of Teaching in the Addictions*. He is retiring from Essex County College in Newark, NJ where he was Professor and Coordinator of the Addiction Counselor Training Program, and is Adjunct Assistant Professor of Human Services at the New York City College of Technology, CUNY.

A Century of Research

Peter L. Myers, PhD

INTRODUCTION

This monograph is a centennial volume on the study of ethnicity and psychoactive substance use. At the dawn of the 20th Century, explorer-ethnographers cataloged not only pottery and basketry, but also the earliest scientific descriptions of ethnic-specific use of mind-altering chemicals.[1] Waldemar Jochelson (1906) published the results of his late 19th Century fieldwork among the Turkic-speaking Yakut tribe of Siberia, especially the myth and ritual surrounding the avid consumption of fermented mare's milk in festivals dedicated to the deities, as well as in daily living. Fermentation instructions were, in fact, provided by a deity. Anthropologists saw many societies in which drinking, and shamanistic drug use, was seamlessly woven into the fabric of society, as opposed to the problem usage that we most often focus upon in this journal.

If ethnography is the marker, we are due a centennial celebration. However, many might postulate the genesis of our subfield to be the 1940's, when scientific models of the relationship of culture to drug use were formulated . Explanatory models of alcohol use begin with Donald Horton, whose essay on "The functions of alcohol use in primitive societies" (Horton, 1943) is a footnote in all historical reviews of alcohol research. Horton postulated that alcohol use functions to relieve anxiety, which can arise from intranicene feuding, warfare, marginal subsistence

[Haworth co-indexing entry note]: "A Century of Research." Myers, Peter L. Co-published simultaneously in *Journal of Ethnicity in Substance Abuse* (The Haworth Press, Inc.) Vol. 6, No. 2, 2007, pp. 1-9; and: *21st Century Research on Drugs and Ethnicity: Studies Supported by the National Institute on Drug Abuse* (ed: Peter L. Myers) The Haworth Press, 2007, pp. 1-9. Single or multiple copies of this article are available for a fee from The Haworth Document Delivery Service [1-800-HAWORTH, 9:00 a.m. - 5:00 p.m. (EST). E-mail address: docdelivery@haworthpress.com].

Available online at http://jesa.haworthpress.com

doi:10.1300/J233v06n02_01

techniques, and disruptive culture contact with Europeans and Americans. In his view, the amount of drunkenness obtained via drinking is proportional to the strengths of dangers facing the society. However, alcohol use creates a new problem, that of dealing with drunken aggression and unleashed sexual impulses, and these societies create institutions to channel and limit aggression and sexuality. The other most cited pioneer is Robert Bales, who first compared and explained differential patterns of drinking among ethnic groups, in his study of Irish and Jewish drinking (1946). Bales described Irish agricultural economics and inheritance patterns that kept men at home as bachelors and "boys" well into their forties, consorting in same-sex tavern groups, where it was normative if not encouraged to engage in heavy drinking to facilitate conviviality, as well as to ameliorate their sexual and economic frustration. In contrast, Bales stated that Jews drank at home, with families, in a ritualistic context, and developed temperate habits. Religiosity and animosity to drunkenness also played a large part in Jewish sobriety. Finally, Bales cited a low level of alcohol abuse among the Balinese, who released tension through trance states rather than in inebriety.

Acculturative stress/strain, a prominent research theme in ethnicity/drug research, also stems from this period. Horton (1943) not only gave us the first attempt at a scientific theory of drunkenness, but was one of the first to consider acculturative stress in substance abuse, based on subsistence anxieties. The other earliest mention came the year before, in the work of the three Chopras (1942) in describing the weakening of strictures against drunkenness as people left traditional rural communities of India.

We are happy to be able to compile, in this volume, some of the important research on ethnicity and substance use supported by the National Institute on Drug Abuse over the last several years, that has been accepted for publication in the *Journal of Ethnicity in Substance Abuse*. In these parlous budgetary times, it is gratifying to observe that a governmental entity can facilitate such a multiplicity of research projects covering so many areas of study in this important interdisciplinary subfield, that will contribute to the effort to deliver effective and appropriate treatment and prevention services to all Americans. NIDA special populations research has been featured throughout the history of this journal, and in its predecessor publication, *Drugs & Society*. Fifteen years ago, Haworth published *Ethnic and Multicultural Drug Abuse: Perspectives on Current Research* (Trimble et al., eds. 1992), a monograph that had appeared as a special issue of *Drugs & Society* with support from a NIDA grant. In a review article, Howard Rebach (1992) conducted a methodological critique with caveats that hold true today. He cautioned against using student or patient groups as samples, as some populations are less likely to seek treatment, and are more likely to drop out of school and be omitted from study. One thought-provoking declaration made by Rebach challenged us to abandon ethnic membership as a variable for study, but rather, consider ethnicity as a marker for a host of variables including family structures, male-female relations, child-rearing practices, and of course a host of issues regarding alcohol and drug use. Both Rebach (1992) Collins (1992), and Chavez and Swain (1992) all writing in the same volume remind us that it is difficult to generalize about an ethnic group due to huge intra-group variation, pre and post immigration, in degree of acculturation, socioeconomic status, gender, age, urban-rural and regional differences, which this writer has dubbed as "six-dimensional epidemiology."

Seven years later, our predecessor publication spun off the monograph *Conducting Drug Abuse Research with Minority Populations–Advances and Issues,* in 1999. The lead editor was Mario R. De La Rosa, who is the lead author of an article in this volume. In that compilation, William Vega and Andres Gil (1999), investigating drug use behavior among Hispanic adolescents, cast doubt on the rosy promises of assimilation. They point to assimilation to any of a variety of local cultures, some of which are gang and drug-ridden, with weakening of traditional family structures. Here, one might even find worsening of grades and educational aspirations as a concomitant of assimilation, hardly the American Dream. Dr. De La Rosa also edited, with Lori K. Holleran and Shulamith L. A. Straussner (2005), a Haworth volume on Substance Abusing Latinos.

Increasingly, researchers seek to differentiate between ethnic value systems and economic situations as either protective or risk factors for substance use; we will cast a brief look at studies of Dominican substance use. Andrew Gordon, a member of the Editorial Board of this journal, authored a classic study of Hispanic heterogeneity, in his look at Dominicans, Guatamalans, and Puerto Ricans in Newton, Massachusetts. (Gordon, 1978, 1981). Dominicans drank less after migration, which they related to their efforts to integrate into the local economy, which was abetted by a kind of work ethic. Men are expected to correspond to the ideal of the "hombre serio," conscientious and responsible, concerned about the future. Gross drunkenness was considered "indecente," failing to show respect. In contrast, about one-third of Guatamalan males in Newton drank to excess and drunkenness, and drank more than they did in Guatamala. Drunkenness was glamorized and sentimentalized; the drinker is roguish, sad, picaresque, as seen in the exchange "Como esta?" "Un poco jodido de chupar" (a little wrecked from drinking). Dominican upward mobility described by Gordon in Newton, Massachusetts also obtained in New York City in the 1990's, where, for example, 80 percent of bodegas were Dominican-owned. Twenty-one years after Gordon's study, Michelle Shedlin and Sherry Deren (2002) reported on their ethnographic research in the Dominican community of Washington Heights in this journal. They found that "getting ahead" for economic stability and family support were still important values. Moreover, "control and self-control . . . emerged as the most important attribute to be maintained in life . . . control of the family . . . future . . . behavior . . . resources . . . mind and body, are all seen as necessary for success and the respect of the family, of friends, and the community here and in the Dominican Republic" (p. 78). What had intriguing implications for treatment was that these values persist even among drug users. A common expression among drug users was "I am trying to dominate/control the drug(s)." Crack use in particular was seen as loss of control, but even crack users evaluated themselves as relatively in or out of control in their use of that substance. Treatment providers working with clients totally immersed in addictive lifestyles can appeal to cultural values in their facilitation of clients' motivational and decisional balance. Using several screening instruments, Drohan and colleagues (1997) found a lifetime prevalence of alcohol abuse and alcohol dependence at 22% for Dominicans, 41% for Central Americans, and 47% for Puerto Ricans in their sample, findings that are in line with other such studies. In another recent Haworth monograph on Latino alcohol use, Annecy Baez (2005) refers to the transnational identity of Dominicans–their ambivalence about national identity, their returns and visits to DR, and financial attachments–and their settlement in a small number of close-knit communities, as slowing acculturation and assimilation, and forming, to some extent, a protective barrier against alcohol abuse/addiction among Dominican adults. On the other hand, there are high rates of poverty among Dominicans, and there is a subset of depressed, unemployed males, who have "dishonorably" failed to provide for their families, in the proclaimed goal of upward mobility and respectability, and who then separate from their families and drift into alcoholism.[2]

The *Journal of Ethnicity in Substance Abuse* accepted ten NIDA-supported studies in its short history, prior to this volume that features nine manuscripts.[3] The current volume shows the wide range of subjects supported by NIDA. The first article (Redko et al., 2007) was exciting in that it compared professional models of treatment readiness, such as in the Stages of Change transtheoretical model, and Motivational Enhancement, with folk models of clients, what another discipline might call a mental map of recovery. Another analysis of how client culture matches treatment culture follows in the work of Michael Villanueva, J. Scott Tonigan, and William Miller (Villanueva et al., 2007). This article continues the work of the Center on Alcoholism, Substance Abuse, and Addictions at the University of New Mexico, which has produced several looks at Project MATCH data vís-a-vís ethnicity. In previous work, they had found that Hispanic clients attended AA less frequently, but were more involved in and committed to the AA program than whites (Tonigan et al., 1998). This may be related to the greater religiosity of Hispanic clients, which resonates with the spirituality of AA and Twelve-Step Facilitation (Arroyo et al., 2002) The current article is one of the first to examine native American clients response to modern treatment modalities, and suggests that they respond better to Motivational Enhancement Therapy than to the other Project MATCH treatment methods, Twelve Step Facilitation and Cognitive-Behavioral Therapy. The third article (McCabe et al., 2007) revisits the field of collegiate drug prevention. Readers may remember when a large federal initiative, the Drug Prevention Programs in Higher Education, Fund for the Improvement of Post-Secondary Education, U.S. DOE, supported hundreds of institutional efforts and created ninety regional prevention consortia. In this article, McCabe and colleagues remind us that ethnicity forms attitudes about drugs before college, and keeps us current on rates of drug use among racial/ethnic groups at colleges in the 21st Century. Valdez and colleagues (2007) examine the complexities of acculturation as pertains to injecting drug use behaviors. It is interesting to contrast this research with the research thread on Dominicans that we summarized above. They hone in on a traditional, older *tecato* chronic injecting heroin user subculture, as opposed to younger, more acculturated non-injecting heroin users. Thus, this sample reverses the usual "acculturated, more at-risk" Hispanic population in that the acculturated are removed from an injecting subculture. The same "exceptionalism" was also demonstrated by Rodriguez and colleagues (2007) in the very next article, in which dually diagnosed adolescents in treatment had more substance use problems when less acculturated. This sample was approximately one-half Cuban, ramifications of the Cuban immigrant experience were mentioned. This is followed by an article by Alvarez and colleagues (2007) who review problems of treatment underutilization by Latinos/Latinas, and also accent the need to reconceptualize acculturation and its many dimensions.

Fernandez and colleagues (2007) experiment with new electronic venues to recruit the "hidden" populations of Hispanic men who have sex with men to prevention studies. Continuing in our quest for culturally competent strategies for data collection, Mario de La Rosa and colleagues (De La Rosa, 2007) outlined methods to approach and elicit information from Latino women. Finally, we end on a hopeful note with a study of American Indian youth in Phoenix, for whom neighborhood disorganization was less of a risk factor for drug use in comparison with non-American Indian youth. Their resiliency was related back to close familial organization and ethnic pride, and leads to a consideration of best culturally competent practices with American Indian youth.

NOTES

1. Before scientific investigation of ethnicity and substance use, awareness of any link between these phenomena were limited to nativist and xenophobic currents embedded in temperance and Prohibition politics. Starting with the arrival of Germans and Irish in 1840's, many viewed immigrant groups as drunkards and threats. Later, Southern Prohibitionists linked their cause to racist imaginings about African-American males, and Chinese immigrants were impugned as opium-smoking "dope fiends," the so-called "Yellow Peril." Ethnic stereotypy, often aimed at Hispanics, featured in the 1930's Reefer Madness period of Harry Anslinger zealotry. Ethnophobias and stigmatization of drug users are both examples of demonization of "outsiders" who bring pollution and danger to native purity (Kinder, 1992, Douglas, 1966). Here, the categories neatly intersected.

2. A challenge in doing quantitative analyses among acculturating peoples is that they are standing on a variety of bridges. Two classic ethnographic portraits of this phenomenon were by William Madsen (1967) among Mexican-Americans in South Texas and George and Louise Spindler's (1971) study of the Menomini. They identified subgroups who abandoned traditional culture but were not successfully acculturated, in limbo and at risk for addictions. The Texas subgroup were reviled by traditionalists as "agringados" (gringo-fied). Others may be successfully adapted to a bicultural status and behavior, happily "code-switching" as situations demand. Then again, they may occupy a cultural space best categorized as a blended or creolized culture. To provide a graphic example, Puerto Rican clients the author worked with in New York City used many words that blended Spanish and English. "Spanglish" words include "rufo" for roof, "eleavador" instead of "ascensor" for elevator, "daime" for dime. Furthermore, they partially acculturated to urban African-American sensibilities.

3. Bibliography of NIDA-Supported Research in *Journal of Ethnicity in Substance Abuse*, 2002-2006.

Alvarez, J., Jason, L.A., Davis, M.I., & Ferrari, J.R. (2004). Latinos and Latinas in Oxford Houses: Perceptions of barriers and opportunities. *Journal of Ethnicity in Substance Abuse, 3*(4), 17-32.

Broman, C.L., Reckase, M.D., & Freedman-Doan, C.R. (2006). The role of parenting in drug uses among Black, Latino, and White adolescents. *Journal of Ethnicity in Substance Abuse, 5*(1), 39-50.

Brown, E.J. (2003). Double Whammy: Accessing, Recruiting and Retaining the hidden of the hidden. *Journal of Ethnicity in Substance Abuse, 2*(1), 43-51.

Chen, K.W., & Killeya-Jones, L.A. (2006). Understanding differences in marijuana use among urban Black and suburban White high school students from two U.S. community samples. *Journal of Ethnicity in Substance Abuse, 5*(2), 51-73.

Isralowitz, R.E., Straussner, S.L.A., & Rosenblum, A. (2006). Drug abuse, risks of infectious diseases and service utilization among former Soviet Union immigrants: A view from New York City (Brief Research Report). *Journal of Ethnicity in Substance Abuse, 5*(1), 91-96.

Johnson, H.D., & Young, S. (2002). Addiction, Abuse, and Family Relationships: Childhood Experiences of Five Incarcerated African-American Women. *Journal of Ethnicity in Substance Abuse, 1*(4), 29-47.

Reynolds, G.L., Wells, R.S., Fisher, D.G., & Cagle, H.H. (2004). Health services usage by Alaskan injection drug users. *Journal of Ethnicity in Substance Abuse, 3*(4), 61-73.

Rinehart, C.S., Bridges, L.J., & Seligman, C.K. (2006). Differences between Black and White elementary school children's orientation towards alcohol and cocaine: A three-study comparison. *Journal of Ethnicity in Substance Abuse, 5*(3), 75-102.

Sexton, R.L., Carlson, R.G., Siegal, H.A., Leukefeld, C.G., & Booth, B.M. (2006). The role of African-American clergy in providing informal services to drug users in the rural South: Preliminary ethnographic findings. *Journal of Ethnicity in Substance Abuse, 5*(1), 1-21.

Slesnick, N., Vasquez, C., & Bittinger, J. (2002). Family Functioning, Substance Use and Related Problem Behaviors: Hispanic vs. Anglo Runaway Youths. *Journal of Ethnicity in Substance Abuse, 1*(4), 83-101.

Strycker, L.A., Duncan, S.C., & Pickering, M.A. (2003). The social context of alcohol initiation among African-American and White youth. *Journal of Ethnicity in Substance Abuse, 2*(1), 35-42.

REFERENCES

Alvarez, J., Jason, L.A., Olson, B.D., Ferrari, J.R., & Davis, M.I. (2007). Substance abuse prevalence and treatment among Latinos and Latinas. *Journal of Ethnicity in Substance Abuse, 6*(2), 115-141.

Baez, A. (2005). Alcohol use among Dominican Americans: An explanation. Chapter 4 in Delgado, M. (ed.). *Latinos and Alcohol Use/Misuse Revisited.* Binghamton, NY: The Haworth Press.

Bales, R. (1946). Cultural differences in rates of alcoholism. *Quarterly Journal of Studies on Alcohol, 6*, 480-499.

Chavez, E.L., & Swaim, R.C. (1992). Hispanic Substance Use: Problems in Epidemiology, pp. 211-230 in Trimble, J.E., Bolek, C., & Niemcryk, S.J. eds. *Ethnic and Multicultural Drug Use: Perspectives on Current Research.* Binghamton, NY: The Haworth Press.

Chopra, R.N., Chopra, G.S., & Chopra, I.C. (1942). Alcoholic beverages in India. *Indian Medical Gazette, 77*, 225-230.

Collins, R. L. (1992). Methodological issues in conducting substance abuse research on ethnic minority populations. pp. 59-77.

De La Rosa, M.R., Holleran, L.K., & Straussner, S.L.A. (2005). Substance Abuse Latinos: Current Research on epidemiology, prevention, and treatment. NY: The Haworth Press.

De La Rosa, M., Rahill, G.J., Rojas, P., & Pinto, E. (2007). Cultural adaptions in data collections: Field experiences. *Journal of Ethnicity in Substance Abuse, 6*(2), 163-180.

Douglas, M. (1966). Purity and danger: An analysis of concepts of pollution and taboo. New York: Frederick A. Praeger.

Fernandez, M.I.,Warren, J.D.,Varga, L.M., Prado, G., Hernandez, N., & Bowen, G.S. (2007). Cruising in cyber-space: Comparing internet chat room vs. community venues for recruiting Hispanic men who have had sex with men to participate in prevention studies. *Journal of Ethnicity in Substance Abuse, 6*(2), 143-162.

Horton, D. (1943). The functions of alcohol in primitive societies: A cross-cultural study. *Quarterly Journal of Studies on Alcohol, 4*, 199-320.

Juarez, P., Miller, W.R., & Tonigan, J.S. (2002). AA utilization of hispanic and non-Hispanic white clients. Center on Alcoholism, Substance Abuse, and Addictions, University of New Mexico. http://casaa.unm.edu/posters.html

McCabe, S.E., Morales, M., Cranford, J.A., Delva, J., McPherson, M.D., & Boyd, C.J. (2007). Race/ethnicity and gender differences in drug use and abuse among college students. *Journal of Ethnicity in Substance Abuse, 6*(2), 75-95.

Rebach, H. (1992). Alcohol and Drug Use among American Minorities. pp. 23-57. In Trimble, J.E., Bolek, C., & Niemcryk, S.J., eds. *Ethnic and Multicultural Drug Use: Perspectives on Current Research.* Binghamton, NY: The Haworth Press.

Redko, C., Carlson, R.G., & Rapp, R.C. (2007). A folk model of treatment readiness among drug users in Ohio. *Journal of Ethnicity in Substance Abuse, 6*(2), 15-40.

Rodriguez, R.A., Henderson, C.E., Rowe, C.L., Burnett, K.F., Dakof, G.A:, & Liddle, H.A. (2007). Acculturation and drug use among dually diagnosed Hispanic adolescents. *Journal of Ethnicity in Substance Abuse, 6*(2), 97-113.

Tonigan, J.S., Connors, G.J., & Miller, W.R. (1998). Special Populations in Alcoholics Anonymous. *Alcohol Health and Research World, 22*(4), 281-285.

Trimble, J.E., Bolek, C., & Niemcryk, S.J. (eds.) (1992). Ethnic and Multicultural Drug Use: Perspectives on Current Research. Binghamton, NY: The Haworth Press.

Valdez, A., Neaigus, A., & Cepeda, A. (2007). Potential risk factors for injecting among Mexican-American non-injecting heroin users. *Journal of Ethnicity in Substance Abuse, 6*(2), 49-73.

Vega, W. A., & Gill, A.G. (1999). A model for explaining drug use behavior among Hispanic adolescents. pp. 57-74. In De La Rosa, M.R., Segal, B., & Lopez, R. (eds.) *Conducting drug abuse research with minority adolescents*. NY: The Haworth Press.

Villanueva, M., Tonigan, J.S., & Miller, W.R. (2007). Response of Native American clients to three treatment methods for alcohol dependence. *Journal of Ethnicity in Substance Abuse*, *6*(2), 41-48.

Yakibu, S.T., Rayle, A.D., Okamoto, S.K., Marsiglia, F.F., & Kulis, S. (2007). The Effect of Neighborhood Context on the Drug Use of American Indian Youth of the Southwest. *Journal of Ethnicity in Substance Abuse*, *6*(2), 181-204.

doi:10.1300/J233v06n02_01

Introduction

Lula A. Beatty, PhD

Epidemiologic data have consistently shown over the years that overall drug use in the United States varies little by race/ethnicity. That is, most racial/ethnic minority populations report lifetime use of substances at about the same rate as their respective representation in the population (SAMHSA, 2002) There are, however, variations in patterns of drug use among racial/ethnic minority groups. For example, whites are more likely to use methamphetamine than African Americans, and African Americans appear to differ from other groups in their age of first drug use and progression to problem use. These variations carry important implications for our understanding of drug abuse and addiction and designing appropriate and effective prevention, treatment, and services for these populations.

Although prevalence rates are similar across population groups, the impact of drug use and addiction on the health and well-being of racial/ethnic minority populations is strikingly different. Racial/Ethnic minority groups are more likely to experience consequences that result in more disease, mortality and poorer quality of life. An example of these differences in consequences is the disproportionate rates of HIV/AIDS and incarceration/criminal justice involvement related to drug use experienced by African Americans and Hispanics. (See, for example, Beatty, Jones, & Doctor, 2005.) Another example is the high rate of suicide among Native

---

Dr. Lula Beatty is Chief of the Special Operations Office in the Office of the Director at the National Institute on Drug Abuse.

[Haworth co-indexing entry note]: "Introduction." Beatty, Lula A. Co-published simultaneously in *Journal of Ethnicity in Substance Abuse* (The Haworth Press, Inc.) Vol. 6, No. 2, 2007, pp. 11-13; and: *21st Century Research on Drugs and Ethnicity: Studies Supported by the National Institute on Drug Abuse* (ed: Peter L. Myers) The Haworth Press, 2007, pp. 11-13. Single or multiple copies of this article are available for a fee from The Haworth Document Delivery Service [1-800-HAWORTH, 9:00 a.m. - 5:00 p.m. (EST). E-mail address: docdelivery@haworthpress.com].

Available online at http://jesa.haworthpress.com

doi:10.1300/J233v06n02_02

Americans related to drug use. It is these gaps in differential consequences that characterize much of NIDA's health disparities priorities.

NIDA's mission is to "lead the nation in bringing the power of science to bear on drug abuse and addiction." We accomplish this through supporting and conducting research across a broad range of disciplines and disseminating research results to improve prevention, treatment and policy. We have long recognized that in order to fully achieve our mission we need to encourage and support work that addresses drug abuse and addiction in racial/ethnic minority populations. For many years, we have addressed the concerns of underrepresented groups through a variety of activities and programs designed both to increase research studies on minority concerns in drug abuse and addiction in all of our program areas and to increase the number of researchers investigating these issues. In 2000 the Surgeon General identified Eliminating Health Disparities as a public health priority. The National Institutes of Health responded by requiring that all institutes develop a health disparities strategic plan. NIDA developed its Health Disparities Strategic Plan in 2000 (revised in 2004; available at http://www.drugabuse.gov/StrategicPlan/HealthStratPlan.html), describing the research, research capacity development, and outreach priorities and activities that we consider critical to advancing the field.

Our research priority areas of emphasis are epidemiology of drug abuse, health consequences and infectious diseases among minority populations; prevention of drug abuse and addiction; treatment and health services research; and racial/ethnic disparities in basic and clinical neurosciences. Within these areas, are propose specific research questions that should be explored. In addition, we routinely assess the status of communities and science to remain responsive to current needs and opportunities, and we have made health disparities a cross-cutting research area to be addressed in all of our research studies, where appropriate.

We need investigators involved in health disparities research. Having investigators who are knowledgeable about the issues, conceptual frameworks, and methodological approaches is essential to our goal of increasing the quantity and quality of studies in this area. To that end, we have sponsored a number of programs and activities to stimulate interest and provide research training and career development opportunities for both new and established researchers.

We are extremely pleased to see the progress we are making in drug abuse health disparities research as reflected in the collection of articles appearing in this volume. The articles demonstrate variety in researchers, subject populations, research support mechanisms, and range of topic areas. Findings reported emanate not only from R01 research grants but also from career development awards, center grants, institutional development awards, and small grants suggesting that the authors represent early career investigators as well as established investigators. Moreover, the investigators themselves are from diverse population groups. The population groups of study include Native Americans, Latinos and Latinas, Asians, African Americans, and Whites. Topics addressed include treatment readiness, risk factors, acculturation, and methodological concerns and innovations.

There is still a great amount of research to be done. We encourage the authors of these articles to continue their work as researchers and mentors. We also encourage new and established investigators to consider expanding their research to include minority health disparities using the resources of NIDA and other NIH institutes.

REFERENCES

Beatty, L., Jones, D., & Doctor, L. (Eds.) (2005). *Journal of health care for the poor and underserved, 16*(4), Supplement B.

Substance Abuse and Mental Health Services Administration. (2002). *Results from the 2001 national household survey on drug abuse: Volume I. Summary of national findings.* DHHS Publication No. (SMA) 02-3758. Rockville, MD: Office of Applied Studies, SAMHSA.

doi:10.1300/J233v06n02_02

A Folk Model of Treatment Readiness Among Drug Users in Ohio

Cristina Redko, PhD
Robert G. Carlson, PhD
Richard C. Rapp, MSW

SUMMARY. Despite the benefits of substance abuse treatment, only a small proportion of drug users enter treatment. Understanding "readiness" is critical for engaging drug users in treatment and for involving them in the recovery process. This paper reports on ethnographic interviews

Cristina Redko, Robert G. Carlson, and Richard C. Rapp are affiliated with Center for Interventions, Treatment, and Addictions Research (CITAR), Wright State University, Boonshoft School of Medicine, 3640 Colonel Glenn Highway, Dayton, OH USA 45435.

Address correspondence to: Cristina Redko, PhD, Center for Interventions, Treatment and Addictions Research (CITAR), Wright State University, Boonshoft School of Medicine, 3640 Colonel Glenn Highway, Dayton, OH USA 45435 (E-mail: cristina.redko@wright.edu).

A preliminary version of this article was presented at the Meetings of the Society for Applied Anthropology in Santa Fe, New Mexico, April 2005. Research was supported by the National Institute on Drug Abuse (NIDA) for a study entitled "Reducing Barriers to Drug Abuse Treatment Services," grant number DA15690. Richard Rapp, Principal Investigator; Robert G. Carlson, Co-Principal Investigator. Special gratitude to the late Harvey A. Siegal, former Principal Investigator, and founder of CITAR. The authors thank Tracy D. Daus for qualitative interview transcription. The views expressed in this paper do not necessarily reflect those of NIDA or any government agency.

[Haworth co-indexing entry note]: "A Folk Model of Treatment Readiness Among Drug Users in Ohio." Redko, Cristina, Robert G. Carlson, and Richard C. Rapp. Co-published simultaneously in *Journal of Ethnicity in Substance Abuse* (The Haworth Press, Inc.) Vol. 6, No. 2, 2007, pp. 15-40; and: *21st Century Research on Drugs and Ethnicity: Studies Supported by the National Institute on Drug Abuse* (ed: Peter L. Myers) The Haworth Press, 2007, pp. 15-40. Single or multiple copies of this article are available for a fee from The Haworth Document Delivery Service [1-800-HAWORTH, 9:00 a.m.–5:00 p.m. (EST). E-mail address: docdelivery@haworthpress.com].

Available online at http://jesa.haworthpress.com

doi:10.1300/J233v06n02_03

conducted with 35 active drug users as they were entering treatment services, to describe how they perceive readiness for treatment. Drug users expressed readiness for treatment in terms reflective of twelve step programs, a folk model of treatment. A better understanding of drug users' perceptions can help to inform interventions designed to improve readiness for treatment. doi:10.1300/J233v06n02_03 *[Article copies available for a fee from The Haworth Document Delivery Service: 1-800-HAWORTH. E-mail address: <docdelivery@haworthpress.com> Website: <http://www. HaworthPress.com>*

KEYWORDS. Treatment readiness, substance abuse treatment, ethnography

INTRODUCTION

The effectiveness of substance abuse treatment is widely recognized, yet the majority of drug users do not enter treatment (Battjes, Onken, Delany, 1999). Many drug users who enter treatment leave prematurely or relapse soon after treatment (Prendergast, Podus, Chang, & Urada, 2004; Hubbard, Craddock, & Anderson, 2003); therefore, multiple treatment episodes are often required to achieve long-term recovery (Hser, Anglin, Grella, Longshore, & Prendergast, 1997: Anglin, Hser, & Grella, 1997). Motivation to seek help and "readiness" for treatment are key factors in predicting success in linking, engaging, and during the longer-term recovery process (Simpson, Joe, Dansereau, & Chatham, 1997; Sia, Dansereau, & Czuchry, 2000; Broome, Knight, Hiller, & Simpson, 1997; Hiller, Knight, Leukefeld, & Simpson, 2002).

Readiness to take action (or motivation to change) and confront a substance abuse problem is a complex and dynamic process. From the perspective of professional models, readiness refers to the personal considerations, commitments, reasons, and intentions that move individuals to perform certain behaviors, in this case, entering substance abuse treatment (DiClemente, Schlundt, & Gemmell, 2004).

High levels of readiness predict both engagement and retention across the major treatment modalities–outpatient methadone, outpatient drug free, long-term residential programs (Joe, Simpson, & Broome, 1999)–and among a heterogeneous sample of substance abusing clients (Joe, Simpson, & Broome, 1998; Simpson, Joe, Rowan-Szal, & Greener, 1995). As such, interventions that enhance readiness for treatment have also been developed, including motivational interviewing (Miller, Rollnick, & Conforti, 2002).

Much of our understanding about treatment readiness and how people change derives from professional models, that is, from clinical and scientific models. In contrast, other members of society, and particularly drug users, have their own interpretations about what being ready for treatment means. These folk models differ from professional models in that they represent underlying attitudes and belief systems which drive specific behaviors. Michael Agar's (1985) seminal paper comparing folk and professional models of drug use emphasizes the significance of understanding both folk and professional models prior to developing and implementing treatment interventions. By analogy, understanding folk models of readiness may contribute to improved interventions designed to increase the level of readiness among drug users who are engaging in treatment or in the recovery process.

The purpose of this paper is to describe the ways drug users express being ready for treatment soon after having gone through substance abuse assessment and referral at a centralized intake unit in Dayton, Ohio. The paper is based on ethnographic interviews conducted with 35 drug users who had been assessed at the centralized intake unit. During interviews, participants spontaneously emphasized how "being ready" was a critical factor influencing their decision to link with treatment. Ethnographic studies that describe and examine the process of treatment engagement are still very limited (Reisinger, Bush, Colom, Agar, & Battjes, 2003; Duroy, Schmidt, & Perry, 2003). To contextualize our study, we provide a brief review of professional models of treatment readiness, as well as the perspective of Alcoholics Anonymous.

Professional Models of Treatment Readiness

Several professional models have been developed to describe the process of individual change with respect to substance misuse. The most influential approach has been Prochaska and DiClemente's *transtheoretical model* indicating how change occurs as individuals move (or do not move) through the five successive stages of precontemplation, contemplation, preparation, action, and maintenance (Prochaska, DiClemente, & Norcross, 1992; DiClemente & Prochaska, 1998). The stages represent how people progress towards recovery by realizing that their substance use is a problem, by preparing to take and then taking specific actions to stop using drugs, and by using a variety of cognitive strategies to ensure that positive change is maintained. Except for the pre-contemplative stage, the concept of readiness is implied throughout the model.

Readiness for treatment models represent a conceptual shift from the broadly defined motivation for change models because they try to demonstrate how people engage in treatment for their substance abuse problems. Researchers at Texas Christian University developed the *treatment process model* which recognizes readiness as a key component of the change process leading to treatment engagement. The treatment process is conceptualized in discrete phases (outreach, induction, engagement, treatment, and aftercare) allowing for specialized intervention and evaluation strategies (Simpson, 2004; Simpson, 2001). In this model, treatment readiness is preceded by problem recognition and desire for help (Joe et al., 1998; Simpson & Joe, 1993).

Another professional model that addresses readiness is De Leon's *integrative recovery model,* the first model that differentiated readiness for change from readiness for treatment (1996; De Leon, Melnick, & Tims, 2001). This model describes ten stages of recovery including six pre-treatment stages (denial, ambivalence, external motivation, internal motivation, readiness for change, and readiness for treatment) and four treatment-related stages (deaddiction, abstinence, continuance, integration and identity change). Since De Leon's model was initially proposed to describe the treatment experience that takes place in therapeutic communities, it highlights change in social and personal identity as the distinctive marker of the final integration stage.

In sum, treatment readiness refers to an individual's level of preparedness to actively engage in the cognitive and behavioral changes required during the treatment process. Most treatment interventions are designed for clients who are already motivated to take action, and for this reason they may be inappropriate for those clients unmotivated for or ambivalent about change (Battjes et al., 1999; DiClemente, 1999).

Twelve Step Programs and a Folk Model Approach to Readiness

In addition to professional models of readiness, Alcoholics Anonymous (AA) and other twelve step programs provide a folk model approach to readiness to change. AA was first established in 1935 by a small group of alcoholics who shared their experiences about how to stay sober. The product of this experience is contained in the Twelve Steps of the "Big Book" (Alcoholics Anonymous, 1976) and in the Twelve Traditions (Alcoholics Anonymous, 1953) resulting in a flexible democratic fellowship that has spread around the world. For those who want to "work the steps" the only requirement for membership is a desire to stop drinking, an expression of readiness. The model has one primary purpose: "to carry its message to the alcoholic who still suffers." For recovery to occur, readiness and sobriety must take place "one day at a time" through a long-term process of change (Fiorentine & Hillhouse, 2000; Chappel & DuPont, 1999).

The structure of twelve step programs differs from formal treatment programs in many ways, including the freedom from any financial motivation, because participation is free and the leaders of the groups are unpaid. Participation is accomplished by merely attending the meetings; membership lists are not kept. Members are encouraged to help themselves by helping others–by sharing experiences, listening to stories, and by telling their own stories (Cain, 1991; Swora, 2001). Study participants frequently described their readiness for treatment framed by AA's language of *hitting rock bottom* and *being sick and tired.*

METHODS

The paper is based on baseline ethnographic interviews conducted as part of the Reducing Barriers to Drug Abuse Treatment Services Project (Reducing Barriers). Reducing Barriers is a clinical trial designed to assess the relative effectiveness of motivational interviewing and strengths-based case management, compared to a standard of care control, in linking clients with treatment services and subsequently engaging them in services. Eligible subjects had to: (1) be over 18 years of age; (2) be diagnosed as having a substance abuse and/or dependence disorder using criteria from the Diagnostic and Statistical Manual (DSM-IV-TR); (3) not have schizophrenia or any other psychotic disorder; and (4) be referred to either residential or outpatient substance abuse services. Alcohol-abusing or dependent individuals without other substance disorders were not eligible.

Reducing Barriers is located in Dayton Ohio with a county population of 552,000. Participants for the project are recruited from a centralized intake unit (CIU), the county's only point of entry for uninsured individuals seeking treatment for substance abuse and mental health problems. Assessment therapists conduct psychosocial, mental health, and substance abuse assessments to determine the nature and extent of clients' problems. Clients are referred to an appropriate level of care within the community treatment system based on ASAM (American Society of Addiction Medicine) (2001) criteria and situational factors such as treatment availability and client preference. Referrals are made to eight state-certified, specialty substance abuse treatment programs.

Clients generally do not contact the treatment program immediately after the assessment, but must wait to get a specific date from the CIU, which may take from several days to over a week after the assessment. Clients who are admitted to the trial receive either the typical services provided by the CIU while awaiting substance abuse treatment, or are randomized into one of the clinical trial's two experimental arms: motivational interviewing or strengths-based case management.

The project ethnographer (first author) selected a convenience sample from the clinical trial population while attempting to diversify the sample in terms of gender, ethnicity, age, and primary substance used. Audiotape recorded interviews averaging 90 minutes were conducted by the project ethnographer at the CIU. The interview protocol covered history of substance use, abstinence and help-seeking attempts, history of substance abuse treatment, barriers to treatment, treatment engagement, and interactions with health services and study interventions. Individuals were compensated $20 for their time. Participants completed an informed consent form approved by the University's Institutional Review Board. Throughout this article, case examples of drug users are provided under fictitious names to protect the anonymity of research participants.

Ethnographic interview audiotapes were transcribed verbatim and coded by the project ethnographer using NVivo®, a program designed for qualitative data analysis (Richards, 1999). Research codes for pre-defined and emergent categories were generated to index segments of text that referred to specific themes. This process is called open coding in the grounded theory approach to the analysis of ethnographic data (Glaser & Strauss, 1967; Strauss & Corbin, 1998; Fielding & Lee, 1998). For example, open codes identifying sections of text in which participants discussed readiness for treatment were coded as *being ready*. A coding system was created while examining the correspondence among various themes (open codes), by investigating relationships between themes, and by discovering unanticipated relationships. The next step in this kind of analysis is to look for significant recurrences, repetitions, and contradictions between and within themes. This step often leads to the emergence of other sub-themes that opens ground to explore the data in new and unexpected ways.

The ethnographic interviews were also clustered together whenever it was suspected that correlations between themes would be better understood in relation to a major attribute. Thus, the narratives of those drug users who had previous treatment experience were contrasted to those who had none or very little treatment experience. This was done to examine whether previous treatment experience influenced participants' attitudes and concerns regarding their perceived readiness for treatment.

RESULTS

Characteristics of the Ethnographic Study Participants

Twenty-five men (71.4%) and ten women (28.6%) who were assessed for substance abuse treatment at the CIU agreed to be interviewed. Qualitative interviews took place in a private office at the CIU between May 2004 and February 2005. Regarding drug of choice: 60% (21) of participants preferred to use crack or powdered cocaine; 28.6% (10) used heroin and/or pharmaceutical opioids; while 11.4% (4) had a preference for marijuana. About one quarter of participants, 25.7% (9) were court-ordered for the CIU assessment; 25.7% were initially referred for assessment by another health care provider; and the remaining 45.7% (16) arrived at the CIU on their own.

Eighteen of the 35 study participants were African-American (51.4%), and 16 were white (45.7%). In addition, one participant was Native American (2.9%). Forty percent (14) had completed high school or had a GED, while 31.4% (11) had some college education, and the remaining 28.6% (10) had less than a high school education. Over half of the participants, 51.4% (18), were unemployed during the six months prior to the assessment. The average age was 39 (SD = 11.67), and about 29% (10) were less than 30 years old.

The majority of the participants, 71.4% (25), had previously been in some form of substance abuse treatment. Of those, 25.7% (9) had been to treatment once, and 46.7% (16) had multiple treatment episodes. Most of these participants, 68% (25) had been in treatment within the past three years. Of all 35 participants, 28.6% (10) had no previous treatment experience. Table 1 indicates age, sex, ethnicity, drug of choice, and number of times each participant engaged in treatment in the past.

Eighty percent (28) of the participants had attended a self-help meeting, and 62.8% (22) had attended more than 10 meetings. Those participants with multiple treatment episodes were also more likely to have attended more AA meetings. Since Alcoholic Anonymous (AA) meetings are more ubiquitous than NA, these participants had more opportunities to attend AA, compared to NA.

TABLE 1. Sample Characteristics, Drug of Choice, Previous Treatment Engagement

Participants	Age	Sex	Ethnicity	Drug of Choice	Treatment
No Treatment					
Javier	18	M	African-American	marijuana	00
Darryl	22	M	White	heroin/opiates	00
Allan	27	M	White	marijuana	00
Julia	35	F	White	crack/cocaine	00
Lara	39	F	White	crack/cocaine	00
John	41	M	African-American	crack/cocaine	00
Maurice	45	M	White	crack/cocaine	00
Gigi	45	F	African-American	crack/cocaine	00
Jason	45	M	African-American	crack/cocaine	00
Daniel	45	M	African-American	crack/cocaine	00
One Previous Treatment					
Lilian	19	F	White	heroin/opiates	01
Karina	24	F	White	heroin/opiates	01
Mark	25	M	White	marijuana	01
Martha	29	F	White	crack/cocaine	01
Vincent	43	M	African-American	crack/cocaine	01
Beatrice	44	F	African-American	crack/cocaine	01
Rick	49	M	African-American	crack/cocaine	01
Ned	53	M	African-American	crack/cocaine	01
Walter	55	M	White	crack/cocaine	01
Two or More Previous Treatment Episodes					
Alex	20	M	White	heroin/opiates	02
Brian	22	M	White	heroin/opiates	03
Larry	30	M	African-American	marijuana	10
Wilson	36	M	White	heroin/opiates	03
Karl	37	M	African-American	crack/cocaine	03
Louise	40	F	African-American	crack/cocaine	04
Steve	42	M	Native-American	crack/cocaine	02
Jack	42	M	African-American	crack/cocaine	12
Jacob	44	M	African-American	crack/cocaine	12
Matt	46	M	White	heroin/opiates	02
Erasmus	46	M	African-American	crack/cocaine	03

TABLE 1 (continued)

Participants	Age	Sex	Ethnicity	Drug of Choice	Treatment
Leah	48	F	White	heroin/opiates	05
Ralph	50	M	African-American	crack/cocaine	02
Ted	51	M	White	heroin/opiates	08
Elvis	54	M	African-American	heroin/opiates	05
Holly	64	F	African-American	crack/cocaine	02

Context of CIU Assessment

Most participants expressed a strong desire to enter treatment. They had overcome barriers to completing a CIU assessment, the first step toward engaging in substance abuse treatment. Several participants commented that they had stopped using any drugs for a few days or weeks before the ethnographic interview, although this abstinence was more common among those participants who were self-referred, and were not court-ordered. They identified this commitment to abstinence during the time of the CIU assessment as an unmistakable sign of their treatment readiness. This short-term abstinence also helped them feel more confident that they were capable of stopping drug use. This abstinence prior to treatment engagement evoked two different attitudes. Most participants interpreted their abstinence as a positive starting point for treatment readiness and engagement. This was particularly helpful because most treatment settings focus on abstinence as a major treatment outcome. In contrast, some participants showed signs of ambivalence regarding their need of treatment, because they had already achieved abstinence on their own. As such, they had diminished interest to link and engage in treatment services (Rosengren, Downey, & Donovan, 2000). They reasoned that treatment was only necessary for those who were still using, and were not capable of quitting on their own.

Although most participants emphasized their determination to stop using drugs, a few participants mentioned that reasons for treatment engagement are not always related to stopping drug use and maintaining abstinence. Some participants who were court-ordered to treatment reasoned that going to treatment was better than jail. A few women were forced into treatment because Children Services threatened to take their children away. Other participants had other intentions for the CIU assessment, like taking care of mental health, gaining disability status, maintaining driver's license, and holding a job. In some situations, individuals just wanted some time off from the "street life" and the drug addict lifestyle (Carlson, 2006). Koester, Anderson and Hoffer (1999) have described reasons for treatment participation that may include controlling and reducing drug use, substituting the drug of choice for another one perceived as less harmful, or changing the method of administration, such as transitioning from injection to smoking, of heroin, for example.

Below, we describe the most common ways participants expressed their readiness for treatment in relation to their determination to stop using, often by talking in terms of "being ready," "being sick and tired," or "hitting rock bottom."

Being Ready

Most participants endorsed *being ready* for treatment and recovery in some way or other. Ted, a 51 year old heroin user who had attended several methadone clinics, was very emphatic: "You got to be ready to quit; if you're not ready you're wasting your time." Larry, a 30 year old marijuana user, described the notion of being ready by making an analogy with a footrace. If the runner is not ready to run, he will not win the race, but "if you're ready, it will work." Larry also offered some advice for treatment success:

> You got to be motivated for it to work; you got to be willing and open . . . Once you get into a mind state to be able to look in a mirror and say "OK" and open yourself up and look and say "OK, this is me, and I'm ready to change," then that's when you're ready, when you're able to look . . .

Participants also described readiness as having the courage to look at oneself and accept the need for change. For some readiness evoked openness, honesty, and truthfulnes. Karl, a 37 year old crack user, described this state of openness: "When I'm ready, and it's just like listening to all the positive things. When you listen to the positive things, everything else will work out."

Karl abused crack on-and-off for more than fifteen years. He had attended formal treatment three times in the past, as well as attended AA meetings. After his first interview, Karl expressed a desire to be interviewed multiple times. He hoped that talking frequently about his drug use problems would help him maintain his sobriety until the start of treatment. This is a strategy that he learned in AA which he was trying to apply in his current context. Talking about the problem whenever possible was a strategy employed by several participants. This talking about drug dependence with friends, relatives, and sometimes even an ethnographer, complemented a series of small actions and changes needed to achieve readiness: preparation. Mark, a 25 year old marijuana user, mentioned how his ethnographic interview became part of this process of preparation:

> It's all about preparation. You got to prepare yourself; this is part of my preparation . . . Talking to people like you and the case manager . . . This is my preparation because I don't want to smoke weed no more.

Talking openly about one's readiness to quit drugs is very different from just talking about drugs, as the 49 year old crack user Rick explained:

> Anytime you talk about it [using drugs] on a constant basis you're not ready to put it down. If you're constantly talking about it you're gonna pick [it] up . . . Your mind [is] already telling you to go pick up while you're talking about it because you're steady talking about it, and next thing you're gone to get some crack.

Rick was referred to the CIU by a local homeless shelter. He expressed the ambivalence he was experiencing regarding treatment because he honestly enjoyed smoking crack, although it was making him feel miserable. He questioned whether it was possible to deal with life's emotions and troubles without crack:

> No need to be putting me in no program because right now I'm not ready to get through using. I want to, but I'm not really ready, it sounds like a contradiction or whatever, but one part of my mind wants to get off them period, but the other part of it just enjoys it so much that I can't let it, I'm just not really ready to let it go, yet, all the way. I got mixed feelings about it, and then dealing with life without it.

Rick believed that his "spiritual part"–representing his relationship with God–was "ready," but that his decision-making-self was not ready, so he continued to smoke crack. He used the analogy of a person divided in two parts who needed to become whole again before quitting drugs:

> The part that's ready is the spiritual part of me . . . because I know I shouldn't do it. And I know God doesn't allow that, and the temple is his body, so where I go I take the holy spirit with me, which is the spirit of God, if I go smoke crack, so he's right there with me, but you know that should be a scary thing to me. But I still go smoke crack. The other part of me is the self part of me, my own decision to pick up or not to pick up.

While some participants described how readiness for treatment emerged slowly through preparation, such as talking to people about problems related to their drug use, other participants believed that readiness came abruptly, like a "switch that clicks on" indicating the urgent need for help, especially in circumstances of major breakdowns. Either way, they initially had to acknowledge they had a problem. For Alex, a 20 year old heroin user, this acknowledgment emerged when he realized he was living together with his "dope dealer" instead of living with his family in their middle class suburban home: "You have to admit that drugs have taken over your life, that it's gotten out of control, you have to admit that yourself . . . I have lost total control over it, and I need help."

Another dimension of *being ready* is determined by acknowledging the consequences of changing or not changing, as Leah, a 48 year old user of heroin and cocaine described:

> I would love to still be getting high everyday in my life, no doubt about it. I just can't suffer the consequences anymore. Going out doing shit that's illegal, going to jail, because I mean, that's the only way you're going to get high is do illegal stuff.

A broader definition of being ready for treatment specifies the intention (or desire) to stop using, and includes the consequences, as well as the strategies that will make treatment work. Matt, a 46 year old heroin user, suggested that by weighing the pros and cons of drug use, it is possible to recognize the negative consequences and conclude that quitting is the only option.

> Ready, fed up with the sickness, the abuse, the trouble you get into, hurting others, hurting yourself. When you're done with that and you want to give it up, you got to want to be off of this stuff. You got to weigh all the facts and look at things it's done to you, things it's causing around you. Destroying your life, destroying your family life.

Participants alluded to different strategies for attaining readiness throughout the process of treatment engagement and recovery. For instance, Beatrice, a 44 year old crack user, understood readiness as a work-in-progress: "You have to have tools to work with to keep you on the right track." Jason, a 45 year old crack user, associated strategies with the creation of a plan for stopping drug use. He also suggested that this plan would have to cover other aspects of life:

> I've got to come up with a plan for getting clean. You don't just quit doing drugs and say "OK," and then wait for your life to get better. Our lives are so messed up!

Almost 50% of all interviewees had at least two prior treatment experiences. For them readiness was perceived in the context of a prolonged process encompassing successes and failures, rather than a one time success. Putting it differently, further levels of readiness can fluctuate over time. For instance, Ted perceived himself as the inveterate "junkie" who had already experienced treatment in all types of facilities: "You're just going through the motions. OK, 'cause I've done it the right way before and I've done it the wrong way before." As another example, Jack, a 42 year old crack user, attended residential treatment more than seven different times during the last fifteen years. All the occasions that he remained clean from drugs occurred during a short period of time after treatment discharge: "I believe that I can change my life and turn it around . . . that's why it is important for me to get back into treatment. What am I missing, not grasping, and not doing?"

Participants with previous treatment experiences reasoned they needed a few previous treatment experiences before engaging in a serious attempt to stop using drugs. They believed that each previous treatment experience contributed to the current readiness to stop drugs. Initially they only wanted to control their drug use by taking a "time out" or because they were forced by family or the court system to go to treatment. Only after these initial experiences did they feel they were ready to commit to treatment.

Maturing Out

Several participants associated readiness for treatment with the number of years a person had already used drugs. From this perspective, long-time drug users frequently considered themselves much more receptive to quitting compared to beginners or to young users. Beatrice observed that "some have been there long enough to know it is time to quit, and some just getting started and ain't ready to quit." Other participants perceived readiness as a normal part of their life cycle–they were *maturing out* of addiction: "I've seen people do it, they just get older, more mature and get tired of it and just quit" [Matt, 46 year old heroin user]. Another group of participants related readiness with the normal life cycle because they linked it with specific situations or life events. Allan elaborated, "Something is going to have to happen that's going to be either traumatic or involve the law, or I'm going to have to hit rock bottom again" [Allan, 27 year old marijuana user].

When the narratives of younger participants (18-29) were contrasted to the narratives of older participants (older than 30), the connotations of maturing out were somewhat different. Younger participants, like Lilian, often understood maturing out of addiction as their rite of passage to a more fulfilling adulthood:

> You sort of have to snap back to reality and it's not . . . I can't get high my whole life! I can't do that and have a regular job, I can't do that and go to school (. . .) I'm [at] that step right now and I'm not even it's like, it's messing up my life. I'm quitting 'cause I mean I'm only 19! I want to do something, I want to go to school. I want to be normal!

Older participants were more inclined to describe maturing out as the natural endpoint in time after enduring many years of chronic drug abuse. For Louise, a 40 year old crack user, maturing out also represented the outgrowth of *being sick and tired* for a prolonged time:

> It's all about me . . . I'm tired I'm ready to get my life together. I'm getting older, not younger. I realized that it's the drugs that's tearing me apart my mind, my body, my health, my strength it was taking me down. I just want to have something for me and my grandkids before I die.

Younger participants understood readiness for treatment more in terms of a necessary condition that would allow the opportunity of building a future like having a normal life, a regular job, education, spouse, and children. Older participants discussed readiness more in terms of recovering some positive aspects of their lives that appeared buried by all the negative consequences of chronic drug abuse. In short, younger participants focused on the positive consequences they would gain with abstinence, while older participants focused on the negative consequences they had suffered with addiction.

The gradual aggravation of negative consequences, including being tired of the drug use lifestyle, was the most prevalent reason for seeking treatment. Nevertheless, a few participants indicated that certain positive consequences also led them to seek treatment. For instance, Karina, a 24 year old OxyContin® user, was raised in an environment where drug use was allowed inside the home. But when her twin babies were born she decided to keep them away from the drug-using lifestyle, and this positive occurrence influenced her perceived readiness for treatment.

Being Sick and Tired

Being sick and tired of addiction was a very common expression that participants linked to treatment readiness. Holly, a 64 year old crack user asserted: "If you're getting sick and tired of getting sick and tired then you're going start doing something, and that's what happened, I got sick and tired of being sick and tired, and I went into rehab." This experience of being sick and tired evokes a feeling of never-ending repetition, that is, a circular or spiral feeling leading nowhere: "I just got tired of doing the same thing day in and day out" [Jason, 45 year old crack user], "You get tired of beating your head up against the wall" [Ralph, 50 year old crack user].

Participants also mentioned how much they had enjoyed the thrills and excitement of the drug lifestyle. When the accumulation of negative consequences emerging from this lifestyle became overwhelming, they expressed this in terms of tiredness. As Lara, a 39 year old crack user explained:

> It's hard to explain, it's just a feeling I have inside that I'm tired, I don't want to do this anymore, I don't want to hurt my family. I don't want to feel bad about myself, I want to try to make up for some of the bad things that I've done in the past year and a half. I want to try to turn it around. Kind of, I don't need that type of excitement in

> my life anymore. Whatever excitement and thrills I was looking for through that drug use, I don't need that anymore.

It usually took participants several years of chronic drug use before they became sick and tired of it all. Older participants (over 30 years) usually had a longer drug use history, and probably for this reason they referred to being sick and tired more often than the younger participants. In some situations the condition of being sick and tired is not associated with prolonged use or the addict lifestyle. It can be related to excessive use, as in the case of drug overdose:

> I did that for just about a solid year. And I got tired of it. I didn't want to be caught up in that no more. Because I almost od'd cause I got over dosed . . . the OxyContin® and the painkillers mix and some alcohol thins your blood too thin and it's hard on your heart at my age. [Matt, 46 year old heroin user]

Participants described how they became sick and tired because of the symptoms and physical reactions related to drug use, for instance, withdrawal symptoms:

> I was sick of getting sick and having to have it, it got to a point to where I couldn't even function, I mean just literally body ache, ill, just like heroin, until one day I just didn't have anything, couldn't find anything, I was just sick of being sick. [Martha, 29 year old crack user]

Hitting Rock Bottom

According to our participants, readiness is about commitment. They claimed that drug users had to be willing to do whatever it takes to quit; they had to be 100% committed, in the same ways they would be to buy the drug. These participants also believed that "some people won't hit that state of mind until they absolutely hit rock bottom" [Alex, 20 year old heroin user]. This expression *hitting rock bottom* is widely used among drug users, even more by those who previously participated in self-help groups (e.g., AA, NA). It evokes a downward movement as a preceding condition for readiness, while treatment engagement is generally perceived as a succeeding upward movement from rock bottom:

> I was hitting rock bottom . . . Yea, 'cause I had nothing, only my clothes that's all that I had, lost everything that I had. I hit rock bottom

> and now I got to climb up. Now I got to accumulate all of the stuff that I used to have, and get a good job and work from there. Take one day at a time. [Brian, 22 year old heroin user]

Some participants declared that participating in self-help groups often provided comfort and reassurance about climbing up from rock bottom. By listening to the stories of other addicts who hit rock bottom, but who climbed up again, they learned that it is possible to be hopeful. Other participants regarded this downward movement as less absolute because as they commented: "people have different bottoms" [Beatrice, 44 year old crack user].

The notion of having different bottom points is illustrated by the two following participants. Leah, 48 years old, decided to go to treatment because she was tired of injecting heroin and cocaine, and of the drug addict lifestyle she maintained, including prostitution, stealing, conning, lying, and other illegal activities in which she was involved. For Leah, the possibility of eventually working in a "regular job" sounded much better. In contrast, Beatrice still loved the feeling she experienced from smoking crack. She worked as a nurse's aid and she could buy crack with her salary. Beatrice was proud that she never had any involvement with Children Services. She believed she always took good care of her kids, despite being addicted to crack. Beatrice decided to quit buying crack with the money that she planned to spend on her kids. She claimed that she would never become homeless or turn to prostitution in exchange for crack. Beatrice finally hit rock bottom when she was caught stealing shoes after she had spent all her money on crack, because she wanted to give the shoes to her kids.

Participants experienced hitting rock bottom in a variety of ways. Metaphorically speaking, Lilian, a 19 year old heroin user, associated it with the experience of walking on a straight line followed by a sudden fall:

> You don't even see it coming . . . It's like little decisions here and there, and then all of a sudden you are at the bottom, and you don't understand how you got there, you don't get it! It's really hard sometimes for people to understand how it happened, because it does, it goes real quick.

Karl described the rock bottom experience as if experiencing a slow downward movement:

> How can you constantly have better dreams but then wake up the next day and still do the 'worser' of life? And that's why it takes

> time to get to the point to where you're actually tired. It's not just going to happen to you overnight. You have to really and truly hit rock bottom.

Apparently Karl combined the repetitive feeling of being sick and tired with the gradual acceptance that he ended up hitting rock bottom. For him, hitting rock bottom was a gradual process that developed very slowly.

According to some participants, facing death or fear of dying was the ultimate rock bottom, the *bottoming out* consequence that led them to seek treatment: "When it boils down you can choose life or you can choose death" [Julia, 35 year old crack user]; "the life I had was pretty much the mirror image of death . . . so I was sick and tired of it" [Steve, 42 year old crack user]; "you've got a couple of choices or you could die, or you could die, or you could die" [Erasmus, 46 year old crack user]; "I am ready to get some help . . . that's why you stop it . . . before it gets towards the end" [Karl, 37 year old crack user]. In this context, readiness for change represented the only possible alternative to more dire consequences. Associating bottoming out with death was more likely to be made by those participants who had multiple treatment episodes or more experience in Alcoholics Anonymous or Narcotic Anonymous.

DISCUSSION

Inspired by Michael Agar's (1985) work contrasting folk and professional models of drug use, this paper describes the various ways drug users expressed readiness for treatment immediately after substance abuse treatment assessment and referral. Although participants told stories that reflected some elements of the professional models of readiness, these stories were largely influenced by AA's folk model.

Limitations

For a variety of reasons, up to 60% of those individuals who receive a CIU substance abuse treatment referral do not engage in treatment. Those participants who did not engage in treatment (within 90 days of the assessment) probably did not maintain the same levels of readiness manifested during the initial ethnographic interview. Some responses may have also been influenced by the study intervention (case management or motivational interviewing) in which interviewees participated.

Given the small sample size of participants who had used particular drugs, it is not possible to describe the relationship of folk or professional models with respect to primary drug. Because in North America most treatment programs incorporate 12 step principles or variations of this model (Laudet, 2003), it is difficult to tease out how much the dominant folk model of readiness reflected intensity of AA participation, rather than treatment program involvement.

Professional Models

When participants described what it meant to be ready for treatment, they did not allude directly to professional models of readiness. For instance, they did not talk in terms of *problem recognition* or *preparation stage*. However, certain scientific concepts related to the professional models, like problem recognition or preparation stage received a lay interpretation. But using their own words, participants explained that recognizing they had a problem with drugs was a very important first step for readiness. Participants also insisted on the intentional nature of *being ready* which they understood as a process of inner transformation, because readiness demanded being truthful, honest, and open with oneself.

Other lay interpretations indicated different strategies for being ready, like the work-in-progress or the need for creating a plan. Participants also interpreted readiness in ways that contradicted the professional models because they did not describe readiness in terms of a sequence of stages, as defined in the *transtheoretical model,* or in the successive phases of the *integrative recovery model.* Participants demonstrated a much more pragmatic attitude by giving more relevance to *what* and *how* readiness for change can happen, instead of *when*, or in which sequence it happens. Participants seemed to give more credence that readiness fluctuates over time, instead of occurring in a specific sequence.

Participants also talked about being ready as a consequence of having *matured out* of the drug-using lifestyle. This concept was first defined by Charles Winick after investigating nation-wide records of the Federal Bureau of Narcotics (1962). It is a process by which people stop using drugs as the problems for which they originally began using become less salient and less urgent. This phenomenon is associated with the normal maturational process in the life cycle of the drug user. It can also be a reflection of the number of years the person is addicted, because of the cycle of the addiction itself.

Clinical impressions concerning age-related changes indicate that older drug users are more likely to either mature out of their addiction without treatment or to bottom out in their addiction and seek treatment (De Leon, Melnick, & Hawke, 2000). Study participants amplified these ideas because they believed that many individuals contemplating treatment were also experiencing maturing out. They also believed that maturing out affected drug users of all ages, independent of the maturational process.

AA's Folk Model of Readiness

AA's folk model of readiness emerged when participants told stories composed of experiences of *being sick and tired* or *hitting rock bottom.* Some stories suggested that sick and tired and rock bottom were interrelated. It is the repetitive circular feeling of being sick and tired that fomented the more downward feeling of hitting rock bottom. Other stories provided a different focus because sick and tired focused on the drug-using lifestyle and the symptoms (e.g., withdrawal), while reaching rock bottom focused more on broader social consequences, like unemployment, homelessness, and criminal justice involvement.

Hitting rock bottom plays an important role in the process of recovery, particularly from alcoholism (Bateson, 1971; Denzin, 1995). It is traditionally associated with step one of AA's 12 step model implying that everyone must first hit bottom before admitting a state of surrender: "We admitted we were powerless over alcohol–that our lives had become unmanageable" (Alcoholics Anonymous, 1953). Conversely, the AA philosophy explains failures by asserting that those individuals who relapsed have not yet hit bottom. However, this image of hitting rock bottom is not absolute because many participants believed that "people have different bottoms."

Beyond framing one's experience in terms of the language of being sick and tired or hitting rock bottom, AA represents a pragmatically structured set of experiences that put the person's desire for change into action. Following this approach, a person goes to meetings, practices the twelve steps, and talks with his/her sponsor. These small actions repeated over and over again, gradually substitute for the urge to use drugs. Constant repetition exemplified by the endless opportunities to talk about one's addiction, or to hear other people talk about theirs, is essential for the success of this model of mutual help (Denzin, 1995). Many participants believed that they benefited from telling their stories over and over again, even when they told these stories outside the context of AA meetings.

The immediacy of the language learned through AA is much closer to the subjective experience of participants and to the stories they tell, than the *why* explanations communicated by most professional models. This difference in language was pointed out by some participants in the following way: Those individuals who are *working the steps* of AA *one day at a time* have more opportunities to express the "here and now" of what they are experiencing, while in many treatment settings, they are largely expected to discover only *why* they have been using drugs, which is not a focus for AA. In sum, the *what* and *how* seems much closer to one's subjective experience, than the rationalizations of *why*.

Such attitudes, of continuously *working the steps* and storytelling, are also reflected in AA's ritual end of meeting slogan: "Keep coming back, it works if you work it." This slogan evokes the idea that readiness will be maintained only if perpetually renewed one day at a time, and every day. In this context, slips and relapses are also acceptable. Since readiness is perceived to fluctuate, when individuals increase their level of readiness and seek help again, they will have another chance: "if you work it, it will work."

In short, AA's folk model reflects the subjective experience of participants through the language of storytelling. According to Rappaport (1993), stories order experience, give coherence and meaning to events, and provide a sense of history and future. Telling and listening to personal stories can be a mediating device for self-understanding, as well as a cultural vehicle for change (Cain, 1991; Davis & Jansen, 1998). Beyond the content of what was being told, it is the ways the stories were being told that allowed participants to reinterpret their personal experience, and in this case, to reinterpret their readiness for treatment.

Folk and Professional Models Together

Participants often interpreted readiness in terms that combined professional models (*being ready* and *maturing out*) and AA's folk model (*being sick and tired* and *hitting rock bottom*). For instance, sometimes the feeling of being sick and tired of drug use triggered the process of maturing out. Some participants commented that all the chances they had to tell their stories constituted the preparation stage for entering treatment.

Elements of folk and professional models were also combined by the "If you're ready it will work" attitude expressed by most participants. Such a mind-set may keep individuals in the pre-contemplative stage of change because it implies the need for being sincerely ready before any change can happen (Carlson, 2006; Carlson, Siegal, Falck, & Wang, 1996). From another standpoint, this attitude works as a self-fulfilling prophecy, since it accommodates the possibility of failure. Those individuals who relapsed did so because they were not ready. But considering AA's folk model, if they are ready the next time they seek help, they have another chance that treatment will work.

Folk and professional models of readiness can also be compared to a spiral. Metaphorically speaking, the expression *being sick and tired of being sick and tired* provides a feeling of never-ending repetition that may resemble a spiral. Surprisingly, the professional model of *stages of change* is also represented by a spiral (Prochaska et al., 1992). People start at the bottom of the spiral and then move through the stages in order, but often relapse to an earlier stage. People may cycle and recycle through the stages before reaching the top of the spiral and achieving successful long-term behavior change. Many participants moved one step beyond this spiral analogy. They believed that previous slips, relapses, and failed treatment episodes were contributing to the readiness of engaging in treatment again.

Recommendations

Participants proposed two main recommendations associated with the concept of being ready. First, they advocated that all those individuals manifesting readiness need to be accepted into treatment immediately. They were concerned with the likelihood of relapse if the waiting period was too long. Other researchers have already suggested that treatment readiness can be a transient state that must be exploited immediately if treatment engagement is to occur (Festinger, Lamb, Kountz, Kirby, & Marlowe, 1995). Our findings suggest that levels of readiness fluctuate over time; that readiness probably "waxes and wanes." Therefore, readiness may require constant stimulation, or may be attained only one day at a time.

Second, some participants advocated the creation of interventions for reaching individuals before they hit rock bottom. According to Bill Wilson, the co-founder of AA, people do not have to hit every possible bottom before they surrender (Alcoholics Anonymous, 1967). However, participants pointed out that most times treatment is readily available only for those drug users who have already hit rock bottom. They pointed out that those individuals who are unemployed, homeless, or in prison have more chances of receiving assistance from the State to cover their treatment, while those individuals who are still working and have health insurance cannot afford to go to treatment because most health insurance plans do not provide substance abuse treatment coverage.

In sum, participants' interpretations of treatment readiness were influenced by both folk and professional models. However, the dominant AA folk model provided the possibility of alternative understandings by allowing participants tell their particular stories. Variability and specificity was always present, even if participants framed their stories as *being sick and tired* and *hitting rock bottom*. It becomes evident that these repeated opportunities to tell one's personal story were the most significant aspect of AA's folk model. It is the telling of one's story, over and over again, that contributes to the process of self-understanding, and consequently, of treatment readiness.

Most research to date has emphasized the association between high levels of readiness and successful treatment outcomes (Joe et al., 1998: De Leon et al., 2001). Analysis of the interviews with participants in the Reducing Barriers project supports the need for creating and delivering interventions that enhance and sustain readiness to seek treatment. We also need to gain a better understanding of how to sustain drug users' readiness for treatment for longer periods of time.

REFERENCES

Agar, M. H. (1985). Folks and professionals: Different models for the interpretation of drug use. *The International Journal of the Addictions, 20*(1). 173-182.

Alcoholics-Anonymous. (1953). *Twelve Steps and Twelve Traditions*. New York: Alcoholics Anonymous World Services Inc.

Alcoholics-Anonymous. (1967). *As Bill sees it: The AA way of life. Selected writings of AA's cofounder*. New York: Alcoholics Anonymous World Services Inc.

Alcoholics-Anonymous. (1976). *Alcoholics Anonymous*. New York: Alcoholics Anonymous World Services Inc.

American Society of Addiction Medicine. (2001). *Patient placement criteria for the treatment of substance-related disorders*. (second ed.). Chevy Chase, MD: American Society of Addiction Medicine.

Anglin, M. D., Hser, Y., & Grella, C. E. (1997). Drug addiction and treatment careers among clients in the drug abuse treatment outcome study (DATOS). *Psychology of Addictive Behaviors, 11*(4), 308-323. doi:10.1037/0893-164X.11.4.308

Bateson, G. (1971). The cybernetics of "self": A theory of alcoholism. *Psychiatry, 34*, 1-18.

Battjes, R. J., Onken, L. S., & Delany, P. J. (1999). Drug abuse treatment entry and engagement: Report of a meeting on treatment readiness. *Journal of Clinical Psychology, 55*(5), 643-657. doi:10.1002/(SICI)1097-4679(199905)55:5<643::AID-JCLP11>3.0.CO;2-S

Broome, K. M., Knight, K., Hiller, M., & Simpson, D. D. (1997). Peer, pressure and motivational issues on drug treatment process and recidivism for probationers. *Journal of Clinical Psychology, 53*, 387-397. doi:10.1002/(SICI)1097-4679(199706)53:4<387::AID-JCLP12>3.0.CO;2-C

Cain, C. (1991). Personal stories: Identity acquisition and self-understanding in Alcoholics Anonymous. *Ethos, 19*(2), 210-253. doi:10.1525/eth.1991.19.2.02a00040 (2)

Carlson, R. G. (2006). Ethnography: Anthropological and Cross-Cultural Factors. In: W. Miller, & K. Carroll (Eds.), *Rethinking Substance Abuse: What Science Shows and What We Should Do About It.* New York: Guilford Publications.

Carlson, R. G., Siegal, H. A., Falck, R. S., & Wang, J. (1996 manuscript). *Exploring the cultural logic of addiction: Drug abuse treatment and engagement in the Midwest.* Invited Paper presented at Treatment Readiness: factors influencing entry and engagement. Organized by Robert Battjess. National Institute on Drug Abuse. Rockville, Maryland, December 3-4.

Chappel, J. N., & DuPont, R. L. (1999). Twelve-step and mutual help programs for addictive disorders. *Psychiatric Clinics of North America, 22*(2), 425-446. doi:10.1016/S0193-953X(05)70085-X

Davis, D. R., & Jansen, G. G. (1998). Making meaning of Alcoholics Anonymous for social workers: Myths, metaphors, and realities. *Social Work, 43*(2), 169-182.

De Leon, G. (1996). Integrative recovery: A stage paradigm. *Substance Abuse, 17*(1), 51-63.

De Leon, G., Melnick, G., & Hawke, J. (2000). The motivation readiness factor in drug treatment: Implications for research and policy. *Advances in Medical Sociology, 7*, 103-129.

De Leon, G., Melnick, G., & Tims, F. (2001). The role of motivation and readiness in treatment and recovery. In: F. M. Tims, C. G. Leukefeld, & J. J. Platt (Eds.), *Relapse and Recovery in Addictions* (pp. 142-171). New Haven, CT: Yale University Press.

Denzin, N. K. (1995). Alcoholic Society: Addiction and Recovery of the Self. New Brunswick, New Jersey: Transaction Publishers.

DiClemente, C. (1999). Motivation for change: Implications for substance abuse treatment. *Psychological Science, 10*(3), 209-213. doi:10.1111/1467-9280.00137

DiClemente, C., & Prochaska, J. (1998). Toward a comprehensive transtheoretical model of change: Stages of change and addictive behaviors. In: W. R. Miller, & N. Heather (Eds.), *Treating Addictive Behaviors* (pp. 49-60). New York: Plenum Press.

DiClemente, C., Schlundt, D., & Gemmell, L. (2004). Readiness and stages of change in addiction treatment. *The American Journal on Addictions, 13*, 103-119. doi:10.1080/10550490490435777

Duroy, T. H., Schmidt, S. L., & Perry, P. D. (2003). Adolescents' and young adults perspectives on a continuum of care in a three year drug treatment program. *Journal of Drug Issues, 33*(4), 801-832.

Festinger, D. S., Lamb, R. J., Kountz, M. R., Kirby, K. C., & Marlowe, D. (1995). Pretreatment dropout as a function of treatment delay and client variables. *Addictive Behaviors, 20*(1), 111-115. doi:10.1016/0306-4603(94)00052-Z

Fielding, N. G., & Lee, R. M. (1998). *Computer Analysis and Qualitative Research.* Thousand Oaks, California: SAGE.

Fiorentine, R., & Hillhouse, M. P. (2000). Drug treatment and 12-step program participation. The additive effects of integrated recovery activities. *Journal of Substance Abuse Treatment, 18*, 65-74. doi:10.1016/S0740-5472(99)00020-3

Glaser, B. G., & Strauss, A. L. (1967). *The Discovery of Grounded Theory: Strategies for Qualitative Research.* Chicago, Illinois: Aldine Publication Company.

Hiller, M. L., Knight, K., Leukefeld, C., & Simpson, D. D. (2002). Motivation as a predictor of therapeutic engagement in mandated residential substance abuse treatment. *Criminal Justice Behavior, 29*, 56-75. doi:10.1177/0093854802029001004

Hser, Y. I., Anglin, M. D., Grella, C. E., Longshore, D., & Prendergast, M. L. (1997). Drug treatment careers: A conceptual framework and existing research findings. *Journal of Substance Abuse Treatment, 14*(6), 543-558. doi:10.1016/S0740-5472 (97)00016-0

Hubbard, R. L., Craddock, S. G., & Anderson, J. (2003). Overview of 5-year follow-up outcomes in the drug abuse treatment outcome studies (DATOS). *Journal of Drug Abuse Treatment, 25*(63), 125-134. doi:10.1016/S0740-5472(03)00130-2

Joe, G., Simpson, D., & Broome, K. (1998). Effects of readiness for drug abuse treatment on client retention and assessment of process. *Addiction, 93*(8), 1177-1190. doi:10.1046/j.1360-0443.1998.93811776.x

Joe, G. W., Simpson, D. D., & Broome, K. M. (1999). Retention and patient engagement models for different treatment modalities in DATOS. *Drug and Alcohol Dependence, 7*, 113-125. doi:10.1016/S0376-8716(99)00088-5

Koester, S., Anderson, K., & Hoffer, L. (1999). Active heroin injectors' perceptions and use of methadone maintenance treatment: Cynical performance or self-prescribed risk reduction? *Substance Use & Misuse, 34*(14), 2135-2153.

Laudet, A. B. (2003). Attitudes and beliefs about 12-step groups among addiction treatment clients and clinicians: Toward identifying obstacles to participation. *Substance Use & Misuse, 38*(14), 2017-2047. doi:10.1081/JA-120025124

Miller, W. R., Rollnick, S., & Conforti, K. (2002). *Motivational Interviewing: Preparing people for change* (second ed.). New York, N.Y.: Guilford Press.

Prendergast, M., Podus, D., Chang, S., & Urada, D. (2004). The effectivenes of drug abuse treatment: A meta-analysis of comparison group studies. *Drug and Alcohol Dependence, 67*, 53-72. doi:10.1016/S0376-8716(02)00014-5

Prochaska, J., DiClemente, C., & Norcross, J. (1992). In search of how people change: Applications to addictive behaviors. *American Psychologist, 47*, 1102-1114. doi:10.1037/0003-066X.47.9.1102

Rapp, R. C. (1997). The strengths perspective and persons with substance abuse problems. In: Saleebey, D. (Ed.), *The Strengths Perspective in Social Work Practice* (pp. 77-96). New York: Longman.

Rappaport, J. (1993). Narrative studies, personal stories, an identity transformation in the mutual help context. *The Journal of Applied Behavioral Science, 29*(2), 239- 256. doi:10.1177/0021886393292007

Reisinger, H. S., Bush, T., Colom, M. A., Agar, M., & Battjes, R. (2003). Navigation and engagement: How does one measure success? *Journal of Drug Issues, 33*(4), 777-800.

Richards, L. (1999). Using NVivo in Qualitative Research. Thousand Oaks: SAGE.

Rosengren, D. B., Downey, L., & Donovan, D. M. (2000). "I already stopped": Abstinence prior to treatment. *Addiction, 95*(1), 65-76. doi:10.1046/j.1360-0443.2000.951657.x

Sia, T., Dansereau, D., & Czuchry, M. (2000). Treatment readiness training and probationers' evaluation of substance abuse treatment in a criminal justice setting. *Journal of Substance Abuse Treatment, 19*, 459-467. doi:10.1016/S0740-5472 (00) 00139-2

Simpson, D. D. (2004). A conceptual framework for drug treatment process and outcomes. *Journal of Substance Abuse Treatment, 27*, 99-121. doi:10.1016/j.jsat.2004.06.001

Simpson, D. D. (2001). Modeling treatment process and outcomes. *Addiction, 96*, 207-211. doi:10.1046/j.1360-0443.2001.9622073.x

Simpson, D. D., & Joe, G. W. (1993). Motivation as a predictor of early dropout from drug abuse treatment. *Psychotherapy, 30*, 357-368.

Simpson, D. D., Joe, G. W., Dansereau, D. F., & Chatham, L. R. (1997). Strategies for improving methadone treatment process and outcomes. *Journal of Drug Issues, 27*(2), 239-260.

Simpson, D. D., Joe, G.W., Rowan-Szal, G., & Greener, J. (1995). Client engagement and change during drug abuse treatment. *Journal of Substance Abuse, 7*, 117-134. doi:10.1016/0899-3289(95)90309-7

Strauss, A., & Corbin, J. (1998). *Basics of Qualitative Research: Techniques and Procedures for Developing Grounded Theory*. Thousand Oaks, California: SAGE.

Swora, M. G. (2001). Commemoration and the healing of memories in Alcoholics Anonymous. *Ethos, 29*(1), 58-77. doi:10.1525/eth.2001.29.1.58

Winick, C. (1962). Maturing out of narcotic addiction. *Bulletin of Narcotics, 14*, 1-7.

doi:10.1300/J233v06n02_03

Response of Native American Clients to Three Treatment Methods for Alcohol Dependence

Michael Villanueva, PhD
J. Scott Tonigan, PhD
William R. Miller, PhD

SUMMARY. *Objective*: It is well-documented that American Indians suffer disproportionately high rates of alcohol use disorders as well as correspondingly high rates of alcohol based mortality, health, and social problems. Despite these health disparities, anecdotal evidence continues to guide alcohol treatment approaches in Indian Country, in part due to a dearth of clinical trials with Native Americans. Project MATCH, a multisite clinical trial, included 25 Native Americans (1.4% of the total sample) who were randomized to three psychosocial treatments. Based on cultural compatibility, our *a priori* hypothesis was that Native Americans in Motivational Enhancement Therapy (MET) would fare better than those assigned either to Cognitive Behavioral Therapy (CBT) or to Twelve-step Facilitation (TSF).

Michael Villanueva, J. Scott Tonigan, and William R. Miller are affiliated with Center on Alcoholism, Substance Abuse and Addictions (CASAA), The University of New Mexico, 2650 Alamo SE, Albuquerque, NM 87106.

Address correspondence to: Michael Villanueva, PhD, 2650 Alamo SE, Albuquerque, NM 87106 (E-mail: michaelv@unm.edu).

Preparation of this article was supported in part by grants K23-DA00506 from the National Institute on Drug Abuse, and grants K05-AA00133, K02-AA00326-05, and U10-AA08435 from the National Institute on Alcohol Abuse and Alcoholism.

[Haworth co-indexing entry note]: "Response of Native American Clients to Three Treatment Methods for Alcohol Dependence." Villanueva, Michael, J. Scott Tonigan, and William R. Miller. Co-published simultaneously in *Journal of Ethnicity in Substance Abuse* (The Haworth Press, Inc.) Vol. 6, No. 2, 2007, pp. 41-48; and: *21st Century Research on Drugs and Ethnicity: Studies Supported by the National Institute on Drug Abuse* (ed: Peter L. Myers) The Haworth Press, 2007, pp. 41-48. Single or multiple copies of this article are available for a fee from The Haworth Document Delivery Service [1-800-HAWORTH, 9:00 a.m. - 5:00 p.m. (EST). E-mail address: docdelivery@haworthpress.com].

Available online at http://jesa.haworthpress.com

doi:10.1300/J233v06n02_04

Method: Of 25 Native Americans in Project MATCH, 23 (92%) were interviewed at all six assessment points. Four ANOCOVA's were computed to investigate possible differential treatment response.

Results: Despite a small sample, Native Americans assigned to MET reported significantly less drinking intensity relative to those assigned to CBT or TSF, with the highest proportion of abstinent days and lowest drinking intensity at both proximal and distal follow-ups.

Conclusions: These findings suggest a differentially better response to MET than to TSF or to CBT among Native Americans with alcohol dependence. Although this is, to date, the largest randomized trial of treatments for alcohol dependence in Native Americans, the findings require replication. doi:10.1300/J233v06n02_04

KEYWORDS. Native American, treatment, project match, MET, motivational interviewing, 12-Step

INTRODUCTION

Although various authors (Mail, Heurtin-Roberts, Martin, & Howard, 2002; French, 2000; King, Beals, Manson, & Trimble, 1992; Young, 1988) and different federal agencies such as IHS (Indian Health Service, 1977; 1999), NIDA (2003), and NIAAA (Beauvais, 1998) state that American Indians suffer disproportionately high rates of substance use disorders, surprisingly little treatment outcome research has been devoted to this population. There is no substance abuse treatment method with well-documented efficacy for American Indians, and this lack would appear to be one of the nation's clearest unaddressed health disparities. Additionally, to date, few randomized clinical trials in the alcohol field have included a substantial number of Native Americans, and none have evaluated relative response of Native Americans to different treatment methods. The assertion that unique kinds of alcohol treatment are needed for Native Americans has relied upon loosely-based conceptual models (e.g., the construct of intergenerational transmission of trauma blended with Jungian theory; Duran, 1990; Duran & Duran, 1995).

The purpose of this study was to investigate Native American treatment responses within a large multi-site randomized clinical trial that compared three 12-week psychosocial treatments (Project MATCH Research Group, 1997a, 1997b, 1998a, 1998b). Only a few of the prospective matching effects were confirmed, and those effects were modest in size. No significant main effects for treatment were found across a year of follow-up on the primary dependent measures (Babor & Del Boca, 2003). We wondered whether the Native American participants would have a differential treatment response between MET, CBT, and TSF.

The *a priori* hypothesis was that the Native Americans in Motivational Enhancement Therapy (MET), would fare better than those assigned to Cognitive Behavioral Therapy (CBT; Kadden et al., 1992) or to Twelve-step Facilitation (TSF; Nowinski et al., 1992). The hypothesis was derived from the first author's participation in Native American Church ceremonies, sweat lodges, conversations with medicine people, and direct clinical work with American Indians. These cultural experiences suggested that the process by which Native religious leaders communicate and intervene resembles the client-centered style of motivational interviewing (Miller & Rollnick, 2002) much more than the directive style of CBT or TSF.

METHODS

Project MATCH participants were recruited at five outpatient treatment centers (N = 952) and six aftercare treatment centers (N = 774). Clients were interviewed at intake and treatment termination (12 weeks), and subsequently at 3, 6, 9, and 12 months after treatment (Connors et al., 1994).

Twenty-five Native American clients (1.4% of total sample) were randomized in the Project MATCH study, of which 23 (92%) were interviewed at all six assessment points. Most (n = 16) were recruited at outpatient sites, 12 of these in Albuquerque, and among aftercare sites, Seattle contributed 6 of the 9 Native American participants. The 25 Native American participants were evenly distributed across the three treatment groups: 9 in CBT, 8 in MET, and 8 in TSF.

The Form 90 interview (Miller, 1996) was administered at each assessment point to quantify the frequency and intensity of drinking. The Form 90 uses a hybrid of timeline and grid averaging methods, and has demonstrated reliability in assessing both alcohol (Tonigan et al., 1996) and other drug use in clinical populations (Westerberg et al., 1999). Consistent with Project MATCH analyses, two measures of drinking were used in this study: percent days abstinent (PDA), and average drinks per drinking day (DDD), both of which were transformed prior to analyses (PDA: arcsine; DDD: square root).

To compare the Native American sample with the larger MATCH sample, we examined ten baseline measures including the two dependent variables. These included measures of motivation for change, severity of alcohol problems (Miller, Tonigan, & Longabaugh, R., 1995) and dependence using the ADS and the number of days of AA attendance in the prior 90 days (obtained from Form 90).

RESULTS

Table 1 displays the pretreatment characteristics of the 25 Native American clients in Project MATCH, and as a reference point these characteristics are compared with the larger non-Hispanic White Project MATCH clients. As a group, Native Americans were younger ($p < .02$) and reported substantially more abstinent days ($p < .004$) prior to treatment relative to the non-Hispanic White clients. Native American and non-Hispanic White clients, however, were similar on years of education, drinks per drinking day (alcohol intensity), social function impairment, readiness for change, and extent of alcohol related consequences.

Four ANOCOVAs were computed to investigate the predicted differential treatment response among Native Americans in Project MATCH. The between-subject factor was treatment group (3 levels), with pretreatment values of the dependent measure and MATCH study arm (outpatient and aftercare) included as covariates. The two dependent measures were proportion abstinent days and drinks per drinking day, which were

TABLE 1. Pre-Treatment Characteristics of Native American Clients

Intake Variable	Native Americans	Whites	p
Age in years	35.64 (9.20)	41.04 (11.17)	.02
Years education	13.16 (1.37)	13.44 (2.15)	.52
% Female	28% (7)	24% (334)	.84
% Never married	36% (9)	22% (303)	.71
Motivation for change	10.65 (1.45)	10.81 (1.69)	.65
Alcohol-related problems	55.70 (19.73)	51.88 (23.16)	.46
Alcohol dependence	34.06 (8.91)	36.46 (10.72)	.27
AA prior 90-days	.02 (.03)	.04 (.12)	.27
% Days abstinent	.73 (.39)	.50 (.40)	.004
Drinks per drinking day	3.88 (1.0)	3.87 (1.16)	.96

evaluated both at proximal (months 1-6 post-treatment) and distal follow-up (post-treatment months 7-12. Table 2 shows the means and SD's by treatment group for these four drinking measures.

As predicted Native Americans assigned to MET reported the highest proportion of abstinent days and lowest drinking intensity at both proximal and distal follow-ups. Despite low statistical power, one of these four contrasts was significant in the predicted direction: Native Americans assigned to MET reported significantly less drinking intensity at distal follow-up relative to Native Americans assigned to CBT or TSF. Pairwise contrasts indicated that there were no mean differences in proportion abstinent days and drinks per drinking day between Native Americans assigned to TSF and CBT.

Post hoc analyses were conducted to determine whether the differential treatment response could be explained by between-group differences in treatment compliance, engagement, and or satisfaction. Shown in Table 3 are selected measures of these constructs. No mean between-group differences were observed on these measures.

TABLE 2. Native American Treatment Response in Project MATCH (N = 23)

	Proximal Follow-up Months 4-9		Distal Follow-up Months 10-15	
	PDA	DDD	PDA	DDD
CBT (n = 7)	1.23 (.32)	2.19 (1.85)	1.18 (.41)	1.86 (1.74)
MET (n = 8)	1.44 (.18)	1.18 (1.49)	1.48 (.13)	.69 (.87)
TSF (n = 8)	1.13 (.39)	2.21 (1.24)	1.02 (.41)	2.41 (.79)
F statistic (df = 2, 22)	.62, p < .55	2.49, p < .11	1.70, p < .21	3.96, p < .04

TABLE 3. Native American Treatment Compliance, Engagement, and Satisfaction

	CBT	MET	TSF	p
Proportion therapy attended	.66	.72	.61	.85
Therapeutic bond	71.62	70.00	70.71	.93
Agreement with therapy tasks	69.88	72.71	74.00	.61
Agreement with therapy goals	71.00	73.14	73.57	.79
Satisfaction with MATCH treatment	7.38	9.29	6.83	.28

DISCUSSION

A clear limitation of this report is the small sample size and thus low power to detect between-treatment differences. Nevertheless, to this date, twenty-five is the largest randomized trial to date for any alcohol treatment method with Native Americans. In this context, the observed differences in treatment outcome are notable. Given the low power, we are less confident where our findings suggest no significant differences. Other contrasts while not significant indicated a modest effect favoring MET. Where we found the predicted effect, it was large, accounting for 33% of the variance.

It is also noteworthy that the outcome difference emerged on the drinking intensity measure (drinks per drinking day, DDD), rather than on the abstinence variable (percent days abstinent, PDA). As with other indigenous groups, Native Americans tend to abstain more frequently relative to the majority population (Daugherty et al., 2002), a difference that was evident at baseline in this study sample. For populations with an already higher rate of abstinence (PDA), the principal benefits of treatment may be reflected in impact on drinking intensity rather than frequency, and may be missed by focusing on abstinence measures (cf. Miller et al., 2001).

Although our findings suggest a differentially better response to MET than to TSF or CBT among Native Americans with alcohol dependence, Native Americans were no less engaged in TSF or CBT treatment. Obvious mechanisms of change were not supported: No between-treatment differences were found for therapeutic alliance, therapy sessions attended, or overall satisfaction with treatment. In sum, we found no evidence that Native American clients differentially rejected either a TSF or CBT approach, they simply yielded less favorable results when compared with MET. Future research involving quantitative or qualitative methodology with Native Americans should examine what factors, if any, explain treatment engagement.

The enduringly high rates of alcohol abuse among Native Americans suggest that current interventions have at best minimal impact. Few treatment methods have been tested and no evidence-based treatments have been systematically implemented. That is, very little of what works with the more general population has been offered to and tested with Native Americans. As an evidence-based treatment MET seems one sensible component in developing effective interventions for an understudied and underserved population.

REFERENCES

Babor, T. F., & Del Boca, F. K. (Eds.) (2003). Treatment matching in alcoholism. Cambridge, UK: Cambridge University Press.

Beauvais, F. (1998). American Indians and alcohol [Electronic version]. In Alcohol health & research world: Vol. 22. Alcohol use among special populations (pp. 253-259). Bethesda, MD: National Institute on Alcohol Abuse and Alcoholism. Retrieved September 30, 2005, from http://www.niaaa.nih.gov/publication/arh22-4/253.pdf

Behavioral Coping Skills Therapy Manual: A clinical research guide for therapists treating individuals with alcohol abuse and dependence. Rockville, MD: National Institute on Alcohol Abuse and Alcoholism.

Connors, G. J., Allen, J., Cooney, N. L., DiClemente, C. C., Tonigan, J. S., & Anton, R. (1994). Assessment issues and strategies in alcoholism treatment matching research. *Journal of Studies on Alcohol*, Supplement, *12*, 92-100.

Daugherty, M., Love, C. T., James, W. H., & Miller, W. R. (2002). Substance abuse among displaced and indigenous peoples. In W. R. Miller, & C. Weisner (Eds.). Changing substance abuse through health and social systems (pp. 225-239). New York: Kluwer/Plenum.

Duran, E. Transforming the Soul Wound. (1980) Berkeley: Folklore Press.

Duran, E., and Duran, B. Native American Postcolonial Psychology. (1985). Albany: SUNY Books, 1995.

French, L. A. (2000). Addictions and Native Americans. Westport, CT: Praeger.

Indian Health Service, Office of Public Health, Program Statistics Team. (1999). Trends in Indian health: 1998-99. Rockville, MD: U.S. Department of Health and Human Services.

Indian Health Service Alcoholism: A high priority health problem. (1997). (DHEW Publication No. HAS 77-1001). Washington, DC: U.S. Government Printing Office.

Kadden, R., Carroll, K., Donovan, D., Cooney, N., Monti, P., Abrams, D., Litt, M., & Hester, R. (2202). Cognitive-behavioral coping skills therapy manual: A clinical research guide for therapists treating individuals with alcohol abuse and dependence. Rockville, MD: National Institute on Alcohol Abuse and Alcoholism.

King, J., Beals, J., Manson, S. M., & Trimble, J. E. (1992). A structural equation model of factors related to substance use among American Indian adolescents. *Drugs and Society, 6*, 253-268.

Mail, P. D., Heurtin-Roberts, S., Martin, S. E., & Howard, J. (Eds.) (2002). Alcohol use among American Indians: Multiple perspectives on a complex problem (NIAAA Research Monograph No. 37). Bethesda, MD: National Institutes of Health. National Institute on Alcohol Abuse and Alcoholism.

Miller, W. R., Tonigan, J. S., & Longabaugh, R. (1995). The Drinker Inventory of Consequences (DrInC): An instrument for assessing adverse consequences of alcohol abuse. Test Manual, (Volume 4, Project MATCH Monograph series). Rockville MD: National Institute on Alcohol Abuse and Alcoholism.

Miller, W. R. Manual for Form 90: A structured assessment interview for drinking and related behaviors. (1996). (Volume 5, Project MATCH Monograph Series). Rockville, MD: National Institute on Alcohol Abuse and Alcoholism.

Miller, W. R., & Rollnick, S. (2002). Motivational interviewing: Preparing people for change. (2nd ed.). New York: Guilford Press.

Miller, W. R., Walters, S. T., & Bennett, M. E. (2001). How effective is alcoholism treatment? *Journal of Studies on Alcohol, 62*, 211-220.

Miller, W. R., Zweben, A., DiClemente, C. C., & Rychtarik, R. G. (1992). Motivational enhancement therapy manual: A clinical research guide for therapists treating individuals with alcohol abuse and dependence. Rockville, MD: National Institute on Alcohol Abuse and Alcoholism.

Nowinski, J., Baker, S., & Carroll, K. (1992). Twelve step facilitation therapy manual: A clinical research guide for therapists treating individuals with alcohol and dependence. Rockville, MD: National Institute on Alcohol Abuse and Alcoholism.

Tonigan, J. S., Miller, W. R., Juarez, P., & Villanueva, M. (2002). Utilization of AA by Hispanic and nonHispanic white clients receiving outpatient alcohol treatment. *Journal of Studies on Alcohol, 63*, 215-218.

Tonigan, J. S., Miller, W. R., & Brown, J. M. (1997). The reliability of Form 90: An instrument for assessing alcohol treatment outcome. *Journal of Studies on Alcohol, 58*, 358-364.

Westerberg, V. S., Miller, W. R., & Tonigan, J. S. (1999). Reliability of Form 90D: An instrument for quantifying drug use. *Substance Abuse, 19*, 179-189.

Young, T. J. (1988). Substance use and abuse among Native Americans. *Clinical Psychology Review, 8*, 125-138.

doi:10.1300/J233v06n02_04

Potential Risk Factors for Injecting Among Mexican American Non-Injecting Heroin Users

Avelardo Valdez, PhD
Alan Neaigus, PhD
Alice Cepeda, PhD

SUMMARY. This study examines potential risk factors for resuming and transitioning to injecting among a prospective cohort of 300 Mexican American non-injecting heroin users (NIUs) with distinct injecting histories (i.e., never vs. former injectors). Overall, findings revealed NIUs with an injecting history are more likely to be at greater risk for resuming

Avelardo Valdez is affiliated with University of Houston Office for Drug and Social Policy Research, Graduate College of Social Work, 237 Social Work Building, Houston, TX 77204-4013 (E-mail: avaldez2@uh.edu).

Alan Neaigus is affiliated with Institute for International Research on Youth at Risk, National Development and Research Institutes, Inc. & Department of Epidemiology, Mailman School of Public Health, Columbia University, 71 West 23rd Street, 8th Floor, New York City, NY 10010 (E-mail: alan.neaigus@ndri.org).

Alice Cepeda is affiliated with University of Houston, Office for Drug and Social Policy Research & Department of Sociology, 237 Social Work Building, Houston, TX 77204-4013 (E-mail: acepeda2@uh.edu).

The study was funded by the National Institutes of Health, National Institute on Drug Abuse (5 R01 DA13560) "Hispanic Heroin Users, Transitions to Injecting and HIV." The authors are grateful to John Alvarado, Richard Arcos, Ronald Cardenas and Pauline Solis for their work on this research study.

[Haworth co-indexing entry note]: "Potential Risk Factors for Injecting Among Mexican American Non-Injecting Heroin Users." Valdez, Avelardo, Alan Neaigus, and Alice Cepeda. Co-published simultaneously in *Journal of Ethnicity in Substance Abuse* (The Haworth Press, Inc.) Vol. 6, No. 2, 2007, pp. 49-73; and: *21st Century Research on Drugs and Ethnicity: Studies Supported by the National Institute on Drug Abuse* (ed: Peter L. Myers) The Haworth Press, 2007, pp. 49-73. Single or multiple copies of this article are available for a fee from The Haworth Document Delivery Service [1-800-HAWORTH, 9:00 a.m. - 5:00 p.m. (EST). E-mail address: docdelivery@haworthpress.com].

Available online at http://jesa.haworthpress.com

doi:10.1300/J233v06n02_05

injecting practices. Of interest, scoring high on acculturation decreased the risk of being a former injector. The present analysis supports previous research, and more importantly further identifies potential risk factors for injecting that are unique to the cultural and social context of the Mexican American community. doi:10.1300/J233v06n02_05

KEYWORDS. Non-injecting heroin, transitioning, injecting, Mexican Americans, acculturation

INTRODUCTION

Existing research has documented the numerous social and health consequences associated with injection drug use (IDU). For instance, injecting drug use has been associated with such health and social consequences as depression, suicidal ideation, incarceration, homelessness, Hepatitis C and of most consequential risk, HIV infection (Campbell et al., 2006; Chitwood et al., 2000; Des Jarlais et al., 1999; Havens, Sherman, Sapun, & Strathdee, 2006; Ochoa et al., 2005; Waldrop-Valverde, Ownby, & Kumar, 2005; Wood et al., 2005). Of the 33,132 cases of HIV infection reported in 2004, 12 percent of adults and adolescents were IDU associated (Centers for Disease Control and Prevention, 2004). Specifically, those most widely affected by IDU associated HIV infection are racial and ethnic minority populations in the United States. In 2004, injection drug use HIV infection accounted for 23 percent of cases among Hispanics and 11 percent among African Americans compared to 6 percent among white adults and adolescents. One of the important new precursors of injecting use is sniffing or smoking heroin, a popular route among young Hispanic polydrug users. This paper explains the potential risk factors associated with Mexican American non-injectors embedded in a community with a long history of injecting heroin use.

Rapid growth in non-injecting heroin use (NIU) has been reported in highly diverse cultural populations and social settings (Griffiths, Gossop, Powis, & Strang, 1992). This route of heroin administration has included different forms of non-injecting use, such as "sniffing," smoking in cigarettes mixed with tobacco/cannabis and *shabanging* ("spraying" a mix of heroin and water into nasal cavities using a syringe). Among IDUs the increase in this new route of administration (NIU) may represent a decline in the spread of HIV among this population. Conversely, NIU may be a precursor to initiating injecting drug use among those who have never injected or through resuming the practice among those who are former injectors. Thus, the increase in transitioning to injecting has serious consequences for the epidemic spread of HIV and other blood borne pathogens into a cohort of heroin users at risk of initiating or resuming injecting practices.

Recently, a growing body of research has focused on the risks associated with making a transition to injecting among NIUs (Chitwood et al., 2000; De La Fuente, Barrio, Royuela, & Bravo, 1997; Des Jarlais et al., 1999; Neaigus et al., 2006; Neaigus et al., 2001). Many of these studies have found that former injectors are at greater risk of making a transition to injecting compared to those who have never injected. Factors associated with these former injectors resuming and transitioning to injecting include such characteristics as being older male users, younger age of first heroin use, longer duration of use, and greater heroin dependence (Des Jarlais, Casriel, Friedman, & Rosenblum, 1992; Griffiths, Gossop, Powis, & Strang, 1994; Neaigus et al., 2001; van Ameijden, van den Hoek, & Coutinho, 1994). This same research has also identified having drug and sexual networks that include injectors as factors associated with transitioning. Furthermore, individual susceptibility such as personal traumatic events, fear of HIV/AIDS, not being afraid of needles and attitudes about injectors have been identified as important risks for making a transition (Bravo, Barrio, & de la Fuente, 2003; Casriel, Des Jarlais, Rodriguez, Friedman, & Khurl, 1990; Neaigus, Atillasoy, & Friedman, 1998; Sotheran, Goldsmith, Blasco, & Friedman, 1999).

Among Hispanics who comprise a heterogeneous population by ethnicity, generation, and region of residence only limited research has been done on non-injecting heroin users. Two existing studies have included sub-samples of Hispanic NIUs including Puerto Ricans in New York City (37%) and Puerto Ricans and Dominicans in Miami (26%) (Chitwood et al., 2000; Neaigus et al., 2001). These studies have begun to provide evidence of the association of ethnicity and injection history. For instance, in New York City, Puerto Rican NIUs were found to be overrepresented among frequent former injectors (Neaigus et al., 2001).

More recently, Mexican Americans in San Antonio have experienced an increase in non-injecting heroin use among a drug-using population that has consistently been characterized by high rates of drug injecting (ADAM, 1998; Desmond & Maddux, 1984; DUF, 1995, 1996). Before the 1990's, heroin use in this city as in others was almost exclusively by injection (Bullington, 1977; Casavantes, 1976; Desmond & Maddux, 1984; Moore, 1978). Much of this was associated with a distinct heroin subculture developed over the last fifty years in Southwestern cities and towns, including San Antonio among Mexican American users or *tecatos*. The term tecato tends to denote a chronic or career injecting heroin user with a criminal orientation and repeated involvement with the criminal justice system. As a result, in these communities tecatos have developed a distinct street identity that revolves around a "pachuco" lifestyle characterized by heroin use, criminality, incarceration, and distinct style of dress, tattoos, and street-based social networks.

In the early 90's there was evidence of changes in heroin and other drug markets that led to increases in the supply, accessibility, and purity of powdered "brown" heroin that could be used non-intravenously (Valdez & Sifaneck, 2004). Previously, Mexican black tar was the heroin most available in this market, however, it requires an extensive process in preparing it for non-intravenous use. This new form of administration has increased the relatively young Mexican American heroin using population that tended to reject the traditional tecato lifestyle or were adverse to injecting. This young NIU population is at risk for potentially transitioning or resume injecting especially within the context of a poly-drug using low-income Mexican American barrio. These behaviors increase the number of Mexican American and other Hispanic IDUs at risk of acquiring or transmitting HIV and other blood-borne diseases.

Among NIUs, those with a history of injecting, Hispanics have the highest risk of transitioning to injecting. Given this and the health consequences, there is a considerable need to assess the extent to which Hispanic NIUs with a history of being former injectors are at risk of resuming injecting practices. In this analyses, we examine potential risk factors for transitioning to injecting including heroin use patterns, drug and sex IDU partners, personal susceptibility, perceived susceptibility and attitudinal factors by injecting history differences (i.e., never vs. former). As importantly, we will examine how acculturation may be a distinct risk factor among Mexican Americans. These risk factors may be different from other populations of NIUs, given the long history and cultural context of heroin use among Mexican-Americans. Furthermore, of significance, is that by conducting the present research among Mexican Americans in San Antonio this analysis will enhance the generalizability of the study to a larger and more diverse population of Hispanic NIUs and newly transitioned injectors in the U.S.[1]

METHODS

Study Design

Data for this analysis are from baseline structured interviews with 300 Mexican American non-injecting heroin users in San Antonio. The purpose of the study is to investigate the incidence and risk factors for making a transition to injecting and the prevalence and incidence for infection with blood borne and sexually transmitted infections (HIV, HBV and HCV). The prospective cohort study design consists of a baseline interview with two follow up interviews at six-month intervals. The present analysis focuses on injecting history at baseline defined as either never injectors (those who have never injected) or former injectors (those who were former IDU, have not injected in prior 6 months and are currently non-injectors).

Study Setting

San Antonio, Texas is located 140 miles from the U.S.-Mexico border. The population in 2000 was estimated at 1.2 million, with approximately 60 percent of Mexican descent (U.S. Bureau of the Census, 2000). The city's economic base is centered on service and tourism, and is sustained by one of the lowest wage structures in the United States. Compared to other cities, San Antonio has one of the largest populations of "working poor." Poverty is largely a Mexican-American phenomenon with 28% of that group below the poverty line compared to 19% of the total general population (U.S. Bureau of the Census, 2001). Among cities with large U.S. Mexican populations, San Antonio is one of three cities with a relatively low percentage of foreign-born Hispanics.

Sampling

The study used an adaptive sampling methodology that included a combination of several techniques that the authors have employed in prior studies of non-treatment populations. It combines elements of a field-intensive outreach methodology with a targeted respondent-driven sampling design (Booth, Watters, & Chitwood, 1993; Broadhead, Heckathorn, Grund, Stern, & Anthony, 1995; Carlson, Wang, Siegal, Falck, & Guo, 1994; Clatts, Davis, & Atillasoy, 1995; Heckathorn, 1997; Kaplan & Korf, 1987; Sifaneck & Neaigus, 2001; TenHouten, 1992; Watters & Biernacki, 1989; Yin, Valdez, Mata, & Kaplan, 1996).

Respondents were recruited from the South and West sides of San Antonio. The study was delimited to these two areas of the city, which are the centers of commerce and residency for San Antonio's Mexican American population. The areas also have the highest concentration of poverty and delinquent behavior including street gang activity (Kasarda, 1993). During the summer of 2001, outreach specialist began social mapping of these two areas by identifying potential recruitment locations including heroin acquisition and using sites. During different times of the day and week, outreach specialist conducted regular sweeps of the neighborhoods identifying potential respondents, key informants and contacts. In conducting this initial fieldwork, outreach specialists were able to establish "an ethnographic presence" (Sifaneck & Neaigus, 2001) and maintain a high visibility within the targeted neighborhoods to help legitimize the project in the community. After this was accomplished, the outreach specialists began to make contacts with the non-injecting heroin users, gain their trust, and obtain access to their social networks. The primary goals of the field workers were to establish rapport with the NIUs, maintain non-judgmental attitudes, and to promote candid and accurate reporting by respondents during data collection and the interview process. During the course of recruiting respondents, outreach specialists documented observations in weekly fieldnotes that were discussed with the research team.

In addition to the field intensive outreach methodology, the study also recruited respondents using respondent-driven sampling. Incentives Sothers. Potential respondents were identified in the network section of the questionnaire in which respondents were asked to nominate individuals who are members of their heroin-using networks. Within this network, respondents were asked whether the network member is a current (last 30 days) non-injecting heroin user. First names or "street" names of these nominated individuals were collected. Respondents were then given a numbered coupon for each potentially eligible network member and asked to help recruit one or more identified members to take part in the study. In order to prevent biasing the sample with respondents who are referred by index subjects with large networks, the number of referrals per index subject was limited to two. Finally, the respondent-recruiter was rewarded if the potential respondent came to the research field office to be screened and was eligible for the study.

Inclusion criteria for entry into the baseline cohort were 16 years of age through 40 years for females and 35 years for males, self-report Mexican American ethnic background, no participation in formal drug treatment in 30 days prior, used noninjected heroin 30 days prior, and either never injected drugs or if a former injector, had not done so in the prior 6 months. Biological confirmation was conducted using the Varian On-Trak Test Stik (Mor) or hair toxicology tests to detect opiate use in the past 30 days. Trained paraprofessional outreach specialists conducted informal field screening of potential subjects in the field. For instance, since most IDUs inject in their arms, respondents were asked to show arms to staff for signs of fresh venipunctures or scarring. If staff observed evidence of recent injecting, subjects were rendered ineligible.

Study Variables

The face-to-face interviews were administered in private by trained interviewers using a modified version of the New York structured questionnaire. The interview was between 2-3 hours in duration and collected self-report data on demographic characteristics, drug use and injecting behavior history, medical history, drug markets, social and risk networks and other personal susceptibility measures. Participants were compensated $35 for their time and effort at the completion of the baseline interview.

For the purposes of this analysis, the injection drug use history variable was obtained by asking subjects to report how many times they had injected drugs in their lifetime. As a preface to this question, subjects were informed that injecting included intravenous (injecting into the veins), intramuscular (injecting into muscles) and subcutaneous (skin popping) injecting by themselves or by someone else. The injection of legally prescribed drugs was excluded from the definition. Given that it would be highly unlikely that subjects could provide the precise number of times they had injected, six fixed categorical choices were provided ranging from never to 1000 times or more. From these, two groups representing the drug injecting history were developed and coded as 0 = never injector and 1 = former injector (former IDU who reported injecting one or more times during their lifetime).

The two injecting experience groups were compared on selected variables associated with possible risk factors for transitioning to injecting. Duration of heroin use variable was constructed by subtracting the age at which heroin was first used from current age. The mean age of initiation of heroin use was also used as a measure for prior history. Heroin use, drug market experiences and characteristics of heroin use and sexual partners were measured for the 30 days prior to the baseline interview. Perceived severity of heroin dependence was measured in the month prior to the baseline using the Severity of Dependence Scale

(SDS) (Gossop, Griffiths, Powis, & Strang, 1992). A cutoff of 6 or above was used to indicate heroin dependence. The alpha coefficient for the scale among this population was .84.

Several personal susceptibility indicators were included in the analysis. Depression in the 30 days prior to the baseline interview was measured using a shortened eight-item version of the Center for Epidemiological Studies Depression Scale (CES-D) (Melchior, Huba, Brown, & Reback, 1993; Radloff, 1977). Individuals scoring 7 or higher were considered to have clinically significant levels of depressive symptoms. Among this population the alpha coefficient for the scale was .94. Lifetime reports of physical abuse, sexual abuse and attempted suicide were also utilized as personal susceptibility indicators. Perceived susceptibility for HIV, HBV and HCV and engaging in injecting drug use were measured using a five-point scale ranging from 1 to 5.

Finally, the Short Acculturation Scale was administered to the sample (Marin, Sabogal, VanOss Marin, Otero-Sabogal, & Perez-Stable, 1987). The measure is a five point Likert type scale that assesses acculturation among Hispanics as measured by modifications in their values, norms, attitudes and behaviors as a result of exposure to the mainstream cultural patterns of the United States. More specifically, the items address English language proficiency, preference for speaking English versus Spanish, preference for English versus Spanish media, and preferred ethnicity of individuals with whom the respondent interacts. A cut-off score of 2.99 or less is considered to indicate a less acculturated individual while those above 2.99 are considered highly acculturated. The alpha coefficient in previous research has been reported to be .92. In this population the alpha coefficient was .84. While much existing research has provided evidence of the relationship between acculturation as measured by immigration status and illicit drug use, few have focused on differences among U.S. born Hispanics (De La Rosa, Vega, & Radisch, 2000; Vega, Sribney, & Achara-Abrahams, 2003). This research will begin to understand the effect of acculturation as a potential risk factor for transitioning to injecting among U.S. Mexican Americans.

Analysis

Comparisons on the dependent variables were analyzed controlling for age, since this variable was associated with the level of prior injecting experience and thus may be associated with differences between the injecting history groups. For these purposes, a continuous age variable was used as a control. Since women who are former injectors may be more likely to have IDU sex partners and have a history of sexual abuse, depression, and other traumatic events, respective analyses were stratified by gender (Anglin, Hser, & McGlothlin, 1987; Miller, 1999; Nichols, 1985; Prather & Fidell, 1978; Rosenbaum, 1981). Univariate analysis of differences between the injection history groups on dichotomous categorical variables were conducted using chi-square test and multivariate analysis using logistic regression controlling for age. T-tests were used to examine differences between the means of continuous variables. In the multivariate analysis, adjusted odds ratios (AOR) with 95% confidence intervals (95% CI) were estimated. Statistical significance is $p < .05$ and all analyses were conducted using SPSS 13.0.

RESULTS

Sample Characteristics

The sample consisted of 300 non-injecting Mexican American heroin users in San Antonio, Texas. Of these, 79 percent ($n = 238$) were never injectors and 21 percent ($n = 62$) were identified as former injectors. As seen in Table 1, the sample was predominantly male with a larger proportion of them reporting former injecting histories (77%; $p < .033$). Mean age of the sample was 22 years ($SD = 4.9$) with females significantly older (23 years) than males (21 years) ($t = 3.4$, $p < .001$). The mean age of the never injectors (21 years, $SD = 4.4$) was significantly lower than that of the former injectors (24 years, $SD = 6.2$, $t = -4.1$, $p < .000$). The mean number of years for education was 9.7 with 11 percent of the sample currently enrolled in school. Of those not in school ($n = 266$), 14 percent had graduated from high school while the remaining 86 percent had not. The majority of the sample indicated being single (56%) with approximately 31% reporting being in a common law relationship. Over 60 percent of the sample reported having children of their own but there were no differences by injecting history.

Additional demographic characteristics reveal that an overwhelming majority (76%) of the sample are unemployed. Income in the last 30 days ranged from 0 to $999 for 63 percent of the sample. While only 39 percent of their income came from a job, the remaining reported their sources of income from family, illegal activities, i.e., drug selling and public assistance. A unique characteristic of this NIU sample is the percentage of respondents who did not identify as current gang members (85%). Compared with former injectors, a larger proportion of never

TABLE 1. Mexican American Non-injecting Heroin Users by Injecting History

	Total	Never (n = 238)		Former (n = 62)		
Variable	%	N	%	N	%	P-value
Sex						.033
Male	(66)	150	(63)	48	(77)	
Female	(34)	88	(37)	14	(23)	
Age						.012
≤ 20	(50)	127	(53)	22	(36)	
≥ 21	(50)	111	(47)	40	(64)	
Graduated high school						.511
Yes	(14)	31	(13)	10	(16)	
No	(86)	205	(87)	51	(84)	
Marital status						1.00
Single	(56)	133	(56)	35	(57)	
Married	(5)	12	(5)	3	(4)	
Separated/Divorced	(8)	19	(8)	5	(8)	
Common Law	(31)	74	(31)	19	(31)	
Have Children						.200
Yes	(62)	142	(60)	42	(69)	
No	(38)	95	(40)	19	(31)	
Employment status						.326
Employed	(24)	61	(26)	12	(20)	
Not employed	(76)	176	(74)	49	(80)	
Current member of gang						.007
Yes	(15)	29	(12)	16	(26)	
No	(85)	209	(88)	46	(74)	
Current parole/Probation						.071
Yes	(26)	32	(23)	16	(36)	
No	(74)	109	(77)	28	(64)	
Lifetime parole/Probation						.052
Yes	(60)	136	(57)	44	(71)	
No	(40)	101	(43)	18	(29)	
Income past month						.926
$0 - $999	(63)	150	(63)	39	(64)	
$1000 or more	(37)	87	(37)	22	(36)	

injectors did not self-identify as gang members. Furthermore, 60 percent reported having been on parole or probation at least once during their lifetime with 26 percent currently in this status. A significantly larger proportion of former injectors reported lifetime parole/probation status (71%; $p < .052$).

Heroin Use and Related Variables

Selected heroin and other related variables are presented in Table 2. Prior history of heroin use was examined using two measures. The first, mean number of years since starting to use heroin, was positively associated with injecting experience with former injectors using heroin for a significantly longer period of time (6.9 years vs. 3.3) $p < .000$. Having used heroin for 4 or more years increased the risk of being a former injector (AOR = 3.7, 95% CI = 1.6, 8.7). A second measure although not significant indicated that former injectors initiated heroin use at a slightly younger age (17.5 years) than never injectors (18.2 years, $p < .228$). Furthermore, approximately 54 percent of the respondents reported daily use of heroin during the past month. However, no significant differences were observed by injecting experience categories for frequency and volume of current (prior 30 days) heroin use. Similarly, no differences were found by injecting experience with route of heroin administration, with over 80 percent in each group reporting using heroin always through sniffing during the 30 days prior to the interview.

Over 30 percent of the respondents reported a score of 6 or higher on the SDS scale, indicating perceived dependence on heroin. No significant differences by injecting experience were observed, however. Overall, the mean SDS score for this population of Mexican American non-injecting heroin users was 4.2 (SD = 3.7, range = 0 to 14, median = 3).

In regards to heroin market experience, seventy-five percent of the sample reported the quality of heroin as being "good" or "very good." Of interest, the never injectors (78%) were slightly more likely to provide a more positive assessment of the quality of heroin compared to the former (66%) injectors. The quantity of heroin available on the street was apparently not an issue for almost all respondents. Overall, 96 percent reported that it was "enough" or "more than enough" with no differences found by injecting experience. Findings associated with the Short Acculturation Scale revealed significant differences by injecting history. The mean score of the never injectors (3.4) was significantly higher, indicating high acculturation in comparison to that of the former injectors (2.9, SD = .7, $t = 4.8$, $p < .000$). Furthermore, analyses revealed

...age at first heroin use 18 or older	45	48	1.0
...se (prior 30 days)			
...ser	54	52	1.0
...gs per day	32	32	1.0
...g (intranasal) always	83	82	1.0
...of heroin dependence (prior 30 days)			
...ty of heroin dependence score ≥ 6 on SDS scale	34	32	1.0
...arket experience (prior 30 days)			
...is good or very good	75	75	1.0
...ty available on the street is enough ...e than enough	96	96	1.0
...e			
...ana	83	83	1.0
...tion			
...3 and Above on Short Acculturation Scale***	71	77	1.0

...l.

...re adjusted for age.

that being highly acculturated decreased the risk of being a former injector (AOR = 0.3, 95% CI = 0.2, 0.7).

Heroin Use Networks and Sex Networks with IDUs

Table 3 shows the extent to which the NIU sample reported using heroin or having sex with IDUs in the prior 30 days. Former injectors were more likely to have used non-injecting heroin with an ever IDU ($\chi^2 = 18.3$, $p < .000$). Those who reported using noninjected heroin with an ever IDU were almost three times more likely to be former injectors (AOR = 2.7, 95% CI = .09, 8.1; $p < .05$). Further analysis revealed that twenty-one percent indicated using non-injecting heroin with current IDUs, but this did not differ by injecting history.

Stratified analysis by gender for the relationship between injection experience and having IDU sex partner were conducted. Women were more likely than men to report having a sex partner who had ever injected (18% vs. 3%, $\chi^2 = 18.1$, $p < .000$) and who was a current IDU sex partner (9% vs. 1%, $\chi^2 = 8.6$, $p < .003$). In the stratified analysis for women, those who reported having a sex partner who was an "ever" IDU were significantly more likely to be former injectors compared to those who did not report this type of partner (AOR = 10.5, 95% CI = 2.0, 54.6; $p < .00$).

Personal Susceptibility

Indicators of personal susceptibility, stratified by gender are presented in Table 4. Women were much more likely to report having been sexually abused, with 33 percent reporting such abuse compared to 8 percent of men ($\chi^2 = 31.2$, $p < .000$). A similar trend was observed for physical abuse with 20 and 11 percent for women and men, respectively ($\chi^2 = 3.9$, $p < .046$). The prevalence for attempted suicide was substantially high for both female and male samples. However, although not statistically significant, the men were more likely to report that they had tried to commit suicide compared to females (39% vs. 36%). Based on the short version of the CES-D scale, a substantial percentage scored 7 or above for the prior 30 days, indicating that they were clinically depressed. Women were more likely than men to report being depressed with 53 percent scoring at or above the cut-off point compared to 24 percent of men ($\chi^2 = 24.8$, $p < .000$). Among the male sample, having been exposed to sexual abuse and attempted suicide increased the risk of being a former injector. For the female sample, with the exception of

Ξ 3. Heroin Use with IDUs by Injecting History, and Sex Partners with IDUs by Injecting
an American Non-Injecting Heroin Using Women

	Total %	Never Injectors %	AOR[a]	Former
	N = 300	N = 238		N
use with IDUs				
non-injected heroin with ever IDUs*	25	20	1.0	47
non-injected heroin with current IDUs	21	16	1.0	39
rtners with IDUs (women)	N = 102	N = 88		N = 14
partner is an ever IDU**	18	13	1.0	46
partner is a current IDU	9	8	1.0	15

01. *p < .05
are adjusted for age.

E 4. Personal Susceptibility Indicators by Injecting History and Stratified by Gender Am
:an Non-Injecting Heroin Users

	Total %	Never Injectors %		Forme
			AOR[a]	
	N = 102	N = 88		
abused sexually	33	30	1.0	54
abused physically	20	18	1.0	29
try suicide	36	29	1.0	64
ession score is ≥ 7 on CES-D scale (prior 30 days)	53	47	1.0	86
	N = 198	N = 150		
abused sexually	8	6	1.0	13
abused physically	11	10	1.0	17
try suicide	39	35	1.0	48
ession score is ≥ 7 on CES-D scale (prior 30 days)	24	23	1.0	27

are adjusted for age.

physical abuse, the presence of the identified personal susceptibility factors increased their risk for being a former injector.

Perceived Susceptibility for Acquiring HIV, HBV and HCV

As shown in Table 5, perceived susceptibility for acquiring HIV, HBV and HCV were more prevalent among former injectors than among those NIUs who have never injected. For instance, former injectors were almost twice as likely to report that they thought they had a "medium" or "very high" chance of getting infected with HIV. Significant differences by injecting history were only observed for getting infected with HCV or HBV. That is those that reported they thought they had a "medium" or "very high" chance of getting infected with HBV or HCV were more than four times as likely to be former injectors (AOR = 4.3, 95% CI = 1.9, 10.1; $p < .001$).

Attitudes About Needle Use and Injecting Drugs

Table 6 presents a strong, positive association between injection history and not being afraid of injecting one self with needles (AOR = 13.9, 95% CI = 6.2, 31.4; $p < .000$). Among former injectors 51 percent were not at all afraid of injecting themselves compared to six percent of never injectors. Thirteen percent of former injectors reported that their friends think that injecting drugs is acceptable. Thirteen percent of the former injectors also reported perceiving their chances of injecting drugs in the next 6 months as "medium" or "very high." Those that reported they felt "quite worried" or "extremely worried" about injecting drugs in the next 6 months were more likely to be former injectors (AOR = 18.3, 95% CI = 4.3, 77.9; $p < .000$).

DISCUSSION

The present analysis supports previous findings on risk to injecting, and further identifies potential risk factors that are unique to the cultural and social context of the Mexican American community. Early studies have found that acculturation has been widely associated with higher rates of drug use among Hispanics (Vega, Zimmerman, Warheit, & Andres, 2002). In this analysis, however, acculturation was a protective factor for engaging in injecting heroin use practices. That is, being

E 5. Perceived Susceptibility for HIV Among Mexican American Non-Injecting Heroin User
ositive, by Injecting History

	Total %	Never Injectors %	AOR[a]	F
	N = 300	N = 238		
believes that his\her chances of getting infected V are "medium" or "very high"	22	16	1.0	45
is "quite worried" or "extremely worried" about infected with HIV	23	20	1.0	32
believes that his\her chances of getting infected CV or HBV are "medium" or "very high"**	29	21	1.0	65
is "quite worried" or "extremely worried" about infected with HCV or HBV	23	19	1.0	38

LE 6. Attitudes About Needle Use and Injecting Drugs by Injecting History Among Me
Injecting Heroin Users

	Total %	Never Injectors %	AOR[a]	Former
	N = 300	N = 238		N =
ct is "not at all afraid" of injecting self with needles***	15	6	1.0	51
ct perceives friends as thinking that it is "OK" to drug	6	4	1.0	13
ct perceives his\her chances of injecting drugs in the 6 months as "medium" or "very high"	3	1	1.0	13
ct is "quite worried" or "extremely worried" about ng drugs in the next 6 months***	5	1	1.0	21

< .001.
l are adjusted for age.

highly acculturated was found to decrease the risk of being a former injector among this population of Mexican American NIUs.

Within this context, the association between acculturation and injecting history may be influenced by the distinct *tecato* subculture that is deeply embedded in traditional styles of dress, language and a street orientation. Never injectors may be less acculturated because of their exposure to the tecatos subculture's adaptation and use of Spanish "slang" language and highly identifiable religious/cultural symbols (i.e., *Virgen de Guadalupe*, Mexican flag, etc.). Contributing to this process is that former injectors were older and have a longer history of injecting heroin use and may be insulated within this subculture. By contrast, the more acculturated never injectors may be less committed to these cultural values associated with the *tecato* lifestyle.

Another factor contributing to this acculturation phenomena is the relatively young age of this Mexican American NIU population. Older former injectors have been found to be more likely to have initiated use earlier, longer history of use and early adoption of injecting practices as route of administration (Neaigus et al., 2001). In contrast, the present analysis reveals a relatively young (early twenties) Mexican American NIU population. These relatively younger NIUs may view sniffing as opposed to injecting, as a way in which to use heroin and avoid the adverse negative association with this lifestyle (i.e., addiction, criminal involvement, incarceration, HIV infection, etc.) and to a lesser extent their ethnicity. This young age is reflective of the distinct socio-historical experiences with heroin in this community that has resulted to some extent in the generational transmission of heroin use. This study's findings reveal that the risk of being a former injector increases if the individual used heroin for four or more years. Thus, the longer history of continued use confounded by the relatively young age makes this former injector NIU population highly susceptible for resuming injecting practices.

Another cultural characteristic of the Mexican Americans that may potentially contribute to increase the risk of former injectors resuming injecting heroin is the traditional value of fatalism. This refers to the belief among more traditional Hispanics that one's destiny is determined by fate and is therefore inevitable (Medina, 1987). Former injectors in this study were more likely to not be afraid of injecting themselves with needles, concerned for becoming infected with HCV, and expressed a strong belief they will resume injecting practices in the near future. These attitudes were in contrast to the younger, less acculturated NIUs who were not former injectors. The former injectors' perceived susceptibility and attitudes about injecting have created a sense of fatalism that points to the resumption of injecting practices.

Prior research has indicated, former injectors are more likely to have IDUs in their networks and are thus subject to the influence of resuming injection practices (Des Jarlais, Casriel, Friedman, & Rosenblum, 1992; Strang, Grif, Powis, & Gossop, 1999; van Ameijden, van den Hoek, Hartgers, & Coutinho, 1994). A similar pattern was observed in this Mexican American population. Because of the greater likelihood of having former IDUs in their heroin use network, former injectors are more likely to resume injecting practices. Within a community with a relatively high density of injecting drug users, these NIU drug networks are more likely to have IDUs.

For females, there was a greater likelihood for former injectors to have former IDUs as sex partners thus potentially increasing the risk for resuming injecting. This is particularly important in light of the the fact that the introduction and initiation of heroin use through male sex partners has been well documented in existing studies of Hispanic female addicts (Moore, 1990; Valdez, Kaplan, & Cepeda, 2000). Mexican American women NIUs thus, may be more prone to the influence of IDU sex partners in transitioning or resuming injecting practices than other non-Hispanic women. This may be reinforced by the importance Hispanic women place on the cultural norm of "connectedness" or maintaining relationships with men (Amaro, 1995). This research has found that women's need for connection with men prevents them from negotiating safer sex practices that are characteristic of non-traditional female gender roles that put them at increased risk for sexually transmitted infections (i.e., HIV, gonorrhea, etc.).

Lastly, these NIUs are embedded within a socio-economic environment that is an exposure risk, independent from the risks stemming from their injecting history. The scarcity of meaningful employment and social opportunities within the community shapes the behaviors of these drug users. Within this context, economic realities necessitate that these non-injectors create and maintain bonds and share resources among the existing drug networks that oftentimes include former injectors. Thus, the potential risk factors that may help to explain former injectors' susceptibility of resuming and making a transition to injecting needs to be taken into account given the social, economic and cultural context of these San Antonio neighborhoods.

The findings in this paper are subject to some key limitations. Respondents were street-recruited and cannot be generalized to other non-injecting heroin populations. While injecting history was based on self-report and observational methods, there remains the possibility that some prior injectors may have reported to be never injectors. Self-reports, however, have been found to have good reliability and validity in reporting HIV risk behaviors in previous research (McElrath, Chitwood, Griffin, & Comerford, 1994; Neaigus et al., 2001).

This research contributes to existing studies on NIUs in that it begins to identify cultural and community norms that may potentially promote or prevent a transition to injecting that are unique to this Hispanic population. Future research on NIUs needs to take into consideration the cultural context in which the risk for transitioning is occurring in order to develop intervention strategies culturally appropriate for the Mexican American population.

NOTE

1. This research is a replication of a study entitled "HIV Risk and Transitions from Non-Injecting Heroin Use" conducted in New York City that included a subsample of Puerto Ricans.

REFERENCES

ADAM. (1998). *Annual report on drug use among adult and juvenile arrestees1998.* National Institute of Justice.

Amaro, H. (1995). Love, sex, and power: Considering women's realities in HIV prevention. *American Psychologist, 50*(6), 437-447.

Anglin, M. D., Hser, Y.-I., & McGlothlin, W. H. (1987). Sex differences in addict careers: 2. Becoming addicted. *American Journal of Drug & Alcohol Abuse, 13*(1 & 2). 59-71.

Booth, R. E., Watters, J. K., & Chitwood, D. D. (1993). HIV Risk-related Sex Behaviors Among Injection Drug Users. Crack Smokers, and Injection Drug Users Who Smoke Crack. *American Journal of Public Health, 83*(8), 1144-1148.

Bravo, M., Barrio, G., & de la Fuente, L. (2003). Reasons for Selecting an Initial Route of Heroin Administraton and for Subsequent Transitions During a Severe HIV Epidemic. *Addiction, 98*, 749-760.

Broadhead, R. S., Heckathorn, D. D., Grund, J. C., Stern, L. S., & Anthony, D. L. (1995). Drug Users versus Outreach Workers in Combatting AIDS: Preliminary Results of a Peer-Driven Intervention. *Journal of Drug Issues, 25*(3), 531-564.

Bullington, B. (1977). *Heroin Use in the Barrio.* Lexington, MA: Lexington Books.

Campbell, J. V., Hagan, H., Latka, M. H., Garfein, R. S., Golub, E. T., Coady, M. H. et al. (2006). High prevalence of alcohol use among hepatitis C virus antibody positive injection drug users in three US cities. *Drug and Alcohol Dependence, 81*(3), 259-265.

Carlson, R. G., Wang, J., Siegal, H. A., Falck, R. S., & Guo, J. (1994). An ethnographic approach to targeted sampling: Problems and solutions in AIDS prevention research among injenction drug and crack-cocaine users. *Journal of the Society for Applied Anthropology, 53*(3), 279- 286.

Casavantes, E. J. (1976). *El Tecato: Cultural and Sociologic Factors Affecting Drug Use Among Chicanos*. Washington, D.C.: National Coalition of Spanish Speaking Mental Health Organizations.

Casriel, C., Des Jarlais, D. C., Rodriguez, S., Friedman, B. S., & Khurl, E. (1990). Working with Heroin Sniffers: Clinical issues in Preventing Drug Injection. *Journal of Substance Abuse Treatment, 7*, 1-10.

Centers for Disease Control and Prevention (Cartographer). (2004). *HIV/AIDS Surveillance Report Vol 16.*

Chitwood, D. D., Sanchez, J., Comerford, M., Page, J. B., McBride, D. C., & Kitner, K. R. (2000). First injection and current risk factors for HIV among new and long-term injection drug users. *AIDS Care, 12*(3), 313-320.

Clatts, M., Davis, W. R., & Atillasoy, A. (1995). Hitting a Moving Target: The Use of Ethnographic Methods in the Development of Sampling Strategies for the Evaluation of AIDS Outreach Programs for Homeless Youth in New York City.

De La Fuente, L., Barrio, G., Royuela, L., & Bravo, M. J. (1997). The transition from injecting to smoking heroin in three Spanish cities. The Spanish Group for the Study of the Route of Heroin Administration. *Addiction, 92*(12), 1749-1763.

De La Rosa, M., Vega, R., & Radisch, M. A. (2000). The role of acculturation in the substance abuse behavior of African-American and Latino adolescents: Advances, issues, and recommendations. *Journal of Psychoactive Drugs, 32*(1), 33-42.

Des Jarlais, D. C., Casriel, C., Friedman, S. R., & Rosenblum, A. (1992). AIDS and the transition to illicit drug injection–results of a randomized trial prevention program. *British Journal of Addiction* (Vol. 87, pp. 493): Blackwell Publishing Limited.

Des Jarlais, D. C., Friedman, S. R., Perlis, T., Chapman, T. F., Sotheran, J. L., Paone, D. et al. (1999). Risk Behavior and HIV Infection among New Drug Injectors in the Era of AIDS in New York City. *Journal of Acquired Immune Deficiency Syndromes and Human Retrovirology, 20*, 67-72.

Desmond, D. P., & Maddux, J. F. (1984). Mexican-American heroin addicts. *American Journal of Drug & Alcohol Abuse, 10*(3), 317-346.

DUF. (1995). *Annual report on adult and juvenile arrestees.* Washington, D. C.: U. S. Department of Justice.

DUF. (1996). *Annial report on adult and juvenile arrestees.* Washington, D. C.: U. S. Department of Justice.

Gossop, M., Griffiths, P., Powis, B., & Strang, J. (1992). Severity of dependence and route of administration of heroin, cocaine and amphetamines. *British Journal of Addiction, 87*, 1527-1536.

Griffiths, P., Gossop, M., Powis, B., & Strang, J. (1992). Extent and nature of transitions of route among heroin addicts in treatment–preliminary data from the Drug Transitions Study. *British Journal of Addiction, 87*(3), 485-491.

Griffiths, P., Gossop, M., Powis, B., & Strang, J. (1994). Transitions in patterns of heroin administration: A study of heroin chasers and heroin injectors. *Addiction, 89*(3), 301-309.

Havens, J. R., Sherman, S. G., Sapun, M., & Strathdee, S. A. (2006). Prevalence and Correlates of Suicidal Ideation Among Young Injection vs. Noninjection Drug Users. *Substance Use & Misuse, 41*(2), 245-254.

Heckathorn, D. D. (1997). Respondent-driven sampling: A new approach to the study of hidden populations. *Social Problems, 44*(2), 174-199.

Kaplan, C. D., & Korf, D. (1987). Temporal and social contexts of heroin-using populations. An illustration of snowball sampling technique. *Journal of Nervous and Mental Disease* (175), 566-574.

Kasarda, J. D. (1993). Urban Underclass Database: An Overview and Machine-Readable File Documentation. New York: Social Science Research Council.

Marin, G., Sabogal, F., VanOss Marin, B., Otero-Sabogal, R., & Perez-Stable, E. J. (1987). Develpment of a Short Acculturation Scale for Hispanics. *Hispanic Journal of Behavioral Sciences, 9*(2), 183-205.

McElrath, K., Chitwood, D. D., Griffin, D. K., & Comerford, M. (1994). The consistency of self-reported HIV risk behavior among injection drug users. *American Journal of Public Health, 84*, 1965-1970.

Medina, C. (1987). Latino culture and Sex Education. *SIECUS Report, 15*(3), 1-4.

Melchior, L. A., Huba, G. J., Brown, V. B., & Reback, C. J. (1993). A Short Depression Scale Index for Women. *Educational and Psychological Measurement, 53*, 1117-1125.

Miller, M. (1999). A Model to Explain the Relationship Between Sexual Abuse and HIV Risk Among Women. *AIDS Care, 11*(1), 3-20.

Moore, J. (1990). Mexican-American women addicts: The influence of family background. In R. Glick & J. W. Moore (Eds.). *Drugs in Hispanic communities* (pp. 127-153). New Brunswick: Rutgers University Press.

Moore, J. W. (1978). *Homeboys: Gangs, drugs, and prison in the barrios of Los Angeles*. Philadelphia, PA: Temple University Press.

Neaigus, A., Atillasoy, A., & Friedman, S. R. (1998). Trends in the Non-Injected use of Heroin and Factors Associated with the Transitioning to Injecting. In J. Inciardi & L. Harrison (Eds.), *Heroin in the Age of Crack-Cocaine*. Thousand Oaks, CA: Sage Publications.

Neaigus, A., Gyarmathy, A., Miller, M., Frajzyngier, V. M., Friedman, S. R., & Don, C. D. J. (2006). Transitions to Injecting Drug Use Among Noninjecting Heroin Users. *JAIDS: Journal of Acquired Immune Deficiency Syndromes, 41*(4), 493-503.

Neaigus, A., Miller, M., Friedman, S. R., Hagen, D. L., Sifaneck, S. J., Ildefonso, G. et al. (2001). Potential risk factors for the transition to injecting among non-injecting heroin users: A comparison of former injectors and never injectors. *Addiction, 96*, 847-860.

Nichols, M. (1985). Theoretical Concerns in the Clinical Treatment of Substance Abusing Women: A Feminist analysis. *Alcoholism Treatment Quarterly, 2*, 79-90.

Ochoa, K. C., Davidson, P. J., Evans, J. L., Hahn, J. A., Page-Shafer, K., & Moss, A. R. (2005). Heroin overdose among young injection drug users in San Francisco. *Drug & Alcohol Dependence, 80*(3), 297-302.

Prather, J. E., & Fidell, L. S. (1978). Drug Use and abuse Among Women: An Overview. *International Journal of the Addictions, 13*, 863-885.

Radloff, L. (1977). The CESD Scale: A Self-Report Depression Scale for Research in the General Population. *Applied Psychosocial Measurement, 1*, 385-401.

Rosenbaum, M. (1981). *Women on heroin* (2nd ed.). New Brunswick, NJ: Rutgers University Press.

Sifaneck, S. J., & Neaigus, A. (2001). The Ethnographic Accessing, Sampling and Screening of Hidden Populations: Heroin Sniffers in New York City. *Addiction Research and Theory, 9*, 519-543.

Sotheran, J. L., Goldsmith, D., Blasco, M., & Friedman, B. S. (1999). Heroin Sniffing As Self-Regulation Among Injecting and Non-Injecting Heroin Users. *Journal of Drug Issues, 29*, 401-.

Strang, J., Grif, P., Powis, B., & Gossop, M. (1999). Heroin Chasers and Heroin Injectors: Differences Observed in a Community Sample in London, UK. *The American Journal on Addictions, 8*, 148-160.

TenHouten, W. D. (1992). Generalization and statistical inference from snowball samples. *Bulletin de Methodologie Sociologique, 37*(December), 25-40.

U.S. Bureau of the Census. (2000). Quick Tables: QT-PL. Race, Hispanic or Latino, and Age: 2000 for San Antonio city, Texas. Retrieved July 16, 2003, 2003, from http://factfinder.census.gov

U.S. Bureau of the Census. (2001, September 23, 2002). Annual Demographic Survey March Supplement: Table 2. Age, Sex, Household Relationship, Race and Hispanic Origin by Ratio of Income to Poverty Level: 2001. Retrieved July 17, 2003, 2003, from http://ferret.bls.census.gov/macro/032002/pov/new02_001.htm

Valdez, A., Kaplan, C. D., & Cepeda, A. (2000). The process of paradoxical autonomy and survival in the heroin careers of Mexican American women. *Contemporary Drug Problems, 27*(Spring, 2000), 189-212.

Valdez, A., & Sifaneck, S. J. (2004). "Getting High and Getting By": Dimensions of Drug Selling Behaviors Among American Mexican Gang Members in South Texas. *Journal of Research in Crime and Delinquency, 41*(1), 82-105.

van Ameijden, E. J., van den Hoek, J. A., & Coutinho, R. A. (1994). Injecting risk behavior among drug users in Amsterdam, 1986 to 1992 and its relationship to AIDS. *American Journal of Public Health* (Vol. 84, pp. 275): American Public Health Association.

van Ameijden, E. J., van den Hoek, J. A., Hartgers, C., & Coutinho, R. A. (1994). Risk factors for the transition from noninjection to injection drug use and accompanying AIDS risk behavior in a cohort of drug users. *American Journal of Epidemiology, 139*(12 (Print)), 1153-1163.

Vega, W., Zimmerman, R., Warheit, G., & Andres, G. (2002). Acculturation, Stress and Latino Adolescent Drug Use. In A. Maney & J. Ramos (Eds.), *Socioeconomic Conditions, Stress and Mental Disorders: Toward a New Synthesis of Research and Public Policy*. Washington, DC: Mental Health Statistical Improvement Program, National Institute of Mental Health.

Vega, W. A., Sribney, W. M., & Achara-Abrahams, I. (2003). Co-Occuring Alcohol, Drug, and Other Psychiatric Disorders Among Mexican-Origin People in the United States. *American Journal of Public Health, 93*(7), 1057-1064.

Waldrop-Valverde, D., Ownby, R. L., & Kumar, M. (2005). Influence of depression and HIV serostatus on the neuropsychological performance of injecting drug users. *Psychiatry & Clinical Neurosciences, 59*(4), 372-378.

Watters, J. K., & Biernacki, P. (1989). Targeted sampling: Options for the study of hidden populations. *Social Problems, 36*(4), 416-430.

Wood, E., Li, K., Small, W., Kerr, T., Montaner, J. S., & Schechter, M. T. (2005). Recent Incarceration Independently Associated with Syringe Sharing by Injection Drug Users. *Public Health Reports, 120*(2), 150-156.

Yin, Z., Valdez, A., Mata, A. G., & Kaplan, C. D. (1996). Developing a field-intensive methodology for generating a randomized sample for gang research. *Free Inquiry-Special Issue: Gang, Drugs and Violence, 24*(2), 195-204.

doi:10.1300/J233v06n02_05

Race/Ethnicity and Gender Differences in Drug Use and Abuse Among College Students

Sean Esteban McCabe, PhD, MA, MSW
Michele Morales, PhD, MA, MSW
James A. Cranford, PhD
Jorge Delva, PhD, MSW
Melnee D. McPherson, PhD, MA, MSW
Carol J. Boyd, PhD, MSN, FAAN

Sean Esteban McCabe is Research Associate Professor, University of Michigan, Substance Abuse Research Center, 2025 Traverwood Dr., Suite C, Ann Arbor, MI 48105-2194.

Michele Morales is Research Associate, University of Michigan, Substance Abuse Research Center, 2025 Traverwood Dr., Suite C, Ann Arbor, MI 48105-2194.

James A. Cranford is Research Assistant Professor at University of Michigan, Substance Abuse Research Center, 2025 Traverwood Dr., Suite C, Ann Arbor, MI 48105-2194.

Jorge Delva is Associate Professor, University of Michigan, School of Social Work, 1080 S. University, Ann Arbor, MI 48109-1106.

Melnee D. McPherson is Postdoctoral Fellow, University of Michigan. Substance Abuse Research Center, 2025 Traverwood Dr., Suite C, Ann Arbor, MI 48105-2194.

Carol J. Boyd is Professor and Director, University of Michigan, Institute for Research on Women and Gender, 204 S. State Street, Ann Arbor, MI 48109-1290.

Address correspondence to: Sean Esteban McCabe, University of Michigan, Substance Abuse Research Center, 2025 Traverwood Drive, Suite C, Ann Arbor, MI 48105-2194 (E-mail: plius@umich.edu).

This study was supported by a research grant R03 DA 018239 (PI: Sean Esteban McCabe) from the National Institute on Drug Abuse, National Institutes of Health.

[Haworth co-indexing entry note]: "Race/Ethnicity and Gender Differences in Drug Use and Abuse Among College Students." McCabe, Sean Esteban et al. Co-published simultaneously in *Journal of Ethnicity in Substance Abuse* (The Haworth Press, Inc.) Vol. 6, No. 2, 2007, pp. 75-95; and: *21st Century Research on Drugs and Ethnicity: Studies Supported by the National Institute on Drug Abuse* (ed: Peter L. Myers) The Haworth Press, 2007, pp. 75-95. Single or multiple copies of this article are available for a fee from The Haworth Document Delivery Service [1-800-HAWORTH, 9:00 a.m. - 5:00 p.m. (EST). E-mail address: docdelivery@haworthpress.com].

Available online at http://jesa.haworthpress.com

doi:10.1300/J233v06n02_06

SUMMARY. This study examines race/ethnicity and gender differences in drug use and abuse for substances other than alcohol among undergraduate college students. A probability-based sample of 4,580 undergraduate students at a Midwestern research university completed a cross-sectional Web-based questionnaire that included demographic information and several substance use measures. Male students were generally more likely to report drug use and abuse than female students. Hispanic and White students were more likely to report drug use and abuse than Asian and African American students prior to coming to college and during college. The findings of the present study reveal several important racial/ethnic differences in drug use and abuse that need to be considered when developing collegiate drug prevention and intervention efforts. doi:10.1300/J233v06n02_06 *[Article copies available for a fee from The Haworth Document Delivery Service: 1-800- HAWORTH. E-mail address: <docdelivery@haworthpress.com> Website: <http://www.HaworthPress.com>*

KEYWORDS. Race/ethnicity, gender, illicit drugs, prescription drugs, drug abuse

INTRODUCTION

The use of marijuana and other illicit drugs has increased significantly among college students in the U.S. over the past decade, according to national epidemiological studies (e.g., Gledhill-Hoyt et al., 2000; Johnston et al., 2005a; Mohler-Kuo et al., 2003; Strote et al., 2002). American young adults between 18 to 29 years of age have the highest past-year prevalence rates of marijuana use, abuse and dependence relative to older age groups (Compton et al., 2004; Johnston et al., 2005a). In addition, American young adults 18 to 25 years of age report the highest prevalence of illicit use of prescription drugs relative to other age groups (Johnston et al., 2005a; SAMHSA, 2004a). According to the 2003 data from the *National Survey on Drug Use and Health (NSDUH)*, young adults 18 to 25 years of age report the highest rates of lifetime (60.5%), past year (34.6%) and past month (20.3%) use of any illicit drug. Most notably, the prevalence of past year illicit drug use by college students 18 to 22 years of age was comparable to their same-age peers not attending college (Johnston et al., 2005a; SAMHSA, 2005).

Although previous research has documented the general prevalence rates of drug use among college students (Bell et al., 1997; Gfroerer et al., 1997; Johnston et al., 2004; Presley et al., 1996), relatively few studies have examined possible racial/ethnic differences in the use of substances other than alcohol (Delva et al., 2004; Meilman et al., 1995; Mohler-Kuo et al., 2003). Further, while there is considerable knowledge regarding illicit *drug use* among college students (e.g., Gledhill-Hoyt et al., 2000; Johnston et al., 2004; Mohler-Kuo et al., 2003), there is limited information available regarding illicit *drug abuse* among college students.

According to the 2003 NSDUH, 38.2% of White young adults 18 to 25 years of age in the U.S. reported any illicit drug use in the past year, followed by African-American (30.6%) and Hispanic (27.5%) young adults (SAMHSA, 2004a). The same race/ethnicity patterns were observed for the past-year prevalence of marijuana use and marijuana use disorders among individuals 18 to 29 years of age according to data from the 2001-2002 National Epidemiological Survey on Alcohol and Related Conditions (NESARC; Compton et al., 2004). Further, the past-year prevalence of DSM-IV marijuana use disorders increased significantly between 1991-1992 and 2001-2002, with the greatest increases observed among Hispanic and African-American young adults. In contrast, the prevalence of DSM-IV marijuana use disorders for White young adults did not change significantly over this same time period (Compton et al., 2004).

Several investigations using data from the College Alcohol Study (CAS), a nationally representative sample of U.S. colleges and universities, examined the individual and college characteristics associated with marijuana and other drug use (e.g., Mohler-Kuo et al., 2003; Strote et al., 2002; Wechsler et al., 2002). For example, one study found that approximately three in ten American college students reported using marijuana in the past year (Mohler-Kuo et al., 2003). The study also found that the prevalence of marijuana use was highest for White college students, followed by Hispanic, Asian, and African American students. Other national studies based on the CAS data have found similar racial/ethnic differences in ecstasy use (Strote et al., 2002), heavy episodic drinking (Wechsler et al., 2002), and nonmedical use of prescription stimulants, opioids and benzodiazepines (McCabe et al., 2005a, 2005b; McCabe, 2005). In another national study, Meilman and colleagues (1995) compared illicit drug use rates between a sample of 6,129 students attending Historically Black Colleges and Universities (HBCUs) and a sample of 6,129 students attending predominantly White institutions (Meilman et al.,

1995). The study found that students from HBCUs reported significantly lower rates of marijuana, cocaine, sedatives, hallucinogens, and other illicit drug use than students at non-HBCUs. Despite evidence for racial/ethnic differences in illicit drug use, there is limited information regarding racial/ethnic differences in drug abuse among college students.

Marijuana use disorders in the U.S. were significantly higher among men than women across all age groups in 1991-1992 and 2001-2002 (Compton et al., 2004) and several college-based national studies have also reported higher rates of marijuana use among college men than women (e.g., Bell et al., 1997; Johnston et al., 2005a; Mohler-Kuo et al., 2003). For example, Johnston and colleagues (2005) found that 39.6% of college men as compared to 29.6% of college women reported using marijuana in the past year. In addition to gender differences in marijuana use, U.S. college men are generally more likely than college women to report illicit drug use other than marijuana; Johnston et al. (2005a) reported that 22.1% of college men as compared to 16.5% of college women used illicit drugs other than marijuana. In addition, two national studies and one single institution study showed that undergraduate college men were more likely than women to report nonmedical use of prescription stimulants (Johnston et al., 2005a; McCabe et al., 2005a; Teter et al., 2005).

To date, there is limited information available regarding racial/ethnic and gender differences in collegiate drug use behaviors. Therefore, the main objective of the present study is to examine racial/ethnic and gender differences in the prevalence of drug use and abuse among undergraduate college students.

RESEARCH METHODS

Design and Sample

Upon receiving approval from the Institutional Review Board, the study was conducted during a two-month period in January and February of 2005, drawing on a total undergraduate population of 20,138 full-time students (10,339 women and 9,799 men) at a Midwestern research university. A simple random sample of 5,389 full-time undergraduate students was drawn from the Registrar's Office. In addition, 652 Hispanic, 634 African-American and 244 Asian undergraduate students were selected using stratified random sampling in order to produce reliable prevalence estimates for these racial/ethnic groups. The entire sample was mailed a

$2.00 bill enclosed with a notification letter describing the study and inviting them to self-administer the Student Life Survey (SLS) by clicking on a link to access the Web survey and using a unique password. The Web survey was maintained on an Internet site running under the secure socket layer protocol to ensure privacy and security. Non-respondents were sent up to three reminder e-mails. By participating in the survey, students became eligible for a sweepstakes that included several prizes including cash prizes, travel vouchers, field passes to athletic events, and iPods. The final response rate was 66.2%, which exceeded the average response rate for national college-based alcohol and other drug studies (Wechsler et al., 2002). The proportion of respondents who completed the entire survey was 97.4% (completion rate). Similar Web survey design and procedures are described in more detail elsewhere (McCabe et al., 2002; McCabe, 2004).

The final sample consisted of 4,580 undergraduate students and the demographic characteristics of the random sample closely resembled the characteristics of the overall student population. The proportion of women was slightly higher in the random sample than the overall undergraduate student population (55% vs. 51%) while the racial/ethnic, class year and age distributions between the random sample and the population closely resembled each other. The average age of the students in the sample was 20 years old.

Instrument and Measures

The Student Life Survey (SLS) includes items adapted from several national studies of alcohol and other drug use (e.g., Johnston et al., 2003; Wechsler et al., 1995). Demographic measures in the survey included items asking about gender, race/ethnicity, class year, living arrangement, and fraternity and sorority membership.

Illicit drug use was assessed with the following question: "On how many occasions in the past 12 months have you used the following types of drugs?" There were separate questions for each of the following eight drugs: Marijuana or hashish, cocaine, LSD, other psychedelics, crystal methamphetamine, heroin, inhalants, and ecstasy. The response scale for each drug was (1) No occasions, (2) 1-2 occasions, (3) 3-5 occasions, (4) 6-9 occasions, (5) 10-19 occasions, (6) 20-39 occasions, and (7) 40 or more occasions.

Illicit use of prescription drugs was assessed with the following question: "On how many occasions in the past 12 months have you used the following types of drugs? Do not include drugs used under a doctor's prescription." There were separate questions for each of the following four drugs: sleeping medication (e.g., Ambien, Halcion, Restoril, temazepam, triazolam), sedative/anxiety medication (e.g., Ativan, Xanax, Valium, Klonopin, diazepam, lorazepam), stimulant medication (e.g., Ritalin, Dexedrine, Adderall, Concerta, methylphenidate) and pain medication (e.g., opioids such as Vicodin, OxyContin, Percocet, Darvocet, morphine, hydrocodone, oxycodone). The response scale for each drug was the same as for illicit drug use.

Drug abuse was assessed with a modified version of the Drug Abuse Screening Test (DAST-10), a self-report instrument that can be used in clinical and non-clinical settings to screen for abuse and dependence on a wide variety of substances other than alcohol (Skinner, 1982). The DAST is a well validated instrument developed in North America that was originally adapted from the MAST, which focuses primarily on alcohol. The two scales are very similar, and the original 28-item version and the more recent 20-item version of the DAST have almost identical psychometric properties, with a correlation of r = 0.99 (Skinner, 1982). In addition, the DAST has been shortened to a 10-item version (DAST-10) which has similar psychometric properties to the other two versions (Cocco & Carey, 1998).

Using Web-based skip logic, respondents who reported past year illicit use of any of the following drugs received the DAST-10 items: marijuana or hashish, cocaine, LSD, other psychedelics, crystal methamphetamine, heroin, inhalants, ecstasy, sleeping medication, sedative/anxiety medication, stimulant medication and pain medication. Respondents were instructed that the DAST-10 questions were about drugs other than alcohol and to answer "Yes" or "No" to each of the DAST-10 items. Respondents were informed that "drug" refers to use of prescription drugs not prescribed to them or in a manner not intended by the prescribing clinician or use of other drugs such as marijuana, cocaine, LSD, ecstasy, etc. The DAST-10 items used in the present study are listed in Table 3. Based on previous research, a cutpoint score of 3 or more DAST-10 items was used to indicate a moderate level of problems related to drug abuse (e.g., Bernstein et al.; French et al., 2001; Skinner, 1982).

Data Analysis

Associations between categorical variables were tested using chi-square and logistic regression analysis. Associations between continuous variables were tested using one-way analysis of variance (ANOVA) and post-hoc pairwise comparisons were conducted using Tukey's Honestly

Significant Difference (HSD) to maintain an alpha level of .05. A series of multiple logistic regression analyses were conducted to assess the main and interactive effects of gender and race/ethnicity on the odds of past 12-month drug use and abuse. Analyses focused on five indicators of past 12-month drug use and abuse: (a) use of illicit or prescription drugs, (b) use of illicit drugs with marijuana, (c) use of illicit drugs without marijuana, (d) illicit use of prescription drugs, and (e) three or more positive items based on the Drug Abuse Screening Test, Short Form. The information for the 5-category race/ethnicity variable was represented with four dummy variables. For gender, the reference group was females, and for race/ethnicity we conducted analyses with African Americans as the reference group.

Procedures outlined by Jaccard (2001) were used to test the interactive effects of gender and race on the odds of past 12-month drug use. A hierarchical logistic regression analyses was conducted with all main effects entered at the first step and all product terms for the Gender × Race interaction entered at the second step. Model fit was evaluated with the chi-square statistic. The finding that Whites and Hispanics had higher levels of illicit drug use and illicit use of prescription drugs was further examined by analyzing race and gender differences in age of onset of marijuana use. For these exploratory analyses, the age of onset variables were dummy coded as 0 = college onset and 1 = pre-college onset.

RESULTS

Prevalence of Illicit Use of Drugs

As shown in Tables 1 and 2, the 12-month prevalence rates of drug use were examined for undergraduate college students based on race/ethnicity and gender. Marijuana was the most commonly used substance followed by opioid analgesics, prescription stimulants and psychedelics. The associations between race/ethnicity and 12-month prevalence rates of substance use were examined for males and females separately using chi-square tests. Among men and women, the use of these substances tended to be higher for Hispanic and White students than for Asian and African American students. As shown in Table 1, 12-month rates of illicit drug use including marijuana were 40.0% for Hispanic women, 38.1% for White women, 20.6% for Asian women, 18.7% for African American women and 32.4% for women from other racial categories ($p < .01$). In

TABLE 1. Race/Ethnicity Differences in 12-month Illicit Drug Use or Illicit Use of Prescription Drugs, Women

	Women					
	Asian n = 310 %	African-American n = 416 %	Hispanic n = 281 %	White n = 1346 %	Other n = 152 %	Chi-square p-value
Illicit or prescription drug[a]	22.9	24.9	44.0	41.8	37.2	**
Marijuana	20.0	18.7	39.9	38.2	32.4	**
Cocaine	0.7	0.7	4.4	3.0	1.4	**
LSD	0.0	0.0	0.4	0.5	0.0	
Other psychedelics	1.3	0.5	2.2	2.9	3.4	*
Crystal methamphetamine	0.3	0.0	0.0	0.3	0.7	
Inhalants	0.7	0.5	1.5	1.4	1.3	
Ecstasy	1.7	0.7	1.5	1.9	1.4	
Heroin	0.0	0.0	0.0	0.2	0.0	
Illicit drug with marijuana[b]	20.6	18.7	40.0	38.1	32.4	**
Illicit drug without marijuana[c]	3.3	1.7	7.3	5.8	6.8	**
Pain medication (opioid)	3.3	6.4	9.8	8.2	6.8	*
Stimulant medication	3.0	0.7	8.0	6.6	2.0	**
Sleeping medication	2.0	1.5	4.0	3.1	4.1	
Sedative/anxiety medication	1.3	1.2	2.9	2.8	2.7	
Any prescription drug[d]	6.3	8.4	18.2	13.8	11.6	**

[a] Includes marijuana, cocaine, LSD, other psychedelics, crystal methamphetamine, inhalant, ecstasy, heroin, pain medication, sedative/anxiety medication, sleeping medication, stimulant medication.

[b] Includes marijuana, cocaine, LSD, other psychedelics, crystal methamphetamine, inhalants, ecstasy, heroin.

[c] Includes cocaine, LSD, other psychedelics, crystal methamphetamine, inhalants, ecstasy, heroin.

[d] Includes pain medication, sedative/anxiety medication, sleeping medication, stimulant medication.

*$p < 0.05$ based on chi-square goodness-of-fit test with df = 4.

**$p < 0.01$ based on chi-square goodness-of-fit test with df = 4.

addition, 12-month rates of illicit use of prescription drugs were 18.2% for Hispanic women, 13.8% for White women, 6.3% for Asian women, 8.4% for African American women and 11.6% for women from other racial categories ($p < .01$).

As shown in Table 2, the racial differences in drug use were similar for undergraduate men. For example, 12-month rates of illicit drug use were 45.1% for Hispanic men, 41.5% for White men, 22.8% for Asian men, 34.1% for African American men and 28.3% for men from other racial categories ($p < .01$). In addition, 12-month rates of illicit use of prescription drugs were 16.2% for Hispanic men, 13.8% for White men, 9.0% for Asian men, 8.6% for African American men and 9.9% for men from other racial categories ($p < .05$).

Prevalence of Drug Abuse

As illustrated in Tables 3 and 4, the 12-month prevalence of DAST-10 items was examined based on race/ethnicity and gender. Similar to drug use, the prevalence of DAST-10 items tended to be higher for Hispanic and White undergraduate students than for Asian and African American undergraduate students. The associations between race and 12-month prevalence rates DAST-10 items were examined for males and females separately using chi-square tests. Results showed significant associations between race and DAST-10. For example, rates of experiencing three or more DAST-10 items were 14.4% for Hispanic men, 14.1% for White men, 6.1% for African American men, 4.9% for Asian men, and 6.6% for men from other racial categories ($p < .01$). In addition, rates of experiencing three or more DAST-10 items were 10.2% for Hispanic women, 9.1% for White women, 3.3% for Asian women, 4.2% for African American women and 6.1% for women from other racial categories ($p < .01$).

Main and Interactive Effects of Gender and Race/Ethnicity on Illicit Use of Drugs

Results from multiple logistic regression analysis for past 12-month illicit use of prescription or illicit drugs revealed that after controlling for race, there was no statistically significant effect of gender (see Table 5). With respect to race, results using African Americans as the reference group showed that, controlling for gender, the odds of past 12-month drug use were statistically significantly higher among Whites (OR = 1.86, $p < .01$) and Hispanics (OR = 2.14, $p < .01$). Additional analyses with Hispanics as the reference category indicated that the odds of past

TABLE 2. Race/Ethnicity Differences in 12-month Illicit Drug Use or Illicit Use of Prescription Drugs, Men

	Men					
	Asian n = 297 %	African-American n = 168 %	Hispanic n = 282 %	White n = 1108 %	Other n = 220 %	Chi-square p-value
Illicit or prescription drug[a]	28.3	36.0	48.0	43.3	29.1	**
Marijuana	22.4	33.5	45.6	41.5	27.8	**
Cocaine	1.7	1.8	6.5	5.1	5.7	*
LSD	0.0	0.0	0.4	1.8	0.0	**
Other psychedelics	2.4	1.8	6.5	7.4	4.2	**
Crystal methamphetamine	0.0	0.0	0.4	0.4	0.0	
Inhalants	0.7	0.6	1.4	2.5	1.9	
Ecstasy	1.0	1.8	2.2	2.1	0.9	
Heroin	0.0	0.0	0.0	0.3	0.0	
Illicit drug with marijuana[b]	22.8	34.1	45.1	41.5	28.3	**
Illicit drug without marijuana[c]	4.8	4.3	11.2	10.6	8.5	**
Pain medication (opioid)	4.5	4.9	8.7	8.5	6.6	
Stimulant medication	3.8	4.9	9.0	7.6	4.7	*
Sleeping medication	1.7	1.2	2.5	1.8	2.3	
Sedative/anxiety medication	0.7	0.6	2.9	2.9	2.3	
Any prescription drug[d]	9.0	8.6	16.2	13.8	9.9	*

[a] Includes marijuana, cocaine, LSD, other psychedelics, crystal methamphetamine, inhalant, ecstasy, heroin, pain medication, sedative/anxiety medication, sleeping medication, stimulant medication.

[b] Includes marijuana, cocaine, LSD, other psychedelics, crystal methamphetamine, inhalants, ecstasy, heroin.

[c] Includes cocaine, LSD, other psychedelics, crystal methamphetamine, inhalants, ecstasy, heroin.

[d] Includes pain medication, sedative/anxiety medication, sleeping medication, and stimulant medication.

*$p < 0.05$ based on chi-square goodness-of-fit test with df = 4.

**$p < 0.01$ based on chi-square goodness-of-fit test with df = 4.

TABLE 3. Race/Ethnicity Differences in the Drug Abuse Screening Test, Women

	Women					
Drug Abuse Screening Test items	Asian n = 301 %	African-American n = 406 %	Hispanic n = 275 %	White n = 1325 %	Other n = 151 %	Chi-square p-value
Have you used more than one drug at a time?	3.3	3.4	7.6	8.0	6.8	**
Have you used drugs other than those required for medical reasons?	13.3	13.8	33.5	30.3	27.7	**
Are you always able to stop using drugs when you want to?	4.3	5.2	5.5	5.1	6.1	
Have you had blackouts or flashbacks as a result of drug use?	1.7	0.7	5.8	4.9	2.0	**
Have you ever felt bad or guilty about your drug use?	7.0	5.4	13.8	12.2	8.8	**
Have family members ever complained about your involvement with drugs?	1.0	0.7	2.9	3.0	1.4	*
Have you stayed away from your family because of your use of drugs?	0.7	0.7	3.3	2.7	2.0	*
Have you engaged in illegal activities in order to obtain drugs?	2.3	1.5	4.4	4.5	1.4	*
Have you had medical problems as a result of your drug use?	0.3	0.2	1.1	1.7	1.4	
Have you ever experienced withdrawal symptoms when you stopped taking drugs?	1.3	1.0	1.8	2.0	2.7	
One or more positive DAST-10 items	17.6	18.2	38.2	34.2	32.4	**
Two or more positive DAST-10 items	8.6	6.9	21.5	18.8	15.5	**
Three or more positive DAST-10 items	3.3	4.2	10.2	9.1	6.1	**

* $p < 0.05$ based on chi-square goodness-of-fit test with df = 4.

** $p < 0.01$ based on chi-square goodness-of-fit test with df = 4.

TABLE 4. Race/Ethnicity Differences in the Drug Abuse Screening Test, Men

	Men					
Drug Abuse Screening Test items	Asian n = 288 %	African-American n = 164 %	Hispanic n = 277 %	White n = 1087 %	Other n = 214 %	Chi-square p-value
Have you used more than one drug at a time?	7.3	6.1	15.2	12.4	8.5	**
Have you used drugs other than those required for medical reasons?	17.7	24.4	37.5	33.7	24.4	**
Are you always able to stop using drugs when you want to?	3.8	5.5	5.8	7.0	3.3	
Have you had blackouts or flashbacks as a result of drug use?	2.1	1.8	5.1	4.8	4.2	
Have you ever felt bad or guilty about your drug use?	6.6	11.0	18.4	16.7	9.4	**
Have family members ever complained about your involvement with drugs?	1.0	3.7	7.2	4.8	1.9	**
Have you stayed away from your family because of your use of drugs?	2.4	1.8	1.8	3.8	0.5	*
Have you engaged in illegal activities in order to obtain drugs?	2.1	4.9	5.8	7.5	2.3	**
Have you had medical problems as a result of your drug use?	0.3	1.2	1.1	1.5	0.5	
Have you ever experienced withdrawal symptoms when you stopped taking drugs?	1.7	1.8	3.2	1.8	0.5	
One or more positive DAST-10 items	21.9	31.7	44.0	39.0	26.8	**
Two or more positive DAST-10 items	13.5	16.5	26.7	24.5	15.5	**
Three or more positive DAST-10 items	4.9	6.1	14.4	14.1	6.6	**

* $p < 0.05$ based on chi-square goodness-of-fit test with df = 4.

** $p < 0.01$ based on chi-square goodness-of-fit test with df = 4.

E 5. Multiple Logistic Regression Analysis of Gender and Race/Ethnicity as Correlates of

	Use of illicit drugs or prescription drugs		Illicit drug use (including marijuana)		Illicit drug use (not including marijuana)		Illicit use of prescription drugs		Three D
	AOR[a]	95% CI[b]	AOR[a]	95% CI[b]	AOR[a]	95% CI[b]	AOR[a]	95% CI[b]	AOR
	—[c]		—[c]		—[c]		—[c]		—[c]
	1.12	0.99 - 1.26	1.20**	1.06 - 1.37	1.80**	1.41 - 2.27	1.00	0.84 - 1.20	1.55*
an	—[c]		—[c]		—[c]		—[c]		—[c]
	1.86**	1.52 - 2.27	2.12**	1.71 - 2.62	3.13**	1.80 - 5.43	1.73**	1.26 - 2.39	2.40*
c	2.14**	1.66 - 2.74	2.37**	1.83 - 3.08	3.57**	1.95 - 6.55	2.25**	1.55 - 3.25	2.57*
	0.84	0.65 - 1.09	0.89	0.67 - 1.17	1.49	0.76 - 2.92	0.89	0.58 - 1.37	0.78
	1.19	0.89 - 1.59	1.35	1.00 - 1.82	2.82**	1.46 - 5.45	1.28	0.81 - 2.00	1.20

: Adjusted odds ratios from multiple logistic regression analyses with gender and race/ethnicity as predictors of illicit drugs or prescription drugs, (b) use of illicit drugs including marijuana, (c) use of illicit drugs not inc : use of prescription drugs, (e) three or more positive items based on the Drug Abuse Screening Test (DAST
:I = 95% confidence interval for the adjusted odds ratio.

12-month drug use were slightly lower among Whites compared to Hispanics, but the difference was not statistically significant (OR = .87, *ns*).

As described in the data analysis section, interactive effects of gender and race on the odds of past 12-month drug use were tested. The chi-square for the main effects model was 112.15 (df = 5), and the chi-square for the interaction effects model was 121.70 (df = 9). The difference between the two χ^2 was 121.70 – 112.15 = 9.55 (df = 4, $p < .05$), which suggests the presence of a statistically significant interaction effect between gender and race. Results showed that the odds ratio for gender was significantly stronger for African Americans compared to Whites (OR = 1.59, $p < .05$) and for African Americans compared to Other Races (OR = 2.44, $p < .01$). Indeed, the effect of gender on past 12-month drug use was statistically significant among African Americans (OR = 1.70, $p < .01$), but not among any of the other racial groups.

Results from multiple logistic regression analysis (see Table 5) for past 12-month use of illicit drugs including marijuana revealed that after controlling for race, there was a significant effect of gender, and the adjusted odds were higher among males compared to females (OR = 1.20, $p < .01$). Results also indicated a main effect for race using African Americans as the reference group. Controlling for gender, the odds of past 12-month drug use were statistically significantly higher among Whites (OR = 2.12, $p < .01$), Hispanics (OR = 2.37, $p < .01$), and Other Races (OR = 1.35, $p = .05$) compared to African Americans. Additional analyses with Hispanics as the reference category showed that the odds of past 12-month illicit drug use were slightly but not significantly lower among Whites compared to Hispanics (OR = .90, *ns*).

Results from a hierarchical logistic regression analyses showed that the chi-square for the main effects model was 135.5 (df = 5), and the chi-square for the interaction effects model was 147.5 (df = 9). The difference between the two χ^2 was 147.5–135.5 = 12.0 (df = 4, $p < .05$), which suggests the presence of a statistically significant interaction effect between gender and race. Results showed that the odds ratio for gender was significantly stronger for African Americans compared to Whites (OR = 1.96, $p < .01$), for African Americans compared to Hispanics (OR = 1.83, $p < .05$), for African Americans compared to Asians (OR = 1.97, $p < .05$), and for African Americans compared to Other Races (OR = 2.74, $p < .01$). No other statistically significant interaction effects were observed.

Results from multiple logistic regression analysis (see Table 5) for past 12-month use of illicit drugs *not* including marijuana revealed that after controlling for race, there was a significant effect of gender, and the adjusted odds ratio were higher among males compared to females (OR = 1.80, $p < .01$). Results also indicated a main effect for race using African Americans as the reference group. Controlling for gender, the odds of past 12-month illicit drug use (not including marijuana) was significantly higher among Whites (OR = 3.13, $p < .01$), Hispanics (OR = 3.57, $p < .01$) and Other Races (OR = 2.82, $p < .01$) compared to African Americans. Results from a hierarchical logistic regression analyses showed that the chi-square for the main effects model was 63.71 (df = 5), and the chi-square for the interaction effects model was 65.30 (df = 9). The difference between the two χ^2 was 65.30 – 63.71 = 1.59 (df = 4, *ns*), which does not support the hypothesis that the effect of gender on past 12-month illicit drug use (not including marijuana) is moderated by race.

Results from multiple logistic regression analysis (see Table 5) for past 12-month illicit use of prescription drugs revealed that after controlling for race, there was no effect of gender. Results also indicated a main effect for race using African Americans as the reference group. Controlling for gender, the odds of past 12-month illicit use of prescription drugs was statistically significantly higher among Whites (OR = 1.73, $p < .01$) and Hispanics (OR = 2.25, $p < .01$) compared to African Americans. Additional analyses indicated that the odds of past 12-month illicit prescription drug use was significantly higher among Hispanics compared to Whites (OR = 1.30, $p < .05$), Asians (OR = 2.52, $p < .01$), and Other Races (OR = 1.76, $p < .01$).

Results from a hierarchical logistic regression analyses showed that the chi-square for the main effects model was 39.22 (df = 5), and the chi-square for the interaction effects model was 41.36 (df = 9). The difference between the two χ^2 was 41.36 – 39.22 = 2.14 (df = 4, *ns*), which does not support the hypothesis that the effect of gender on past 12-month illicit prescription drug use is moderated by race/ethnicity.

Main and Interactive Effects of Gender and Race/Ethnicity on Drug Abuse

Multiple logistic regression analyses were conducted to examine the main and interactive effects of gender and race/ethnicity on reporting three or more DAST-10 items. Results for past 12-month illicit use of prescription drugs revealed that, controlling for race/ethnicity, there was a statistically significant effect for gender, and the odds of reporting three or more drug use-related problems in the past year were higher among males compared to females (OR = 1.55, $p < .01$). Results also indicated a main effect for race/ethnicity using African Americans as the reference group. Controlling for gender, the odds of reporting three or more DAST-10 items was significantly higher among Whites (OR = 2.40, $p < .01$) and Hispanics (OR = 2.57, $p < .01$) compared to African Americans. Analyses with Whites as the reference category showed that the odds of reporting three or more DAST-10 items was not significantly different between Hispanics compared to Whites (OR = 1.07, *ns*). Results from a hierarchical logistic regression analyses showed that the chi-square for the main effects model was 79.3 (df = 5), and the chi-square for the interaction effects model was 80.1 (df = 9). The difference between the two χ^2 was 80.1 – 79.3 = 0.8 (df = 4, *ns*), which does not support the hypothesis that the effect of gender on reporting three or more DAST-10 items is moderated by race/ethnicity.

Our data indicated that the majority of lifetime marijuana users (67.8%) reported using marijuana prior to college. Furthermore, results from multiple logistic regression analyses indicated that the odds of pre-college onset of marijuana use were higher for Whites (OR = 1.44, $p < .05$) and Hispanics (OR = 1.54, $p < .05$) compared to African Americans. Further, the odds of pre-college onset of marijuana use were higher for Whites (OR = 1.75, $p < .01$) and Hispanics (OR = 1.87, $p < .01$) compared to Asians.

DISCUSSION

The present study found higher rates of drug use and drug use related problems among Hispanic and White students relative to their African American and Asian college peers. Indeed, the highest rates of drug use and drug use related problems were generally among Hispanic students. Our data support earlier research that found Hispanic college students have higher rates of marijuana use as compared to Asian and African-American college students (Bell et al., 1997; Gledhill-Hoyt et al., 2000; Mohler-Kuo et al., 2003). The findings of the present study are also in line with past research that has shown White students have higher rates of illicit drug use than African American and Asian college students including marijuana (Bell et al., 1997; Meilman et al., 1995; Mohler-Kuo et al., 2003), ecstasy (Boyd et al., 2003; Strote et al., 2002), and several classes of prescription drugs (McCabe, 2005; McCabe et al., 2005a, 2005b).

We discovered considerable racial differences in *drug abuse* among college students that have not been well-studied to date. Because racial differences in *drug use* among college students do not necessarily reflect racial differences in *drug abuse*, future work is needed to elucidate the underlying causes for the higher rates of drug abuse among Hispanic and White college students. The continued examination of racial differences among young adults is especially important based on the recent increases in past-year prevalence of DSM-IV marijuana use disorders among Hispanic young adults 18 to 29 years of age in the U.S. (Compton et al., 2004).

The illicit use of prescription drugs was second only to marijuana use across both genders and all racial groups; our findings are consistent with an emerging national trend in this age group (e.g., Johnston et al., 2004; McCabe et al., 2007; Mohler-Kuo et al., 2003). In addition, our higher drug use rates among male college students, relative to female college students, support previous work that revealed higher rates of illicit drug use such as marijuana (Bell et al., 1997; Gledhill-Hoyt et al., 2000; Johnston et al., 2004), LSD and other psychedelics (Johnston et al., 2004), inhalants (Johnston et al., 2004), and prescription stimulants (McCabe et al., 2005a) in this population.

The present study was unique in that we explored possible racial differences in the age of initiation of illicit drug use; we found some evidence that the racial differences in illicit drug use were present before college with marijuana use being more prevalent among White and Hispanic students prior to college. Similar racial differences have been observed among secondary school students in the U.S. (Delva et al., 2005; Johnston et al., 2005b); studies have found that the 12-month prevalence of marijuana and cocaine use is significantly higher among Hispanic 8th grade students when compared to non-Hispanic youth. Hispanic students in the present study were found to be at increased risk for severe consequences associated with several drug use behaviors, particularly simultaneous polydrug use (e.g., Cone et al., 2004; SAMHSA, 2004b; Watson et al., 2004). College administrators should be made aware of these racial/ethnic differences and be prepared to offer appropriate screening, referral and treatment options that are racially and ethnically sensitive.

The findings of the present study should be considered in the context of its strengths and limitations. Most notably, a strength is that racial minorities were oversampled enabling calculation of reliable estimates of drug use and drug use related problems for African American, Asian, and Hispanic undergraduate students. Many college-based efforts have lacked the necessary sample sizes of racial minorities to examine drug use and drug use related problems separately across racial categories. Another strength lies in our extension of previous college-based studies to feature the DAST-10 brief screening instrument to detect potential drug abuse. And finally, the present study focused on drug use and drug use related problems for substances (other than alcohol) which represent an understudied topic among college students.

Interpretations of our findings are also constrained by several limitations. First, the findings of the present study may not generalize to other college and non-college populations. Although the demographic characteristics from the sample closely resembled the demographic characteristics of 4-year U.S. colleges and universities nationally (Wechsler et al., 2002), previous research has found rates of illicit drug use vary across U.S. colleges and universities (e.g., Bell et al., 1997; McCabe et al., 2005a, 2005b). Second, the present study did not examine differences between ethnic subgroups (e.g., Cuban American, Mexican American, Puerto Rican) and previous research has found differences in drug use between ethnic subgroups among secondary school students (Delva et al., 2005). Future collegiate studies need to examine possible differences between ethnic subgroups in drug use, especially when considering the higher rates found among Hispanic students. Third, although the DAST-10 has been found to be culturally appropriate in diverse populations, further work should examine the validity of this brief screening instrument for adolescents and across various racial/ethnic groups. Finally, with a response rate of 66%, a non-response bias may have affected our findings. In an effort to assess the possible impact of non-response bias, we conducted a brief telephone survey with a randomly selected sample of students who did not respond to the original survey. A total of 159 students responded to the follow-up effort and we found no significant differences in the rates of alcohol and other drug use for those who responded to the short survey compared to students who completed the original web survey.

Despite these limitations, the present study provides strong evidence from one university that Hispanic and White undergraduate students were at increased risk for drug use and abuse. The heightened risk among Hispanic students is of particular concern when considering the low retention and enrollment rates among Hispanic students in U.S. secondary and postsecondary institutions (U.S. Department of Education, 2003a, 2003b). Institutions of higher education are encouraged to assess illicit drug use on their own campuses while paying particular attention to possible racial/ethnic and gender differences and to consider such differences in the development of prevention and intervention efforts.

REFERENCES

Bell, R., Wechsler, H., & Johnston, L. D. (1997). Correlates of college student marijuana use: Results of a US national survey. *Addiction, 92*, 571-581.

Bernstein, J., Bernstein, E., Tassiopoulos, K., Heeren, T., Levenson, S., & Hingson, R. (2005). Brief motivational intervention at a clinic visit reduces cocaine and heroin use. *Drug and Alcohol Dependence, 77*, 49-59.

Boyd, C., McCabe, S. E., & d'Arcy, H. (2003). Ecstasy use among college undergraduates: Gender, race and sexual identity. *Journal of Substance Abuse Treatment, 24*, 209-215.

Cocco, K. M., & Carey, K. B. (1998). Psychometric properties of the Drug Abuse Screening Test in psychiatric outpatients. *Psychological Assessment, 10*, 408-414.

Compton, W. M., Grant, B. F., Colliver, J. D., Glantz, M.D., & Stinson, F. S. (2004). Prevalence of marijuana use disorders in the United States: 1991-1992 and 2001-2002. *JAMA, 291*, 2114-2121.

Cone, E. J., Fant, R. V., Rohay, J. M., Caplan, Y. H., Ballina, M., Reder, R. F., & Haddox, J. D. (2004). Oxycodone involvement in drug abuse deaths. II. Evidence for toxic multiple drug-drug interactions. *Journal of Analytical Toxicology, 28*, 217-225.

Delva, J., Wallace, J. M. Jr., O'Malley, P. M., Bachman, J. G., Johnston, L. D., & Schulenberg, J. (2005). The epidemiology of alcohol, marijuana, and cocaine use among Mexican American, Puerto Rican, Cuban American, and other Latin American eighth-grade students in the United States: 1991-2002. *American Journal of Public Health, 95*, 696-702.

Delva, J., Smith, M. P., Howell, R. L., Harrison, D. F., Wilke, D., & Jackson, D. L. (2004). A study of the relationship between protective behaviors and drinking consequences among undergraduate college students. *Journal of American College Health, 53*, 19-26.

French, M.T., Roebuck, M.C., McGeary, K.A., Chitwood, D.D., & McCoy, C.B. (2001). Using the Drug Abuse Screening Test (DAST-10) to analyze health services utilization and cost for substance users in a community-based setting. *Substance Use and Misuse, 36*, 927-946.

Gfroerer, J. C., Greenblatt, J. C. & Wright, D. A. (1997). Substance use in the US college-age population: Differences according to educational status and living arrangement. *American Journal of Public Health, 87*, 62-65.

Gledhill-Hoyt, J., Lee, H., Strote, J., & Wechsler, H. (2000). Increased use of marijuana and other illicit drugs at US colleges in the 1990s: Results of three national surveys. *Addiction, 95*, 1655-1667.

Jaccard, J. (2001). *Interaction Effects in Logistic Regression.* Thousand Oaks, CA: Sage.

Johnston, L. D., O'Malley, P. M., & Bachman, J. G. (2003). *Monitoring the Future National Survey Results on Drug Use, 1975-2002. Volume II: College Students and Adults Ages 19-40* (NIH Publication No. 03-5376). Bethesda, MD: National Institute on Drug Abuse.

Johnston, L. D., O'Malley, P. M., Bachman, J. G., & Schulenberg, J.E. (2004). *Monitoring the Future National Survey Results on Drug Use, 1975-2003. Volume II:*

College Students and Adults Ages 19-45. (NIH Publication 04-5508). Bethesda, MD: National Institute on Drug Abuse.

Johnston, L. D., O'Malley, P. M., Bachman, J. G., & Schulenberg, J.E. (2005a). *Monitoring the Future National Survey Results on Drug Use, 1975-2004. Volume II: College Students & Adults Ages 19-45.* (NIH Publication 05-5728). Bethesda, MD: National Institute on Drug Abuse.

Johnston, L. D., O'Malley, P. M., Bachman, J. G., & Schulenberg, J.E. (2005b). *Monitoring the Future National Survey Results on Drug Use, 1975-2004. Volume I: Secondary School Students.* (NIH Publication 05-5727). Bethesda, MD: National Institute on Drug Abuse.

McCabe, S. E. (2004). Comparison of web and mail surveys in collecting illicit drug use data: A randomized experiment. *Journal of Drug Education, 34*, 61-72.

McCabe, S. E. (2005). Correlates of nonmedical use of prescription benzodiazepine anxiolytics: Results from a national survey of U.S. college students. *Drug and Alcohol Dependence, 79*, 53-62.

McCabe, S. E., Boyd, C. J., Couper, M. P., Crawford, S., & d'Arcy, H. (2002). Mode effects for collecting alcohol and other drug use data: Web and U.S. mail. *Journal of Studies of Alcohol, 63*, 755-761.

McCabe, S. E., Knight, J. R., Teter, C. J., & Wechsler, H. (2005a). Non-medical use of prescription stimulants among US college students: Prevalence and correlates from a national survey. *Addiction, 100*, 96-106.

McCabe, S. E., Teter, C. J., Boyd, C. J., Knight, J. R., & Wechsler, H. (2005b). Non-medical use of prescription opioids among U.S. college students: Prevalence and correlates from a national survey. *Addictive Behaviors, 30*, 789-805.

McCabe, S.E., West, B., & Wechsler, H. (2007). Trends in non-medical use of prescription drugs among U.S. college students from 1993 to 2001. *Addiction, 102*, 455-465.

Meilman, P. W., Presley, C. A., & Cashin, J. R. (1995). The sober social life at Historically Black Colleges. *Journal of Blacks in Higher Education, 9*, 98-100.

Mohler-Kuo, M., Lee, J. E. & Wechsler, H. (2003). Trends in marijuana and other illicit drug use among college students. Results from 4 Harvard School of Public Health College Alcohol Study Surveys: 1993-2001. *Journal of American College Health, 52*, 17-24.

Presley, C. A., Meilman, P. W. & Cashin, J. R. (1996). *Alcohol and Drugs on American College Campuses: Use, Consequences, and Perceptions of the Campus Environment*, vol. IV, pp. 1992-1994. Carbondale, IL: Core Institute.

Skinner, H. (1982). The Drug Abuse Screening Test. *Addictive Behaviors, 7*, 363-371.

Strote, J., Lee, J. E., & Wechsler, H. (2002). Increasing MDMA use among college students: Results of a national survey. *Journal of Adolescent Health, 30*, 64-72.

Substance Abuse and Mental Health Services Administration. (2004a). *Overview of Findings from the 2003 National Survey on Drug Use and Health* (Office of Applied Studies, NSDUH Series H–24, DHHS Publication No. SMA 04–3963). Rockville, MD.

Substance Abuse and Mental Health Services Administration. (2004b). *The Dawn Report: Oxycodone, Hydrocodone, and Polydrug Use, 2002.* Office of Applied Studies. Accessed online 8/10/04 http://oas.samhsa.gov/2k4/oxycodone/oxycodone. cfm.

Substance Abuse and Mental Health Services Administration. (2005). *The NSDUH Report: College Enrollment Status and Past Year Illicit Drug Use among Young Adults: 2002, 2003, and 2004*. Office of Applied Studies. Accessed online 12/10/05 http://oas.samhsa.gov/2k5/College/college.pdf.

Teter, C. J., McCabe, S. E., Cranford, J. A., Boyd, C. J., & Guthrie, S. K. (2005). Prevalence and motives for illicit use of prescription stimulants in an undergraduate student sample. *Journal of American College Health, 53*, 253-262.

U.S. Department of Education. (2003a). National Center for Education Statistics. The Condition of Education 2003. Indicator 17: Status drop out rates by race/ethnicity. [Online] http://nces.ed.gov/programs/coe/2003/section3/indicator17.asp [Accessed October 9, 2005].

U.S. Department of Education. (2003b). National Center for Education Statistics. The Condition of Education 2003. Indicator 18: Immediate transition to college. [Online] http://nces.ed.gov/programs/coe/2003/section3/indicator18.asp#info [Accessed October 9, 2005].

Watson, W. A., Litovitz, T. L., Klein-Schwartz, W., Rodgers, G. C. Jr, Youniss, J., Reid, N., Rouse, W. G., Rembert, R. S., & Borys, D. (2004). 2003 annual report of the American Association of Poison Control Centers Toxic Exposure Surveillance System. *American Journal of Emergency Medicine, 22*, 335-404.

Wechsler, H., Lee, J. E., Kuo, M., Seibring, M., Nelson, T. F., & Lee, H. (2002). Trends in college binge drinking during a period of increased prevention efforts. Findings from 4 Harvard School of Public Health College Alcohol Study surveys: 1993-2001. *Journal of American College Health, 50*, 203-217.

Wechsler, H., Dowdall, G.W., Davenport, A., & Castillo, S. (1995). Correlates of college student binge drinking. *American Journal of Public Health, 85*, 921-926.

doi:10.1300/J233v06n02_06

Acculturation and Drug Use Among Dually Diagnosed Hispanic Adolescents

Rosemarie A. Rodriguez, PhD
Craig E. Henderson, PhD
Cynthia L. Rowe, PhD
Kent F. Burnett, PhD
Gayle A. Dakof, PhD
Howard A. Liddle, EdD

Rosemarie A. Rodriguez is Research Associate, Department of Epidemiology and Public Health, Center for Treatment Research on Adolescent Drug Abuse, University of Miami Leonard M. Miller School of Medicine, Miami, FL 33136 (E-mail: rosemarie.a.rodriguez@att.net). Craig E. Henderson is Research Assistant Professor, Department of Epidemiology and Public Health, Center for Treatment Research on Adolescent Drug Abuse, University of Miami Leonard M. Miller School of Medicine, Miami, FL 33136 (E-mail: craightml@sbcglobal.net). Cynthia L. Rowe is Research Assistant Professor, Department of Epidemiology and Public Health, Center for Treatment Research on Adolescent Drug Abuse, University of Miami Leonard M. Miller School of Medicine, Miami, FL 33136 (E-mail: crowe@med.miami.edu). Kent F. Burnett is Associate Professor, Department of Educational and Psychological Studies, University of Miami School of Education, Miami, FL 33124 (E-mail: kburnett@miami.edu).

Gayle A. Dakof is Research Associate Professor, Department of Epidemiology and Public Health, Center for Treatment Research on Adolescent Drug Abuse, University of Miami Leonard M. Miller School of Medicine, Miami, FL 33136 (E-mail: gdakof@med.miami.edu) Howard A. Liddle is Professor, Departments of Epidemiology and Public Health, and Psychology; Director, Center for Treatment Research on Adolescent Drug Abuse, University of Miami Leonard M. Miller School of Medicine, Miami, FL 33136 (E-mail: hliddle@med.miami.edu).

This study was funded by a supplement to Grant DA 11328 from the National Institute on Drug Abuse (NIDA). We gratefully acknowledge Dr. Hua Li for his assistance with data management and we thank Dr. Etiony Aldarondo and Dr. Andrew Wenger for their feedback on earlier drafts.

[Haworth co-indexing entry note]: "Acculturation and Drug Use Among Dually Diagnosed Hispanic Adolescents." Rodriguez, Rosemarie A. et al. Co-published simultaneously in *Journal of Ethnicity in Substance Abuse* (The Haworth Press, Inc.) Vol. 6, No. 2, 2007, pp. 97-113; and: *21st Century Research on Drugs and Ethnicity: Studies Supported by the National Institute on Drug Abuse* (ed: Peter L. Myers) The Haworth Press, 2007, pp. 97-113. Single or multiple copies of this article are available for a fee from The Haworth Document Delivery Service [1-800-HAWORTH, 9:00 a.m. - 5:00 p.m. (EST). E-mail address: docdelivery@haworthpress.com].

Available online at http://jesa.haworthpress.com

doi:10.1300/J233v06n02_07

SUMMARY. With drug abuse among Hispanic youth on the rise, examining cultural factors such as acculturation may provide insight into understanding and addressing this problem. This study examined the relationship between acculturation and severity of drug use among a sample of severely impaired Hispanic adolescents referred for residential substance abuse treatment. As recent studies with clinical samples have found, it was hypothesized that lower levels of acculturation would be associated with higher levels of substance use. Results indicated that youth born outside the United States reported greater frequency of drug use at intake into treatment than those born in the United States, supporting the hypothesis. doi:10.1300/J233v06n02_07 *[Article copies available for a fee from The Haworth Document Delivery Service: 1-800- HAWORTH. E-mail address: <docdelivery@haworthpress.com> Website: <http://www.HaworthPress.com>*

KEYWORDS. Hispanics, acculturation, adolescents, substance use/abuse, drug use/abuse, comorbidity

INTRODUCTION

Drug and alcohol use among Hispanic adolescents is a serious public health concern (Delva, Wallace, O'Malley, Bachman, Johnston, & Schulenberg, 2005; Gil, Wagner, & Tubman, 2004; Szapocznik et al., 1997). Whereas the use of drugs has generally declined among adolescents in recent years, this has not been the case for Hispanic youth, particularly among the youngest cohorts of adolescents (Delva et al., 2005; Johnston, O'Malley, Bachman, & Schulenberg, 2005). In fact, among American teens, Hispanic eighth graders report the highest rates of use for nearly all classes of drugs and alcohol (Johnston, O'Malley, Bachman, & Schulenberg, 2004).

The relatively high prevalence of drug use among Hispanic youths is of concern particularly in the context of recent demographic trends: (a) the Hispanic population in the United States continues to grow rapidly, recently becoming the largest racial and ethnic minority group in the United States (United States Census Bureau, 2001); (b) the Hispanic population is significantly younger than the general population, with the highest fertility rates among all racial and ethnic groups (Downs, 2003; United States Census Bureau, 2000); and (c) Hispanic youth have higher school dropout rates and a higher proportion of families living in poverty than the general population (Bishaw & Iceland, 2003; U.S. Department of Education, 2000). Together, these substance use and sociodemographic trends indicate that a severe drug use problem may be emerging within the Hispanic population.

Examining the impact of cultural factors on substance abuse among Hispanic adolescents may provide important clinical insights about how these problems should be treated. One of the most frequently studied cultural factors associated with substance abuse among Hispanic adolescents is acculturation to the dominant American culture (Gil, Wagner, & Vega, 2000; Gfroerer & De La Rosa, 1993; Szapocznik & Kurtines, 1980). According to Marin (1992), acculturation can be broadly defined as a multidimensional psychosocial phenomenon that is reflected in psychological changes that occur in individuals as a result of their interaction with a new culture (p. 237). Although there are different approaches to conceptualizing acculturation, the consensus is that it is a powerful force shaping individuals' quality of life (Vega, Gil, & Wagner, 1998). Because of the impact of the acculturation process on youths' development, researchers have recently examined the impact of acculturation on adolescent substance use (Vega & Gil, 1999).

Direct relationships between acculturation and drug use have been established in studies conducted with community samples of adolescents. The majority of researchers have found that as Hispanics become more acculturated and their families lose some of their ties to traditional Hispanic cultural mores, frequency of substance use typically increases (Epstein, Botvin, & Diaz, 2000, 2001; Epstein, Margaret, & Botvin, 2003; Khoury, Warheit, Zimmerman, Vega, & Gil, 1996; Lovato, Litrownik, Elder, Nunez-Liriano, Suarez, & Talavera, 1994). These studies suggest that acculturation to dominant American culture may serve as a conduit through which Hispanic youth are placed at risk for substance use through a diminishment of important Hispanic cultural values such as familism (i.e., a strong identification with and loyalty to members of the extended family; Marin, 1993; Vega, 1995). However, the link between acculturation and drug use among clinical samples of Hispanic adolescents has been relatively unexamined. Those few studies that have been conducted have indicated that less acculturated adolescents report more severe drug use problems (Garcia, 1999; Gil, Wagner, & Tubman, 2004), exactly the opposite of what has been observed with community samples. Gil et al. (2004) explain these discrepant findings by suggesting that these teens experience more significant life traumas, more intrafamilial stress, and higher prevalence of comorbid disorders, potentially complicating the acculturation process. More research is needed to fully understand the role of acculturation in substance abuse among clinical samples of Hispanic teens in the United States.

The current study addresses gaps in the research base by examining the relationship between acculturation and severity of drug abuse among a sample of severely impaired adolescents referred for residential substance abuse treatment. In order to examine the possibility that comorbidity helps to explain the inverse relationship between substance abuse and acculturation in clinical samples, the current study was conducted with a sample of substance-abusing teens with comorbid psychiatric disorders. It was hypothesized that among this clinical sample of dually diagnosed Hispanic adolescents, lower levels of acculturation would be positively associated with higher levels of substance use. The potential contributions of the current study include providing more data from clinical samples of Hispanic adolescents with identified substance use disorders (SUD) and testing the generalizability of existing research on clinical samples to those meeting criteria for comorbid psychiatric disorders. Understanding important cultural processes more fully may provide direction for the refinement of existing research-based interventions, extending the current research to dually diagnosed adolescents (i.e., those meeting diagnostic criteria for SUD and other psychiatric disorders).

METHOD

All participants had been clinically referred for residential treatment for substance abuse and recruited into a randomized clinical trial. The study focused on the relationship between acculturation and substance use upon entry into treatment and was conducted exclusively with the Hispanic participants.

PARTICIPANTS

Participants consisted of 76 Hispanic male and female adolescents, between the ages of 13 and 17 ($M = 15.3$, $SD = 1.1$), who met DSM-IV criteria for substance dependence, with problems of sufficient severity to be referred for residential treatment, and who met criteria for at least one comorbid psychiatric condition. Participants were primarily referred from a local adolescent detoxification and stabilization facility (68%, many of whom were referred to this facility from the juvenile justice system), and the juvenile justice system (17%). Current local standards for placement in residential treatment are meeting 6 of the following 8 criteria: (1) substance dependence, (2) family history of addiction, (3) positive toxicology screen at assessment, (4) history of high risk behaviors (e.g., serious violations of parental or school rules, aggressive behavior, destruction of property), (5) lack of family stability (i.e., the family provided insufficient structure to prevent the adolescent from running away or meeting probation conditions), (6) low motivation for treatment (i.e., it is perceived that adolescents are highly unlikely to complete a full course of outpatient treatment), (7) drug related arrests or substance-induced psychiatric symptoms, and (8) a history of at least one failed treatment episode. Please see Table 1 for the demographic and clinical characteristics of the study participants.

MEASURES

Demographic Variables

Participants were administered a demographic and background questionnaire. From this interview, gender, age, family income, mother's education, juvenile justice involvement, and parental substance abuse problems were used as covariates in the study analyses.

Substance Use Measures

Timeline Follow-Back Method (TLFB). The TLFB method obtains retrospective reports of daily substance use by using a calendar and other memory prompts to stimulate recall (Dennis, Funk, Godley, & Waldron, 2004). It gathers daily information on specific substances used and amount of use (number of drinks, hits, rocks, etc). It yields consistently high test-retest correlations over periods up to 1 year (Carey, 1997; Maisto & Connors, 1992), and has been shown to correlate with other self-reports as well as with collateral reports (Sobell & Sobell, 1992). Adolescents reported on their use of several categories of drugs over the previous 30-day period.

Psychiatric Diagnoses

Youth Self Report (YSR). The YSR (Achenbach & Edelbrock, 1979, 1983) measures an array of adolescent behavioral problems and social competencies and was used as a report of internalizing and externalizing symptoms. The YSR is a well-known instrument with excellent reliability and validity with minority populations (Achenbach & Edelbrock, 1983),

TABLE 1. Sample Characteristics

	n (%)	*M (SD)*
Age		15.3 (1.10)
Gender		
Male	56 (74)	
Female	20 (26)	
Ethnicity / Race		
Cuban	35 (46)	
Puerto Rican	10 (13)	
Colombian	9 (12)	
Nicaraguan	9 (12)	
Other	13 (17)	
Birthplace		
United States	56 (74)	
Outside United States	20 (26)	
Years Living in United States		14.5 (2.56)
Family Income		$23,275 ($16,688) Median = $18,300
Mother Education		
<High School	30 (40)	
High School Graduate	20 (27)	
Some College/Post High School	15 (20)	
College Graduate	5 (7)	
Graduate / Professional Degree	3 (4)	
Adolescent on Probation	40 (52)	
Adolescent Pending Adjudication	29 (38)	
Family Structure		
Single Parent	27 (35)	
Two Parent	19 (25)	
Blended	19 (25)	
Extended	11 (15)	
Substance Use Disorders		
Cannabis Dependence	61 (80)	
Cocaine Dependence	14 (19)	
Alcohol Dependence	10 (13)	
Polysubstance Dependence	10 (13)	

TABLE 1 (continued)

Comorbid Psychiatric Diagnoses	
Conduct Disorder	57 (75)
Attention-Deficit/Hyperactivity Disorder	19 (25)
Major Depressive Disorder	15 (22)
Posttraumatic Stress Disorder	11 (16)

and has proven useful for assessing changes in the behavior of conduct-disordered adolescents following therapy (Kazdin, 1990).

Revised Child Behavior Checklist (CBCL). The CBCL (Achenbach & Edelbrock, 1979, 1983) is a parent-report instrument that measures an array of child behavioral problems and social competencies. The CBCL is a well-known instrument that has demonstrated excellent reliability and validity. The CBCL was used as a collateral report of adolescent internalizing and externalizing symptoms.

Level of Acculturation

In order to evaluate level of acculturation of adolescents and their primary caregivers, acculturation proxies included in the assessment battery of the parent project were utilized, consisting of birthplace (U.S. vs. other), number of years living in the United States, and language preference. The acculturation proxies were administered to both adolescents and their parents. A formal measure of acculturation was not administered in the parent project; however, these proxies have been used in several previous studies of adolescent behavior problems and substance abuse (Coatsworth, Pantin, McBride, Briones, Kurtines, & Szapocznik, 2000; Norris, Ford, & Bova, 1996). Utilizing proxies can be advantageous because they are easily added to data collection tools, and they are often present in data sets used for secondary data analysis (Driscoll, Biggs, Brindis, & Yankah, 2001). Further, existing measures of acculturation have been criticized for questionable construct validity (i.e., questions still exist as to the most accurate way to measure acculturation; Norris et al., 1996) as well as inadequate content validity (i.e., the measures may not adequately sample all that is relevant to acculturation; Zane & Mak, 2003).

PROCEDURE

Research staff trained in the protection of human subjects contacted parents and youth to describe study procedures and purpose, and to obtain written informed consent (and assent with the youth), prior to the assessment session. It was emphasized that participation was voluntary and that parents and youth had the right to discontinue participation at any time. A research assessment which took approximately two hours to complete was conducted by research staff within one week of families providing consent to participate in the study. Parents and teens were interviewed separately to encourage open and honest answers.

ANALYSES

Multiple regression procedures were conducted to determine whether level of acculturation was associated with adolescent substance abuse and severity of psychiatric symptoms at entry into treatment. Prior to testing the study hypothesis, diagnostic procedures were employed to assess for multivariate outliers as well as the linearity and normality of the dependent measures (Tabachnick & Fidell, 2001). These analyses yielded no multivariate outliers, and the normality and linearity of the data were found to be within permissible limits. Regression models first adjusted for the effect of the background variables of gender, age, family income, mother's education, juvenile justice involvement, and history of family drug use by adding them as covariates in a hierarchical entry procedure. The background variables were entered as a block, followed by adolescent acculturation.

Separate regressions were conducted for each criterion variable: frequency of substance use, internalizing and externalizing symptoms. Language preference was not included as a predictor, as the adolescents all reported that they preferred communicating in English. In addition, given the large proportion of the sample that was born in the United States (consistent with other studies of acculturation and drug use among clinical samples; Gil et al., 2004), years living in the United States was highly correlated with age, which was already included as a covariate and therefore was not included as a predictor variable.

RESULTS

Descriptive Statistics

As shown in Table 1, the average age of the participants was approximately 15 years (SD = 1.10), and 74% were born in the United States. On average, participants had lived in the United States an average of approximately 14.5 years (SD = 2.56). Seventy-four percent of the participants were male and 26% were female. All participants were Hispanics, but they represented several different Hispanic ethnic backgrounds (46% Cuban, 13% Puerto Rican, 12% Colombian, 12% Nicaraguan, and 17% other Hispanic ethnicities). Consistent with their referrals for residential treatment, they had severe substance abuse problems, with 80% meeting diagnostic criteria for cannabis dependence, 19% for cocaine dependence, 13% for alcohol dependence, and 13% for polysubstance dependence at intake. Ninety-five percent of the participants reported using drugs at least weekly, with 34% using them daily, and 30% reporting more than one drug use episode a day. Seventy-six percent reported at least one failed treatment episode. For study inclusion, all adolescents met criteria for at least one comorbid psychiatric disorder. The most common psychiatric disorders were conduct disorder (75% meeting criteria), attention-deficit/hyperactivity disorder (25%), major depressive disorder (22%), and post-traumatic stress disorder (16%). They also had extensive involvement in the juvenile justice system (i.e., 52% were on community control/probation and 38% were pending adjudication). Finally, the participants also came from homes with extensive family dysfunction. Only 25% were from two-parent families, 57% had family members with alcohol or drug abuse problems, 51% had family members with mental health problems, and 53% had family members involved in the criminal justice system. Median annual family income was approximately $23,000.

ACCULTURATION AND DRUG USE

To assess the association between acculturation of Hispanic adolescents and their substance use, a regression model incorporated the acculturation proxy birthplace as a predictor of drug use. A hierarchical entry procedure was utilized in which age, gender, total family income, and mother's level of education and dichotomous variables representing presence/absence of juvenile justice involvement and family involvement in drug use were entered as covariates in the first step, and birthplace in the second. As shown in Table 2, the covariates accounted for approximately 3% of the variance in intake drug use [$F\,(4, 68) = .429, p = .787$]. Birthplace was found to be a significant predictor of drug use having adjusted for the background covariates, accounting for an additional 6% of the variance [$F\,(1, 64) = 4.262, p = .043$], indicating that those youth born outside the United States reported more substance use.

TABLE 2. Hierarchical Regression Analysis of Birthplace Predicting Substance Use

Variable	*B*	*S.E*	*ß*	*t*	*p*
Step 1					
Age	−2.156	1.813	−.153	−1.189	.239
Patient Gender	.400	4.636	.011	.086	.931
Total Family Income	−1.73E-05	.000	−.019	−.152	.880
Mother's Highest Level of Education	.227	1.690	.017	.134	.894
Number of Lifetime Arrests	−.181	.487	−.048	−.371	.712
Family Prior Drug Use Problems	3.937	4.028	.128	.977	.332
Step 2					
Birthplace	−9.136	4.425	−.269	−2.065	.043

$R = .299$, $R^2 = .089$ ($N = 71$)

ACCULTURATION AND INTERNALIZING AND EXTERNALIZING BEHAVIORS

Separate regression models were conducted for adolescent- and parent-reported internalizing and externalizing behaviors. The same covariates were used as the above analysis, and birthplace again served as the predictor. Together the covariates showed a marginal trend toward predicting the extent of internalizing problems [$F(4, 68) = 1.93, p = .12, R^2 = .10$], with females reporting more internalizing than males ($t = 2.77$, $p = .007$). However, birthplace was not a significant predictor, contributing very little to the prediction of internalizing problems to what was accounted for by the covariates [$F(1, 66) = .862, p = .427, R^2 = .13$]. With respect to adolescent-reported externalizing behaviors, birthplace was not a significant predictor above and beyond the covariates [$F(1, 66) = .037, p = .964$]. However, as with internalizing behavior, gender was a significant predictor ($t = 3.18$, $p = .002$), such that males reported more externalizing behaviors. Parent reports of adolescent internalizing and externalizing symptoms duplicated the same pattern (i.e., birthplace was not a significant predictor of either internalizing or externalizing behavior, and gender was a significant predictor of both).

DISCUSSION

The findings support the importance of acculturation as it relates to drug use in clinical samples of Hispanic adolescents. Contrary to studies from community samples, the findings indicated that less acculturated adolescents had more severe drug problems at entry into treatment than more acculturated adolescents (Epstein et al., 2000, 2001, 2003; Khoury et al., 1996; Lovato et al., 1994). However, the results are consistent with Gil et al. (2004), which utilized a clinical sample of adolescents referred for outpatient substance abuse treatment and demonstrated that less acculturated adolescents had higher rates of substance abuse. The current study extends previous research by replicating Gil's findings with a sample of severely impaired, dually diagnosed adolescents referred for residential substance abuse treatment. Consistent with the type of treatment the adolescents received, the sample for the current study had more pervasive drug abuse and psychiatric problems than Gil et al.'s sample and a similar proportion of youth born in the United States (74% vs. 65%). Because all participants met criteria for at least one comorbid psychiatric diagnosis at intake, the findings support Gil et al.'s proposition that the higher prevalence of comorbidity among clinical samples may in part have explained the discrepancy from previous research conducted with community samples. The process of acculturation has been identified as a crucial factor contributing to psychological distress in immigrant populations (Rivera-Sinclair, 1997). Hence, Hispanic adolescents coping with the stress of acculturating to a new country may be at higher risk for drug use, particularly when the adolescents have other psychiatric problems.

Collectively, these studies (along with Garcia, 1999) suggest that opposed to community populations, among Hispanic adolescents referred for drug abuse treatment, less acculturated adolescents may experience more substance use problems (Gil et al., 2004). However, the process by which this occurs, as well as the explanation for the discrepancies from community populations, is less clear. In addition to increased prevalence of psychiatric comorbidity, other possible explanations include increased familial stress and disruption of family interactions resulting from parent-child acculturation differences (Szapocznik, Santisteban, Kurtines, Perez-Vidal, & Hervis, 1984); however, Lau and colleagues [2005] did not find more extensive substance use among families high in differential acculturation), as well as immigration-related parent-child separations (Santisteban, Muir-Malcolm, Mitrani, & Szapocznik, 2002).

Traumatic immigration experiences may also play a role. If the migration experience to a new country has involved loss, trauma or abuse, traumatic stress may develop (Falicov, 1998). If the adolescent has not developed strong coping skills and if he/she does not have access to appropriate social/mental health services, he/she may cope with the distressful emotions by abusing alcohol and drugs. Recall that over 15% of the sample met criteria for PTSD, and anecdotally, many of the participants in this study experienced highly stressful immigration experiences (e.g., families that had fled Cuba as "rafters"). A third possible explanation is peer induction into drug use (Falicov, 1998; Gil, Tubman, & Wagner, 2001). One way minority teens may feel less isolated and gain a sense of belonging is by making attempts to affiliate with an acculturated peer group. If families live in impoverished neighborhoods in which drugs are readily available, and if delinquency and drug use are common among these peers from the dominant culture, less acculturated adolescents may affiliate with these peers as a way to not be viewed as outsiders (Canino & Spurlock, 1994), and thus be inducted into the drug-using lifestyle. Hence, these less acculturated teens may be more susceptible specifically because they are trying to fit into a dominant culture where drug use is the norm.

LIMITATIONS

The findings from this study should be interpreted in light of some limitations. First, the sample was fairly homogeneous, consisting of 46% Cuban adolescents. It was not a representative sample of Hispanics nationally, which may limit the generalizability of the findings. Future research is needed to determine if the findings generalize to other Hispanic ethnicities living in other regions of the United States. Second, acculturation proxies were used rather than a formal measure of acculturation. Although the use of proxies to measure level of acculturation has been accomplished in several previous studies (e.g., Coatsworth et al., 2000; Norris et al., 1996) perhaps a formal measure of acculturation may have yielded different results. However, it should be noted that existing measures of acculturation have their own limitations (i.e., content validity and adequately representing acculturation as an important psychological construct; Driscoll et al., 2001; Norris et al., 1996; Zane & Mak, 2003). Perhaps more data-intensive methodologies such as qualitative inquiry and video-taped observation methods are needed to provide a richer conceptualization of acculturation and its impact on drug use and therapeutic change (Jackson-Gilfort, Liddle, Tejeda, & Dakof, 2001; Liddle, Jackson-Gilfort, & Marvel, 2006). Finally, our sample size was fairly small, limiting the power to detect statistically significant differences.

CLINICAL IMPLICATIONS

Despite these limitations, the findings from this study have important implications for understanding substance use among Hispanic youth. First, they support the relevance of acculturation as it relates to drug use. Given the success of family-based treatments for adolescent substance abuse (Liddle, 2004), clinical interventions designed to address the process of acculturation in the context of the family are in order, such as addressing possible traumatic experiences and eliciting the family's immigration story, which has been found to be an inroad to further, more challenging work with families (Falicov, 1998). It is promising that well-designed, culturally-sensitive interventions are being developed and receiving empirical support (Gil et al., 2001; Santisteban, Mena, & Suarez-Morales, 2006). Second, these findings underscore the importance of targeted outreach and early intervention strategies designed to intervene with youth before their substance use becomes more firmly established (Liddle, Rowe, Henderson, Dakof, & Ungaro, 2004). However, the findings also suggest that outreach targeting less acculturated Hispanics is needed. This may entail interventions designed to reach less acculturated adolescents in schools (e.g., ESOL programs), in the court system (e.g., juvenile justice, immigration), and in the neighborhoods in which these families live. Along this line, Spence (2005) has highlighted the potential of training "promotores(as)" (a subset of a larger group of health workers known as community health workers [CHWs]) in substance use screening, assessment, and referral.

CONCLUSIONS

Acculturation was examined in a unique and distinct clinical sample. This study calls attention to the fact that acculturation is but one piece of a very complex puzzle with this sample of distressed children and families. The findings warrant additional study with clinical samples, possibly including methods such as qualitative inquiry and longitudinal follow-up, to further explore the relationships between ethnicity, cultural differences, and substance abuse in Hispanic adolescents.

REFERENCES

Achenbach, T. M., & Edelbrock, C. S. (1979). The Child Behavior Profile: II, Boys aged 12-16 and girls aged 6-11 and 12-16. *Journal of Consulting and Clinical Psychology, 47*, 223-233.

Achenbach, T. M., & Edelbrock, C. S. (1983). Manual for the Child Behavior Checklist and Revised Child Behavior Profile. Burlington, VT: University of Vermont Department of Psychiatry.

Bishaw, A., & Iceland, J. (2003). Poverty: 1999 (Census, 2000 Brief). Washington, DC: U.S. Census Bureau. Retrieved August 3, 2005, from http://www.census.gov/prod/2003pubs/c2kbr-19.pdf

Canino, I. A., & Spurlock, J. (1994). *Culturally diverse children and adolescents: Assessment, diagnosis, and treatment.* New York: The Guilford Press.

Carey, K. B. (1997). Reliability and validity of the time-line follow-back interview among psychiatric outpatients: A preliminary report. *Psychology of Addictive Behaviors, 11*, 26-33.

Coatsworth, J. D., Pantin, H., McBride, C., Briones, E., Kurtines, W., & Szapocznik, J. (2000). Ecodevelopmental correlates of behavior problems in young Hispanic females. *Applied Developmental Science, 6*(3), 126-143.

Delva, J., Wallace, J. M., O'Malley, P. M., Bachman, J. G., Johnston, L. D., & Schulenberg, J. E. (2005). The epidemiology of alchol, marijuana, and cocaine use among Mexican American, Puerto Rican, Cuban American, and other Latin American eighth-grade students in the United States: 1991-2002. *American Journal of Public Health, 95*(4), 696-702.

Dennis, M. L., Funk, R., Godley, S. H., Godley, M. D., & Waldron, H. (2004). Cross-validation of the alcohol and cannabis use measures in the Global Appraisal of Individual Needs (GAIN) and Timeline Followback (TLFB; Form 90) among adolescents in substance abuse treatment. *Addiction, 99*(Suppl. 2), 120-128.

Downs, B. (2003). *Fertility of American women: June 2002* (Current Population Reports, P20-548). Washington, DC: U.S. Census Bureau. Retrieved August 2, 2005, from http://www.census.gov/prod/2003pubs/p20-548.pdf

Driscoll, A. K., Biggs, M. A., Brindis, C. D., & Yankah, E. (2001). Adolescent Latino reproductive health: A review of the literature. *Hispanic Journal of Behavioral Sciences, 23*(3), 255-326.

Epstein, J. A., Botvin, G. J., & Diaz, T. (2000). Alcohol use among Hispanic adolescents: Role of linguistic acculturation and gender. *Journal of Alcohol and Drug Education, 45*(3), 18-32.

Epstein, J. A., Botvin, G. J., & Diaz, T. (2001). Linguistic acculturation associated with higher marijuana and polydrug use among Hispanic adolescents. *Substance Use and Misuse, 36*(4), 477-499.

Epstein, J. A., Margaret, D., & Botvin, G. J. (2003). A mediational model of the relationship between linguistic acculturation and polydrug use among Hispanic adolescents. *Psychological Reports, 93*(3), 859-866.

Falicov, C. J. (1998). *Latino families in therapy: A guide to multicultural practice.* The Guilford Press: New York.

Garcia, S. E. (1999). Substance use, acculturation, and alienation among Hispanic adolescents. *Dissertation Abstracts International, 60* (3-B), 1301.

Gfroerer, J., & De La Rosa, M. (1993). Protective and risk factors associated with drug use among Hispanic youth. *Journal of Addictive Diseases, 12*(2), 87-107.

Gil, A. G, Tubman, J. G., & Wagner, E. F. (2001). Substance abuse interventions with Latino adolescents: A cultural framework. In E. F. Wagner & H. B. Waldron (Eds.), *Innovations in adolescent substance abuse interventions* (pp. 353-378). New York, NY: Pergamon.

Gil, A. G., Wagner, E. F., & Tubman, J. G. (2004). Culturally sensitive substance abuse intervention for Hispanic and African American adolescents: Empirical examples from the Alcohol Treatment Targeting Adolescents in Need (ATTAIN) Project. *Addiction, 99*(Suppl. 2), 140-150.

Gil, A. G., Wagner, E. F., & Vega, W. A. (2000). Acculturation, familism, and alcohol use among Latino adolescent males: Longitudinal relations. *Journal of Community Psychology, 28*(4), 443-458.

Jackson-Gilfort, A., Liddle, H. A., Tejeda, M. J., & Dakof, G. A., (2001). Facilitating engagement of African American male adolescents in family therapy: A cultural theme process study. *Journal of Black Psychology, 27*(3), 321-340.

Johnston, L. D., O'Malley, P. M., Bachman, J. G., & Schulenberg, J. E. (2004). *Monitoring the Future national results on adolescent drug use: Overview of key findings, 2003* (NIH Publication No. 04-5506). Bethesda, MD: National Institute on Drug Abuse.

Johnston, L. D., O'Malley, P. M., Bachman, J. G., & Schulenberg, J. E. (2005). *Monitoring the Future national results on adolescent drug use: Overview of key findings, 2004* (NIH Publication No. 05-5726). Bethesda, MD: National Institute on Drug Abuse.

Kazdin, A. E. (1990). Psychotherapy for children and adolescents. *Annual Review of Psychology, 41*, 21-54.

Khoury, E. L., Warheit, G. J., Zimmerman, R. S., Vega, W. A., & Gil, A. G. (1996). Gender and ethnic differences in the prevalence of alcohol, cigarette, and illicit drug use over time in a cohort of young Hispanic adolescents in South Florida. *Women & Health, 24*, 21-40.

Lau, A. S., McCabe, K. M., Yeh, M., Garland, A. F.,Wood, P. A., & Hough, R. L. (2005). The acculturation gap-distress hypothesis among high-risk Mexican American families. *Journal of Family Psychology, 19*(3), 367-375.

Liddle, H. A. (2004). Family-based therapies for adolescent alcohol and drug use: Research contributions and future research needs. *Addiction, 99*(s2), 76-92.

Liddle, H. A., Jackson-Gilfort, A., & Marvel, F. A. (2006). An empirically-supported and culturally specific engagement and intervention strategy for African American adolescent males. *American Journal of Orthopsychiatry, 75*(2), 215-225.

Liddle, H. A., Rowe, C. L., Henderson, C., Dakof, G. A., & Ungaro, R. A. (2004). Early intervention for adolescent substance abuse: Pretreatment to posttreatment outcomes of a randomized controlled trial comparing multidimensional family therapy and peer group treatment. *Journal of Psychoactive Drugs. 36*(1), 2-37.

Lovato, C. Y., Litrownik, A. J., Elder, J., Nunez-Liriano, A., Suarez, D., & Talavera, G. A. (1994). Cigarette and alcohol use among migrant Hispanic adolescents. *Family and Community Health, 16*(4), 18-31.

Maisto, S. A., & Connors, G. J. (1992). Using subject and collateral reports to measure alcohol consumption. In R. Z. Litten & J. P. Allen (Eds.), *Measuring alcohol consumption: Psychosocial and biochemical methods* (pp. 73-96). Clifton, NJ: Humana Press.

Marin, G. (1992). Issues in the measurement of acculturation among Hispanics. In K. F. Geisinger (Ed.), *Psychological testing of Hispanics* (pp. 235-251). Washington, DC: American Psychological Association.

Marin, G. (1993). Influence of acculturation on familialism and self-identification among Hispanics. In M.E. Bernal & G.P. Knight (Eds.), *Ethnic identity: Formation and transmission among Hispanics and other minorities* (pp. 181-196). Albany: State University of New York Press.

Norris, A. E., Ford, K., & Bova, C. A. (1996). Psychometrics of a brief acculturation scale for Hispanics in a probability sample of urban Hispanic adolescents and young adults. *Hispanic Journal of Behavioral Sciences, 18*(1), 29-38.

Rivera-Sinclair, E. A. (1997). Acculturation/biculturalism and its relationship to adjustment in Cuban-Americans. *International Journal of Intercultural Relations, 21*(3), 379-391.

Santisteban, D. A., Mena, M. P. & Suarez-Morales, L. (2006). Using treatment development methods to enhance the family-based treatment of Hispanic adolescents. In H. A. Liddle & C. L. Rowe (Eds.), *Adolescent substance abuse: Research and clinical advances*. London: Cambridge University Press.

Santisteban, D. A., Muir-Malcolm, J. A., Mitrani, V. B., & Szapocznik, J. (2002). Integrating the study of ethnic culture and family psychology intervention science. In H. A. Liddle, D. A. Santisteban, R. F. Levant, & J. H. Bray (Eds.), *Family psychology: Science-based interventions* (pp. 331-351). Washington, DC: American Psychological Association.

Sobell, L. C., & Sobell, M. B. (1992). Timeline follow-back: A technique for assessing self-reported alcohol consumption. In R. Z. Litten & J. P. Allen (Eds.), *Measuring alcohol consumption: Psychosocial and biochemical methods* (pp. 73-96). Clifton, NJ: Humana Press.

Spence, R. T. (2005, July). Drug attitudes and behavior on the US/Mexico border. Paper presented at the National Institute on Drug Abuse, Division of Epidemiology, Services and Prevention Research grantees meeting, Health Disparities and Drug Abuse: What Have We Learned? Where are We Going?, Washington, DC.

Szapocznik, J., & Kurtines, W. (1980). Acculturation, biculturalism, and adjustment among Cuban Americans. In A. M. Padilla (Ed.), *Psychological dimensions on the acculturation process: Theory, models, and some new findings* (pp. 56-78). Boulder, CO: Westview Press.

Szapocznik, J., Santisteban, D., Kurtines, W., Perez-Vidal, A., & Hervis, O. (1984). Bicultural effectiveness training: A treatment intervention for enhancing intercultural adjustment in Cuban American families. *Hispanic Journal of Behavioral Sciences, 6*(4), 317-344.

Szapocznik, J., Kurtines, W., Santisteban, D. A., Pantin, H., Scopetta, M., Mancilla, Y., Aisenberg, S., McIntosh, S., Perez-Vidal, A., & Coatsworth, J. D. (1997). The evolution of structural ecosystemic theory for working with Latino families. In J. G. Garcia & M. C. Zea (Eds.), *Psychological interventions and research with Latino populations* (pp. 166-190). Boston: Allyn and Bacon.

Tabachnick, B. G., & Fidell, L. S. (2001). *Using multivariate statistics.* Needham Heights, MA: Allyn & Bacon.

United States Bureau of the Census (2000). *Statistical abstract of the United States: 1999* (Table 24. Projections of resident population, by age, sex and race: 2000 to 2025, p. 25). Washington, DC: Government Printing Office.

United States Census Bureau (2001). *Overview of race and Hispanic origin: Census, 2000 brief.* Washington, DC: U.S. Department of Commerce, Economics and Statistics Administration.

United States Department of Education, National Center for Education Statistics (2000). *Dropout Rates in the United States: 1999.* (NCES 2001-022). Washington, DC: U.S. Department of Education.

Vega, W. A. (1995). The study of Latino families: A point of departure. In R. E. Zambrana (Ed.). *Understanding Latino families: Scholarship, policy, and practice* (pp. 3-17). Thousand Oaks, CA: Sage.

Vega, W. A., & Gil, A. G. (1999). A model for explaining drug use behavior among Hispanic adolescents. *Drugs & Society, 14,* 55-73.

Vega, W. A., Gil, A. G., & Wagner, E. (1998). Cultural adjustment and Hispanic adolescent drug use. In W. A. Vega & A. G. Gil (Eds.), *Drug use and ethnicity in early adolescence* (pp. 125-148). New York: Plenum Press.

Zane, N., & Mak, W. (2003). Major approaches to the measurement of acculturation among ethnic minority populations: A content analysis and alternative empirical strategy. In K. M. Chun, P. Balls Organista, & G. Marin (Eds.), *Acculturation: Advances in theory, measurement, and applied research* (pp. 39-60). Washington, DC: American Psychological Association.

doi:10.1300/J233v06n02_07

Substance Abuse Prevalence and Treatment Among Latinos and Latinas

Josefina Alvarez, PhD
Leonard A. Jason, PhD
Bradley D. Olson, PhD
Joseph R. Ferrari, PhD
Margaret I. Davis, PhD

SUMMARY. Substance abuse prevalence rates for Latinos/as generally mirror those of the general U.S. population; however, a number of indicators of assimilation to U.S. culture as well as sociodemographic variables predict substance use and abuse among this group. Latinos/as have poorer outcomes in substance abuse treatment programs. Yet there is little empirical evidence that explains the problems these individuals experience in treatment, and there are few studies on the use and effectiveness of

---

Josefina Alvarez, Leonard A. Jason, and Bradley D. Olson are all affiliated with the Center for Community Research at De Paul University, Chicago, IL.

Joseph R. Ferrari is Professor, Department of Psychology, De Paul University, Chicago, IL.

Margaret I. Davis is affiliated with the Department of Psychology, Dickinson College, Carlisle, PA.

Preparation of this manuscript was funded by NIDA grant DA13231-02 and NIAA grant AA12218-02. The authors would like to thank Suzanne L. Rosenberg, Darrin Aase, Andrea Flynn, and Sandra Castro for their help in the preparation of this manuscript.

Address correspondence to: Josefina Alvarez, DePaul University, Center for Community Research, 990 W. Fullerton Avenue, Suite 3100, Chicago, IL 60614-2458 (E-mail: jalvare4@depaul.edu).

[Haworth co-indexing entry note]: "Substance Abuse Prevalence and Treatment Among Latinos and Latinas." Alvarez, Josefina et al. Co-published simultaneously in *Journal of Ethnicity in Substance Abuse* (The Haworth Press, Inc.) Vol. 6, No. 2, 2007, pp. 115-141; and: *21st Century Research on Drugs and Ethnicity: Studies Supported by the National Institute on Drug Abuse* (ed: Peter L. Myers) The Haworth Press, 2007, pp. 115-141. Single or multiple copies of this article are available for a fee from The Haworth Document Delivery Service [1-800-HAWORTH, 9:00 a.m. - 5:00 p.m. (EST). E-mail address: docdelivery@haworthpress.com].

Available online at http://jesa.haworthpress.com

doi:10.1300/J233v06n02_08

mutual help groups among this population. New developments in the conceptualization and measurement of acculturation will lead to a greater understanding of the role of culture in the prevalence and treatment of substance-related problems. doi:10.1300/J233v06n02_08

KEYWORDS. Hispanics, Latinos, alcohol abuse, drug abuse, recovery

INTRODUCTION

The Hispanic/Latin American population of the U.S. has been growing steadily over the last four decades (Casas, Vasquez, & Ruiz de Esparza, 2002) and recent census statistics indicate that 42.7 million Americans identify themselves as Hispanic (U.S. Bureau of the Census, 2006). This group represents a diverse mixture of individuals from various ethnicities, languages, and cultures (Casas et al.; Comas-Diaz, 2001) who trace their origins to several nations. While current literature uses a number of descriptors to identify this diverse group (Comas-Diaz), this paper will use the terms Latino and Latina.

The size of the Latina/o population in the U.S. and projections for its growth require that substance abuse researchers and treatment providers pay greater attention to the prevalence and treatment of drug and alcohol abuse among this group (Delgado, 2005; de la Rosa, Holleran, & Straussner, 2005). Estimates of the rates of substance use and abuse among Latinos/as in the United States have emerged over the past several decades, and these will be reviewed in the section below. This will be followed by a review of empirical information on treatment access and outcome, including mutual help. Although there is a growing literature on substance abuse prevention, and treatment among Latino and Latina youth (de la Rosa et al.), this review will focus on adults.

PREVALENCE

National Household Surveys on Substance Abuse conducted in 1991, 1992, and 1993, indicated that rates of alcohol and other drug use and abuse among Latinas/os did not differ from those of the overall U.S.

population (Substance Abuse and Mental Health Services Administration [SAMHSA], 1998a). One exception was that Latinos/as reported slightly higher 30 day use of crack cocaine in the 1993 survey. However, these higher use rates are likely due to socioeconomic differences (Lillie-Blanton, Anthony, & Schuster, 1993). After a revision of the National Household Survey protocol in 1994, yearly prevalence statistics with national samples of Latinas/os found substance use and abuse rates that mirrored those of the general U.S. population (National Institute on Drug Abuse [NIDA], 1998). These later surveys also included larger samples of Latinos/as, allowing for analyses of national and gender substance use patterns (SAMHSA, 1998b, 1999).

More recent national surveys conducted by SAMHSA continue to indicate that Latinos/as report slightly lower rates of lifetime illicit drug use than European and African Americans. However, rates of past month and past year drug use equal those of other ethnic groups. Additionally, rates of alcohol dependence and binge drinking among this group are similar to those of European Americans and slightly higher than those of African Americans (SAMHSA, 2000, 2001, 2002a, 2003, 2004).

A relatively neglected area involves co-occurring disorders with substance abuse. Early studies involved small samples (Golding, Brurnam, & Wells, 1990, 1992; Kail, Zayas, & Malgady, 2000; Neff, 1993; Wilcox, Briones, & Suess, 1991). However, a number of recent well-designed investigations provide clinically relevant data (Becker, Grilo, Anez, Paris, & McGlashan, 2005; Grilo, Anez, & McGlashan, 2002; Montoya, Covarrubias, Patek, & Graves, 2003; Rios-Bedoya & Gall, 2003; Robles, Matos, Deren, Colon, Sahai, Marrero et al., 2006; Vega, Sribney, & Achara-Abraham, 2003; Vega, Sribney, Aguilar-Gaxiola, & Kolody, 2004). These studies generally document that co-occurring mood and anxiety disorders are common among substance-abusing Latinos and Latinas in the U.S., as they are among the rest of the population. Furthermore, these studies indicate that women and U.S. born Latinos and Latinas have higher rates of co-morbid mood and anxiety disorders than men and foreign-born individuals. Additionally, several studies indicate a relationship between exposure to traumatic events and substance abuse among Latinos and Latinas (Alegria, Vera, Shrout, Canino, Lai, Albizu, Marin et al., 2004; Amaro, Larson, Gampel, Richardson, Savege, & Wagler, 2005; Finch, Catalano, Novaco & Vega, 2003; Lown & Vega, 2001; Vera, Alegria, Pattatucci-Aragon, & Pena, 2005).

A closer examination of prevalence studies reveals a number of variables, which predict rates of substance use and abuse among Latinos/as. Several of these differences reflect assimilation to U.S. culture, while others pertain to sociodemographic variables, including gender. Unfortunately, large-scale surveys of substance use and abuse have failed to measure indicators of assimilation and most have not controlled for demographic variables in their data analyses (SAMHSA, 1998a).

Gender Differences and Cultural Values

National surveys reveal gender differences in prevalence rates of substance use and abuse among all Americans (NIDA, 1998). These differences are especially pronounced between Latinos and Latinas (Black & Markides, 1993; Caetano, 1994; Canino, Burman, & Caetano, 1992; Cervantes, Gilbert, Salgado de Snyder, & Padilla, 1990-1991; Cuadrado & Lieberman, 1998; Guendelman & Abrams, 1994; Hines & Caetano, 1998; Hughes, Day, Marcantonio, & Tropy, 1997; Lee & Markides, 1997; Marin & Posner, 1995; Markides, Ray, Stroup-Benham, & Trevino, 1990; Nielsen, 2000; Parker, Weaver, & Calhoun, 1995; SAMHSA, 1998a; Vega, Alderete, Kolody, & Aguilar-Gaxiola, 1998; Welte & Barnes, 1995). In general, Latinas are more likely than Latinos to abstain from using alcohol and illicit drugs (Amaro, Whitaker, Coffman, & Hereen, 1990; Black & Markides; Caetano; Canino et al.; Hines & Caetano; Lee & Markides; Markides et al.; Nielsen; SAMHSA; Vega et al.), and Latinas are less likely to drink heavily and become dependent on alcohol (Hines & Caetano; Lee & Markides; Markides et al.).

A number of investigators propose that cultural norms that discourage substance use by women may protect Latinas from substance abuse and dependence by promoting abstinence (Canino et al., 1992; Canino, 1994; Moore, 1994; Welte & Barnes, 1995). Indeed, there is empirical support for a relationship between holding U.S. cultural values and substance use among Latinas. For example, results of a national survey of over 1,000 Latinas indicated that those who associated with non-Latinos/as, used English-speaking media, and held U.S. cultural values were less likely to abstain from using alcohol (Caetano, 1994). More recent research has replicated the results cited above (Caetano, Ramisetty-Mikler, & McGrath, 2004). Another study conducted in New York state demonstrated that Latinas who were either U.S.-born, or lived in the U.S. before the age of 18, and held U.S. cultural values were more likely to drink and more likely to drink heavily than Latinas who were foreign-born, spoke Spanish, visited their country of origin regularly, and maintained Latin American values (Welte & Barnes, 1995). In this study, cultural values among Latinos did not predict alcohol or illicit drug use.

One of the hypotheses about cultural mediators of substance use and abuse among Latinos is that traditional gender role attitudes (i.e., "machismo") might encourage Latino substance use. However, two studies have found no relationship between substance use among Latinos and endorsement of traditional gender roles (Cuadrado & Lieberman, 1998; Neff, Prihoda, & Hoppe, 1991). Thus, while cultural values may promote abstinence among Latinas, research has failed to document a relationship between substance use and gender role attitudes among Latinos. Existing literature also supports a relationship between other indicators of cultural assimilation and substance use among Latinos and Latinas.

Language

The strongest support for a relationship between assimilation to U.S. culture and substance use comes from studies that consistently find a positive relationship between English language preference and proficiency and higher rates of alcohol and other drug use, abuse, and dependence among Latinas/os. National epidemiological studies consistently find that Latinos/as who choose to be interviewed in English are more likely to use and abuse substances than those who request to be interviewed in Spanish (Amaro et al., 1990; Black & Markides, 1993; Caetano, 1994; Finch, 2001; NIDA, 1987; SAMHSA, 1998a; Wagner-Echeagaray, Chilcoat, & Anthony, 1994). The relationship between language use/preference and substance use/abuse holds even when data analyses control for socioeconomic status (Amaro et al.; Finch; Wagner-Echeagaray et al.). It should be noted, however, that studies such as SAMHSA's (1998a) analysis of data from three consecutive national surveys (1991, 1992, and 1993) revealed a relationship between English use and illicit drug use as well as self-reported need for drug treatment, but not alcohol use or need for alcohol treatment. Also, analyses of data from SAMHSA's National Household Survey indicated that language use predicted substance use only among Mexican Americans, but not among other Latinas/os (Wagner-Echeagaray et al.).

Smaller regional studies conducted in various parts of the U.S. support national findings on the positive relationship between English proficiency and substance use and abuse (Cuadrado & Lieberman, 1998; Farabee, Wallisch, & Maxwell, 1995; Marin & Posner, 1995; Neff & Hoppe, 1992; Perez-Stable, Marin & Marin, 1994; Vega et al., 1998; Welte & Barnes, 1995) for both Latinos and Latinas.

In the studies reviewed above, language use has been employed as a proxy measure of assimilation to U.S. culture; however, the mediators of the relationship between substance use and abuse and English proficiency are not well understood. Indeed, several researchers propose that English use may represent adaptation to U.S. values and norms such that English-speaking Latinas/os may use substances in ways that are similar to the general American population (Amaro et al., 1990; Black & Markides, 1993; Caetano, 1994; Welte & Barnes, 1995). It is also possible that Spanish-speaking Latinos/as may be more reluctant to report substance use and abuse in response to community surveys due to fears stemming to their lack of familiarity with survey procedures such as confidentiality (Wagner-Echeagaray et al., 1994). Another explanation for the higher rates of substance use among English-speaking Latinas/os involves the loss of connection to family and culture, or to stresses related to minority status among individuals who are committed to becoming part of the mainstream U.S. culture (Castro, Proescholdbell, Abeita, & Rodriguez, 1999; Escobar, Nevi, & Gara, 2000; Ortega, Rosenheck, Alegria, & Desai, 2000). Clearly, there is a need for more research to better understand the factors that mediate the relationship between language preference or proficiency and substance use and abuse.

Place of Birth/Generation in the U.S.

Several investigators have also explored relationships between substance use and abuse and generation in the U.S. The H-HANES demonstrated that U.S. born Latinos and Latinas were more likely to use marijuana and cocaine than men and women who were born in Mexico or Puerto Rico (Amaro et al., 1990). More recently, data from national surveys indicate that Latino/a and other immigrants are less likely to use both alcohol and illicit drugs than individuals born in the U.S. (Abraido-Lanza, Chao, & Flores, 2005; Grant, Stinson, Hasin, Dawson, Chou, & Anderson, 2004; Johnson, VanGeest, & Cho, 2002). Additionally, among Latinos, being born in or residing in the U.S. for 15 years or more has been found to be associated with increased alcohol use (Abraido-Lanza et al.). The National Comorbidity Survey, which included a representative sample of English-speaking Latinos/as, indicated that Mexican Americans who have at least one parent who was born in the United States were more likely to have a substance-related disorder than Mexican Americans whose parents were born in Mexico (Ortega et al., 2000). However, in that study, generation in the 50 states did not predict substance-related disorders among Puerto Ricans.

Regional studies that have examined the relationship between place of birth and substance use or abuse among Latino and Latina samples provide mixed results. Three studies conducted in the West and Southwest found that Latinos and Latinas who were born in the United States reported greater substance use and abuse than either individuals born in Mexico or European Americans (Farabee et al., 1995; Golding, Brurnam, Benjamin, & Wells 1992; Vega et al., 1998). Similarly, Vega, Kolody, Hwang, Noble, and Porter (1997) found that Latinas born outside the U.S. were more likely to abstain from substance use than U.S.-born Latinas. Additionally, Gilbert and Collins (1997) reported that second and third generation Latinas increase their alcohol use such that by the third generation Latinas' drinking patterns resemble those of other women in the U.S. In another study, conducted in New York State, place of birth alone did not predict alcohol use for either men or women in general, but U.S.-born Latinos and Latinas were more likely to use illicit drugs (Welte & Barnes, 1995). Another study conducted in California found that Latinas born outside the U.S. were less likely to report alcohol use than U.S. born Latinas; however, place of birth did not predict self-reported alcohol use among Latinos (Cervantes et al., 1990-1991).

Overall, the studies reviewed above provide some support for a relationship between place of birth, and perhaps generation in the U.S., and substance use and abuse. Contradictory results may be explained by gender, substance(s) of choice, region of the country, age at the time of immigration, language preference, and perhaps cultural values.

Differences Between Latino/a Groups

In addition to addressing language and place of birth, the H-HANES data (NIDA, 1987) highlighted differences in substance use and abuse among the various Latino/a groups. More specifically, the H-HANES indicated that Puerto Rican and Mexican American men were more likely to report lifetime and past year marijuana use than Cuban American men. Among women, Puerto Ricans had the highest rate of both lifetime and past year marijuana use. Lifetime and past year reports of cocaine use indicated that Puerto Rican men and women had higher rates of cocaine use than Mexican and Cuban American men and women. Use of marijuana and cocaine was higher among Puerto Ricans than among European Americans. Other findings from the H-HANES indicate that Puerto Ricans and Mexican Americans are more likely than Cuban Americans to report heavy drinking (Lee & Markides, 1997). Looking specifically at drinking among women, Black and Markides (1993) found that Puerto Rican and Mexican American women surveyed for the H-HANES were less likely to abstain from drinking than were Cuban American women.

Combined prevalence data from the 1991, 1992 and 1993 National Household Surveys revealed differences between "Caribbeans, Central Americans, Cubans, Mexicans, Puerto Rican, and other Hispanics" (SAMHSA, 1998a, p. 7). More specifically, Caribbeans, Cubans, and Central Americans reported rates of illicit drug use that were lower than those of the European American population, while Mexican Americans and Puerto Ricans reported higher rates of illicit drug use and need for drug treatment. Similarly, Mexican Americans had a higher prevalence of heavy alcohol use and alcohol dependence than other Latinos/as and European Americans. SAMHSA's findings also indicated that differences between men and women in heavy drinking and alcohol dependence were particularly large among Mexican Americans and Central Americans. An analysis of the 1993 National Survey on Drug Abuse indicates that Mexican American men are more likely to report heavy drinking than other Latinos (Nielsen, 2000).

Combined data from SAMHSA's 1999 and 2000 National Household Surveys also revealed differences among the various Latino groups. Heavy alcohol use and binge drinking rates for Mexican Americans and Puerto Ricans living in the 50 states were higher than the rates of Central Americans, South Americans, and Cubans living in the U.S. Past year and past month use of illicit drugs was higher among Puerto Ricans in the U.S. than it was among other Latina/o groups as well as European and African Americans (SAMHSA, 2000).

In summary, increasing evidence suggests differences in the rates of substance use and abuse among the various Latino/a groups. More specifically, research indicates that Mexican Americans and Puerto Ricans may be at higher risk of substance abuse and dependence than other Latinas/os, and possibly European and African Americans. These "within group" differences may reflect differences in attitudes about substance use, regional use patterns within the United States, or differences in assimilation/adaptation to U.S. culture, among other factors. Puerto Ricans and Mexican Americans' increased risk for substance use and abuse also may be related to their youthfulness and greater poverty, in comparison to other Latinos/as (U.S. Bureau of the Census, 2000). In fact, research reveals relationships between a number of sociodemographic variables and substance use and abuse among Latinas/os. Unfortunately, with the exception of the analyses conducted on H-HANES data, the national studies reviewed in this section have not controlled for demographic differences among the various Latino/a groups.

Other Sociodemographic Variables

Younger age (18-25) and not being married predict greater substance use among Latinas/os (Black & Markides, 1993; Markides et al., 1990; Nielsen, 2001; Parker et al., 1995; SAMHSA, 1998a; Welte & Barnes, 1995). Married Latinos/as also report fewer alcohol-related problems; however, marital status does not predict the severity of these problems among Mexican-Americans (Nielsen). Additionally, prevalence of drug use, need for drug treatment, heavy alcohol use, and alcohol dependence peak with increasing education between grades 9 and 11 and decrease with increasing education after the 11th grade (SAMHSA).

While having a higher income has been found to predict a greater use of alcohol among Latinos/as (Black & Markides, 1993; Markides et al., 1990; Nielsen, 2000; Parker et al., 1995), being unemployed has been found to predict heavy alcohol use and alcohol dependence (Parker et al.; Nielsen; Parker et al.; SAMHSA; Welte & Barnes, 1995) as well as illicit drug use (Alegria et al., 2004). Increasing poverty has been associated with heavy drinking among Latinas/os (Markides et al.). Similarly, results of a national study indicated that employed Latinos/as and those with higher incomes were less likely to report alcohol-related problems than individuals who were unemployed or had lower incomes (Caetano & Clark, 1998). Finally, a recent study with a large sample of Mexican-origin immigrants in California revealed that job-related experiences of exclusion and discrimination predicted past-year alcohol abuse and dependence. In that study, high levels of social support were not protective among individuals who experienced high to moderate levels of employment frustration (Finch et al., 2003).

Similar relationships between substance use and abuse and variables such as age, marital status, and employment status are found among other ethnic groups as well (SAMHSA, 1998a). Furthermore, census data indicates that there are differences between Latinas/os and other segments of the American population, as well as among the various Latino/a groups in the United States in terms of age, socioeconomic status, and level of education (U.S. Bureau of the Census, 2000). Increasingly it is becoming clear that studies addressing the prevalence of substance use and abuse among Latinas/os need to take into account a number of demographic variables mentioned above. In addition, region of the country and urban or rural residence need to be considered (NIDA, 1998; SAMHSA, 1998a).

Summary of Prevalence Studies

SAMHSA's yearly National Household Surveys now include representative samples of Latinos/as in various parts of the country. Current Latino/a sample sizes allow for data analysis by gender and national group. These surveys conducted since the early 1990's have helped to establish the prevalence of illicit drug use and alcohol use and abuse among Latinos/as. However, prevalence research needs to pay attention to the heterogeneity of the Hispanic/Latino/a population in the U.S. (NIDA, 2003). More specifically, a number of variables need to be taken into account in prevalence research with Latinos/as, including indices of assimilation (language, place of birth and generation in the U.S., cultural values) and sociodemographic indicators (age, marital status, employment status, level of education, income, region of the country, rural/urban residence). The relationships among the variables just mentioned, along with gender and national origin, as predictors of substance use and abuse merit further exploration. A greater understanding of the predictors of substance abuse among this growing segment of the U.S. population will contribute to better treatment and prevention interventions. The association between several indicators of assimilation to U.S. culture (i.e., language, place of birth, generation in the U.S.) deserves particular attention from researchers as the second and third generations of Latinos and Latinas in the U.S. continue to grow.

TREATMENT

Residential and Outpatient Treatment

In contrast to the growing body of knowledge regarding the prevalence of substance use and abuse among Latinas/os, there are fewer studies that identify effective treatment models (Cervantes & Felix-Ortiz, 2004; Vega & Sribney, 2005). Additionally, much of the existing evidence indicates disparities in access to and outcomes in substance abuse interventions for Latinos and Latinas. For example, recent national surveys indicate that Latinas/os have less access than other Americans to substance abuse treatment (SAMHSA, 2001; 2002a) or that they have to wait longer to access such services, and once they enter treatment they are less satisfied with the services they receive (Wells, Klap, Koike, & Sherbourne, 2001). A national survey of Latino/a veterans receiving treatment in VA hospitals indicated that Latinas/os who needed treatment for alcohol abuse were less likely than other veterans to receive such services (Booth, Blow, Bunn, & Fortney, 1992). Recent National Household Surveys on Drug Abuse and Health, however, indicate that Latinos/as are just as likely to report finding substance abuse treatment programs as Americans from other ethnic groups (SAMHSA, 2003; 2004).

Regional studies also provide evidence that Latinos and Latinas underutilize substance abuse treatment. For instance, research conducted with substance abusing individuals involved in the criminal justice system in California indicated that Latinos/as were less likely to express a need for treatment (Longshore, Hsieh, & Anglin, 1993) and less likely to participate in treatment than individuals from other ethnic groups (Anglin, Hser, & Grella, 1997; Longshore, Hsieh, Anglin, & Annon, 1992). Statewide surveys in Massachusetts indicated that Latino/a intravenous drugs users were 1/3 less likely than their European American counterparts to enter residential treatment (Lundgren, Amodeo, Ferguson, & Davis, 2001). Furthermore, a recent study found that Puerto Rican women in Puerto Rico and New York City have less access to substance abuse, medical, and mental health services than men (Robles et al., 2006).

Several regional studies highlight various factors that may facilitate or hinder substance abuse treatment utilization among Latinos/as. For example, the statewide survey of intravenous drug users in Massachusetts indicated that having health insurance and receiving mental health services or being involved with the criminal justice system were associated with greater treatment utilization among women (Lundgren, Amaro, & Ben-Ami, 2005). Other studies conducted in California found that immigrants may be less likely to utilize treatment programs than U.S.-born Latinos/as (Fisher, Reynolds, Moreno-Branson, Jaffe, Wood, Klahn, & Muniz, 2004; Vega & Sribney, 2005). However, Vega and Sribney also reported that U.S.-born Latinos/as were more likely than their immigrant peers to express negative views about treatment services. Finally, qualitative studies with small samples of Latinas/os on the East coast suggest that shame and concerns about disrupting family relationships may prevent at least some Latinos/as from seeking residential treatment for drug and alcohol abuse (Amaro, Nieves, Johannes, & Cabeza, 1999; Kline, 1996).

Additionally, a number of studies have found Latina/Latino ethnicity to be a significant predictor of premature termination of outpatient drug abuse treatment (Agosti, Nunes, & Opecek-Welikson, 1996; Hser, Huang, Teruya, & Anglin, 2005; Kleinman, Kang, Lipton, Woody, Kemp, & Millman, 1992; Simpson, Joe, Rowan-Szal, & Greener, 1995; White, Winn, & Young, 1998). These studies have been conducted in various regions of the country, with individuals using a variety of substances, who sought treatment voluntarily, or were mandated to treatment. Another study conducted on the East coast found that that Latinos/as in treatment for substance abuse were more likely than European or African Americans to drop out of therapeutic communities (DeLeon, Melnick, & Jainchill, 1993). Among individuals in Los Angeles county drug treatment centers, Latina/o ethnicity was found to be a significant predictor of relapse upon termination of services (Brecht, vonMayrhauser, & Anglin, 2000). Finally, a 24-year follow-up of over 500 individuals in a court-mandated substance abuse treatment program, and a survey of treatment centers throughout the U.S., revealed that Latinos and Latinas had poorer outcomes after substance abuse treatment than European Americans (McCaughrin & Howard, 1995; Pendergast, Hser, & Gil-Rivas, 1998).

In contrast to the findings that point to an association between Latina/o ethnicity and premature treatment termination and poorer outcomes, a handful of studies have found that Latinos/as have outcomes that are similar to those of individuals from other ethnic groups. Bell, Williams, Nelson, and Spence (1994) did not find an association between ethnicity and retention in either a 28-day residential or a day treatment program of the same duration. Similarly, evaluations of methadone maintenance programs in California and New York City revealed no relationship between Latino/Latina ethnicity and retention (Hser, Anglin, & Liu, 1990-1991; Mulvaney et al., 1999). Finally, Dansereau, Joe, Dees, and Simpson (1996) found that node-link mapping was more effective for Latinos/as and African Americans than for European Americans in methadone maintenance programs, suggesting that mapping can overcome cultural and educational differences. Two studies, conducted in methadone maintenance programs, also called into question the usefulness of clinician-client ethnic matching for Latinas/os in substance abuse treatment. Maddux and Desmond (1996) found no effect of ethnic matching on treatment outcome, while Fiorentine and Hillhouse (1999) found that clinician/client ethnic matching positively influenced abstinence among women, but not among men.

In response to the contradictory findings reviewed above, several researchers have called for more attention to the impact of cultural variables on substance abuse treatment access, retention, and outcome (Alvarez & Ruiz, 2001; Amaro et al., 1999; Blane, 1993; Caetano, 1993; Castro & Tafoya-Barraza, 1997; Castro et al., 1999; Cervantes & Pena, 1998; de la Rosa, Khalsa, & Rouse, 1990; Gil & Vega, 2001; Institute of Medicine, 1990; Markarian & Franklin, 1998; Medina, 2001; Mora, 1998; Rebach, 1992; Rebhun, 1998; Rothe & Ruiz, 2001; Terrell, 1993). It is likely that differences in terms of cultural values, language, place of birth and generation in the U.S. influence individuals' response to treatment procedures and providers. Since Latinos/as differ in terms of various indices of acculturation, there is a need to document the types of modifications in treatment protocols that may be necessary, and to assess whether such modifications result in improvements in retention and outcomes (Gil & Vega).

Specific cultural values that may play a role in the process and outcome of substance abuse treatment include the value placed on dignity and respect (Ruiz & Langrod, 1992), the tendency to rely on the extended family for support (Castro & Tafoya-Barraza, 1997; Castro et al., 1999; Gil & Vega, 2001; Ruiz & Langrod, 1992; Terrell, 1993), "personalismo" (an emphasis on interpersonal relationships) (Gloria & Peregoy, 1996; Gil & Vega, 2001), "simpatia" (downplaying conflict in relationships) (Gloria & Peregoy, 1996; Gil & Vega, 2001), the value placed on spirituality and religion (Ruiz & Langrod, 1997), and gender roles which emphasize the public appearance of patriarchy (Gloria & Peregoy, 1996; Goldberg, 1997; Mora, 1998; Perez- Arce, 1994).

A number of qualitative studies with small numbers of Latinos and Latinas point to the importance of considering culture in the delivery of substance abuse services (Hohman, 1999; Porter, 1999; Trepper, Nelson, McCollum & McAvoy, 1997). Latinas/os in substance abuse treatment consistently endorsed the positive impact of having Latino/a counselors and peers in their treatment programs, citing the building of trust as an outcome of ethnic similarity. In addition, Trepper and colleagues' interviews with six Latinas in substance abuse treatment echoed many of the culturally specific themes discussed above. One theme included the importance of family and religion/spirituality in recovery. Additional themes involved the need to attend to other cultural values in treatment, such as respect for elders, collectivism, and maintaining the illusion of patriarchy in male-female relationships.

Similarly, a series of reports indicate that culturally-modified therapeutic communities, recovery homes and outpatient programs may lead to greater utilization and better outcome among Latinos and Latinas seeking substance abuse treatment (Cervantes, Kappos, Duenas, & Arellano, 2003; Hohman & Galt, 2001; Waters, Fazio, Hernandez, & Segarra, 2002). However, these findings are based on quasi-experimental studies with small samples and more research is needed to clarify the relationship between cultural affiliation and response to treatment interventions among Latinos and Latinas (Cervantes et al.; Hohman & Galt; Vega & Sribney, 2005).

It is possible that cultural mismatches between client and clinician may account for the higher rates of premature termination and the poorer outcomes of many Latinas/os and Latinas who seek substance abuse services. It is also possible that Latinos/as may have poorer outcomes, lower satisfaction with treatment, and shorter stays in substance abuse programs because of variables unrelated to cultural beliefs, values, and practices. There are only a few studies that document the problems presented by Latinas/os in substance abuse treatment. Arciniega, Arroyo, Miller, and Tonigan (1996) found few differences in alcohol use patterns between Latinos and European American men in alcohol treatment. Latinas, however, reported lower alcohol consumption, fewer symptoms, and less adverse alcohol-related consequences than Latinos and European American men and women. However, a recent analysis of a large national database of individuals in various types of substance abuse treatment programs indicated that Latinas reported more severe medical, psychological and employment problems than Latinos. Additionally, there were no significant differences in reports of alcohol, cannabis, and heroin use between men and women in the 30 days prior to seeking treatment and women reported more days of cocaine use than men during this time period. Furthermore, in terms of lifetime substance use, women reported using alcohol for fewer years than men, but there were no gender differences in years of cannabis, cocaine, and heroin use (Alvarez, Olson, Jason, Davis, & Ferrari, 2004). These findings indicate that Latinas who abuse substances enter treatment with problems that are at least as serious as those of Latinos. These substance-abusing women also need interventions that target medical, employment and co-occurring mental health problems.

Other national surveys indicate that many Latinos and Latinas may bring more serious problems as they enter substance abuse treatment programs, due to their drugs of choice, medical problems and involvement with the criminal justice system. SAMSHA's Drug and Alcohol Services Information System (2002b) reported that nationally, Latinos/as were more likely to be admitted to substance abuse treatment for opiate abuse than non-Latinas/os. Another national survey of substance abuse treatment programs indicated that programs with caseloads that were at least 20% Latino/a served clients who were poorer, more likely to abuse illicit drugs, more likely to have engaged in crime and to be court-referred to treatment, and more likely to be HIV positive or have AIDS (McCaughrin & Howard, 1995). Thus it is likely that the problems that Latinas/os bring to treatment may have an impact on their outcomes (Castro & Tafoya-Barraza, 1997; Hernandez, 2000; Mora, 1998;

Castro et al., 1999; Gil & Vega, 2001). There is a need for more studies that document the types of problems that Latinos/as bring to substance abuse treatment, such as most common drugs of choice, extent of substance use, and substance-related problems, including employment and level of education/job skills. These variables have been found to predict treatment retention and outcome among Latinas/os and others (Agosti et al., 1996; Brecht et al., 2000; Kleinman et al., 1992; Simpson et al., 1995; White et al., 1998). In addition, the effect of perceived discrimination and acculturative stress on treatment outcomes needs to be documented (Hernandez, 2000; Mora, 1998; Castro et al., 1999; Gil & Vega, 2001).

Mutual Help

Latino/Latina participation in 12-step groups such as Alcoholics Anonymous (AA), Narcotics Anonymous (NA), Cocaine Anonymous (CA), and Al-Anon has received less attention than other substance abuse interventions. Another neglected area of research has been the relationship between social support and recovery among Latinas/os (Barerra & Reese, 1993; Delgado & Humm-Delgado, 1993, 1995). Exploration of the relationship between social support and substance abuse recovery among Latinos/as is particularly important given the centrality of social support in substance abuse recovery (Humphreys & Moos, 1996; Humphreys, Moos, & Finney, 1996; Loganbaugh, Wirtz, Beattie, Noel, Stout, & Malloy, 1993).

Research to date indicates that Latinas/os use Alcoholics Anonymous and express agreement with its major principles (Caetano, 1993; Kaskutas, Weisner, & Caetano, 1997; Tonigan, Connors, & Miller, 1998). AA and Al-Anon have spread to Latin America (Caetano), and there are Spanish speaking AA and Al-Anon groups throughout the U.S. (Caetano; Hoffman, 1994). A national survey indicated that Latinos/as utilized AA to address problem drinking (Kaskutas et al.). However, according to AA membership surveys, Latinas/os underutilize this mutual help group (Tonigan et al.). There are no studies of Latino/a participation in Al-Anon, Narcotics Anonymous, or Cocaine Anonymous. Thus, investigations of Latino/a participation in 12 step programs include only individuals seeking help for alcohol abuse. The lack of attention to Al-Anon is particularly surprising given the central role that the family typically plays in Latin American cultures (Marin, 1993).

The few studies that have looked at AA participation have been conducted primarily in Northern New Mexico. Results of these investigations have been mixed. For example, a study in an outpatient treatment center in New Mexico indicated that Latinas/os, in comparison to European Americans, were less likely to report attending AA while in outpatient treatment (Arroyo, Westerberg, & Tonigan, 1998). In contrast, Tonigan, Connors, and Miller (1998) found no differences in AA attendance between Latinos/as and European Americans who attended outpatient substance abuse treatment. However, Tonigan and colleagues found that Latinas/os who received inpatient treatment were less likely to attend AA during the first three months of aftercare, but not nine months later, or at a three year follow-up. Recent studies indicate that Latinos/as in Project MATCH's 12-step facilitation condition were less likely to attend 12-step meetings than European Americans (Arroyo, Miller, & Tonigan, 2003; Tonigan, Miller, Juarez, & Villanueva, 2002). However, no ethnic differences were found for other indicators of 12-step involvement, such has having a sponsor, reading program materials, and working the steps (Tonigan, Miller et al.).

Research on Oxford House, a residential mutual-help recovery intervention, indicates that Latinos and Latinas are underrepresented in this program (Alvarez, Jason, Davis, Ferrari, & Olson, 2004). There is empirical evidence indicating that Oxford House is an effective aftercare intervention (Jason, Davis, Ferrari, & Bishop, 2001; Jason, Olson, Ferrari, & LoSasso, 2006; Jason, Davis, & Ferrari, 2007) and a diverse group of individuals utilize this program (Alvarez, Adebanjo, Davidson, Jason, & Davis, 2006; Majer, Jason, Ferrari, & North, 2002). Additionally, preliminary findings indicate that at least some Latinos/as find Oxford House to be a helpful component of their recovery, and lack of information about the program along with language and cultural barriers may keep many Latinas/os from utilizing this innovative intervention (Alvarez, Jason et al.).

More research is needed on the utilization and effectiveness of mutual-help recovery interventions among larger, more representative samples of Latinos/as. There is a need to document how Latinas/os access 12-step and other mutual-help programs and the factors that may facilitate utilization of these interventions. Research that explores modifications to these groups and the relationship of these changes to access and outcome for Latinas/os differing in terms of cultural affiliation would be particularly helpful (Caetano, 1993). Also, research on mutual help group participation needs to consider factors other than mere attendance, such as commitment and participation in the groups (Tonigan et al., 1998). Because Latinos/as tend to rely on extended family members more than on friends for social support (Schweizer, Schnegg, & Berson, 1998) and they continue to have strong family ties into the third generation in the

U.S. (Marin, 1993), the relationship between reliance on family for support and participation in 12-steps programs needs to be explored.

Summary of Treatment Studies

There is a critical need for research that addresses the impact of various types of substance abuse interventions for Latinos and Latinas. Studies that document modifications to treatment protocols to increase their cultural relevance for Latinas/os varying along various dimensions of acculturation are particularly needed. These studies also need to address the problems that Latinos/as bring to substance abuse treatment and the impact of these problems on retention and outcomes.

Similarly, there is a need for more research on factors that influence mutual help utilization and outcomes among Latinos and Latinas who differ on their substance-related problems and assimilation to U.S. culture. Increasing evidence indicates that 12-step participation plays a key role in recovery (Kelly, 2003), thus the importance of 12-step affiliation among Latinos and Latinas needs to be addressed.

CONCLUSIONS

There is a growing knowledge base in the areas of substance abuse prevalence and treatment among Latinos and Latinas in the United States. National surveys conducted by SAMHSA, which now include large Latino/a samples, provide information on the extent of substance-related problems and more recently, co-occurring mental health conditions. However, research indicates a need to pay closer attention to the heterogeneity of the Latina/o community in the U.S. The association between various indices of acculturation and substance use merits ongoing attention.

There is also a need for more research addressing the impact of various types of interventions on this growing segment of the U.S. population. The influence of cultural affiliation on treatment access, retention, and outcomes merits particular attention, as does the impact of mutual help programs on Latinos/as' recovery.

The multidimensional, bidirectional, and fluid nature of the process of acculturation presents a challenge to both prevalence and intervention research (Cervantes & Felix-Ortiz, 2004; Collins, 1996; Escobar & Vega, 2000; Trimble, 1995). To date, substance abuse researchers have defined acculturation in various ways, most commonly by using proxy measures such as language use, place of birth, and generation in the U.S. New developments in the measurement of acculturation (Berry, 2003; Zane & Mak, 2003) provide researchers with new ways to address the role of culture in the development and treatment of substance-related problems.

REFERENCES

Abraido-Lanza, A. F., Chao, M. T. & Flores, K. R. (2005). Do healthy behaviors decline with greater acculturation? Implications for the Latino mortality paradox. *Social Science & Medicine, 61*, 1243-1255.

Agosti, V., Nunes, E., & Ocepeck-Welikson, K. (1996). Patient factors related to early attrition from outpatient cocaine research. *American Journal of Drug and Alcohol Abuse, 22*, 29-41.

Alegria, M., Vera, M., Shrout, P., Canino, G., Lai, S., Albizu, C., Marin, H., Pena, M., & Rusch, D. (2004).Understanding hard-core drug use among urban Puerto Rican women in high-risk neighborhoods. *Addictive Behaviors, 29*, 643-664.

Alvarez, J., Olson, B. D., Jason, L. A., Davis, M. I., & Ferrari, J. R. (2004). Heterogeneity among Latinos and Latinas entering substance abuse treatment: Findings from a national database. *Journal of Substance Abuse Treatment, 26*, 277-284.

Alvarez, J., Jason, L. A., Davis, M. I., Ferrari, J. R., & Olson, B. D. (2004). Latinos and Latinas in Oxford House: Perceptions of barriers and opportunities. *Journal of Ethnicity in Substance Abuse, 13*, 17-32.

Alvarez, J., Adebanjo, A. M., Davidson, M. K., Jason, L. A., & Davis, M. I. (2006). Oxford House: Deaf-affirmative support for substance abuse recovery. *American Annals of the Deaf, 151*(4), 418-22.

Alvarez, L. R., & Ruiz, P. (2001). Substance abuse in the Mexican American population. In S. L. A. Straussner (Ed.), *Ethnocultural factors in substance abuse treatment* (pp. 111-136). New York: Guilford.

Amaro, H., Whitaker, R., Coffman, G., & Hereen, T. (1990). Acculturation and marijuana and cocaine use: Findings from H-HANES 1982-1984. *American Journal of Public Health, 80*(Supplement), 54-60.

Amaro, H., Nieves, R., Johannes, S. W., & Cabeza, N. M. L. (1999). Substance abuse treatment: Critical issues and challenges in the treatment of Latina women. *Hispanic Journal of Behavioral Sciences, 21*, 266-82.

Amaro, H., Larson, M. J., Gampel, J., Richardson, E., Savage, A., & Wagler, D. (2005). Racial/ethnic differences in social vulnerability among women with co-occurring mental health and substance abuse disorders: Implications for treatment services. *Journal of Community Psychology, 33*, 495-511.

Anglin, M. D., Hser, Y. I., & Grella, C. E. (1997). Drug addiction and treatment careers among clients in the drug abuse treatment outcome study (DATOS). *Psychology of Addictive Behaviors, 11*, 308-311.

Arciniega, L. T., Arroyo, J. A., Miller, W. R., & Tonigan, J. S. (1996). Alcohol, drug use and consequences among Hispanics seeking treatment for alcohol-related problems. *Journal of Studies on Alcohol, 57*, 613-618.

Arroyo, J. A., Miller, W. R., & Tonigan, J. S. (2003). The influence of Hispanic ethnicity on long-term outcome in three alcohol treatment modalities. *Journal of Studies on Alcohol, 64,* 98-104.

Arroyo, J. A., Westerberg, V. S., & Tonigan, J. S. (1998). Comparison of treatment utilization and outcome for Hispanics and non-Hispanic whites. *Journal of Studies on Alcohol. 59,* 286.

Barrera, M., & Reese, F. (1993). Natural social support systems and Hispanic substance abuse. In R. S. Mayers, B. L. Kail, & T. D. Watts (Eds), *Hispanic substance abuse* (pp. 115-130). Springfield, IL: Charles Thomas.

Becker, D. F., Grilo, C. M., Anez, L. M., Paris, M., & McGlashan, T. H. (2005). Discriminant efficiency of antisocial and borderline personality disorder criteria in Hispanic men with substance use disorders. *Comprehensive Psychiatry, 46,* 140-146.

Bell, D. C., Williams, M. L., Nelson, R., & Spence, R. T. (1994). An experimental test of retention in residential and outpatient programs. *American Journal of Drug and Alcohol Abuse, 20,* 331-340.

Berry, J. W. (2003). Conceptual approaches to acculturation. In K. M. Chun, P. B. Organista, & G. Marin (Eds.) *Acculturation: Advances in theory, measurement, and applied research* (pp. 17-38). Washington, D. C.: American Psychological Association.

Black, S. A., & Markides, K. (1993). Acculturation and alcohol consumption in Puerto Rican, Cuban American, and Mexican-American women in the United States. *American Journal of Public Health, 83,* 890-893.

Blane, H. T. (1993). Ethnicity. In M. Galanter (Ed.), *Recent developments in alcoholism (Volume 11)* (pp. 109-122). New York: Plenum.

Booth, B. M., Blow, C. A. L., Bunn, J. Y., & Fortney, J. C. (1992). Age and ethnicity among hospitalized alcoholics: A nationwide study. *Alcoholism: Clinical and Experimental Research, 16,* 1029-1034.

Brecht, M. L., VonMayrhauser, C., & Anglin, M. D. (2000). Predictors of relapse after treatment for metamphetamine use. *Journal of Psychoactive Drugs, 32,* 211-20.

Caetano, R. (1993). Ethnic minority groups and alcoholics anonymous: A review. In B. S. McGrady, & W. R. Miller (Eds.), *Research on Alcoholics Anonymous: Opportunities and alternatives* (pp. 209-231). New Brunswick, NJ: Rutgers Center on Alcohol Studies.

Caetano, R. (1994). Drinking and alcohol related-problems among minority women. *Alcohol Health and Research World, 16,* 233-41.

Caetano, R., & Clark, C. (1998). Trends in alcohol-related problems among Whites, Blacks and Hispanics: 1984-1995. *Alcoholism: Clinical and Experimental Research, 22,* 534-538.

Caetano, R., Ramisetty-Mikler, S., & McGrath, C. (2004). Acculturation, drinking, and intimate partner violence among Hispanic couples in the United States: A longitudinal study. *Hispanic Journal of Behavioral Sciences, 26,* 60-78.

Canino, G. J. (1994). Alcohol use and misuse among Hispanic women: Selected factors, processes, and studies. *The International Journal of the Addictions, 29,* 1083-1100.

Canino, G. J., Burnam, A., & Caetano, R. (1992). The prevalence of alcohol abuse and dependence in two Hispanic communities. In J. E. Helzer & G. J. Canino (Eds.), *Alcoholism in North America, Europe, and Asia* (pp. 131-155). New York: Oxford University Press.

Casas, J. M., Vasquez, M. J. T., & Ruiz de Esparza, C. A. (2002). Counseling the Latina/o: A guiding framework for a diverse population. In P. B. Pedersen, J. G. Draguns, W. L. Lonner, & J. E. Trimble (Eds.), *Counseling across cultures (5th Edition)* (pp. 133-159). Thousand Oaks, CA: Sage Publications.

Castro, F. G. & Tafoya-Barraza, H. M. (1997). Treatment issues with Latinos addicted to cocaine and heroin. In G. G. Garcia & M. C. Zea (Eds.), *Psychological interventions and research with Latino populations* (pp. 191-216). Boston: Allyn & Bacon.

Castro, F. G.; Proescholdbell, R. J., Abeita, L. & Rodriguez, D. (1999). Ethnic and cultural minority groups. In B. S. McGrady & E. E. Epstein (Eds.), *Addictions: A comprehensive guidebook* (pp. 499-526). New York: Oxford University Press.

Cervantes, R. C. & Felix-Ortiz, M. (2004). Substance abuse among Chicanos and other Mexican groups. R. J. Velasquez, L. M. Arellano, & G. W. McNeill (Eds.), *The handbook of Chicana/o psychology and mental health.* (pp. 325-352). Mahwah, NJ: Lawrence Erlbaum Associates.

Cervantes, R., C., Gilbert, M. J., Salgado de Snyder, N., & Padilla, A. M. (1990-1991). Psychosocial and cognitive correlates of alcohol use in younger adult immigrant and US born Hispanics. *The International Journal of the Addictions, 25,* 687-708.

Cervantes, R. C., Kappos, B., Duenas, N., & Arellano, D. (2003). Culturally Focused HIV Prevention and Substance Abuse Treatment for Hispanic Women. *Addictive Disorders & Their Treatment, 2,* 69-77.

Cervantes, R. C. & Pena, C. (1998). Evaluating Hispanic/Latino programs: Ensuring cultural competence. *Alcoholism Treatment Quarterly, 16,* 109-131.

Collins, R. L. (1996). The role of ethnic versus nonethnic sociocultural factors in substance use and misuse. *Substance Use and Misuse, 31,* 95-101.

Comas-Diaz, L. (2001). Hispanics, Latinos, or Americanos: The evolution of identity. *Cultural Diversity and Ethnic Minority Psychology, 7,* 115-120.

Cuadrado, M. & Liberman, L. (1998). Traditionalism in the prevention of substance misuse among Puerto Ricans. *Substance Use and Misuse, 33,* 2737-2755.

Dansereau, D. F., Joe, G. W., Dees, S. M., & Simpson, D. D. (1996). Ethnicity and the effects of mapping-enhanced drug abuse counseling. *Addictive Behaviors, 21,* 363-376.

de la Rosa, M. R. Holleran, L. K., & Straussner, S. L. A. (2005). Substance abuse among U. S. Latinos: A review of the literature. In. M. R. de la Rosa, L. K Holleran, & S. L. A. Straussner (Eds.), *Substance Abusing Latinos: Current research, epidemiology, prevention, and treatment* (pp. 1-20). New York: Haworth.

de la Rosa, M. R., Khalsa, J. H., & Rouse, B. A. (1990). Hispanics and illicit drug use: A review of recent findings. *The International Journal of the Addictions, 25,* 665-691.

DeLeon, G., Melnick, G., Schoket, D., & Jainchill, N. (1993). Is the therapeutic community culturally relevant? Findings on race/ethnic differences in retention in treatment. *Journal of Psychoactive Drugs, 25,* 77-86.

Delgado, M. (2005). Cross-cutting themes and recommendations. In M. Delgado (Ed.), *Latinos and alcohol use/abuse revisited* (pp. 205-212). New York: Haworth.

Delgado, M., & Humm-Delgado, D. (1993). Chemical dependence self-help groups and the Hispanic community. In R. S. Mayers, B. L. Kail & T. D. Watts (Eds), *Hispanic substance abuse* (pp. 145-156). Springfield, IL: Charles Thomas.

Delgado, M., & Humm-Delgado, D. (1995). Hispanic natural support systems and alcohol and other drug services: Challenges and rewards for practice. *Alcoholism Treatment Quarterly, 12,* 17-31.

Escobar, J. I., Nervi, C. H., & Gara, M. A. (2000). Immigration and mental health: Mexican Americans in the United States. *Harvard Review of Psychiatry, 8,* 64-72.

Escobar, J. I., & Vega, W. A. (2000). Mental Health and Immigration's AAAs: Where are we and where do we go from here? *Journal of Nervous and Mental Disease, 188,* 736-740.

Farabee, D., Wallisch, L., & Maxwell, J. C. (1995). Substance use among Texas Hispanics and non-Hispanics: Who's using, who's not and why. *Hispanic Journal of Behavioral Sciences, 17,* 523-536.

Finch, B. K. (2001). Nation of origin, gender, and neighborhood differences in past year substance use among Hispanics and non-Hispanic Whites. *Hispanic Journal of Behavioral Sciences, 23,* 88-101.

Finch, B. K., Catalano, R. C., Novaco, R. W., & Vega, W. A. (2003). Employment frustration and alcohol abuse/dependence among labor migrants in California. *Journal of Immigrant Health, 5,* 181-186.

Fiorentine, R. & Hillhouse, M. P. (1999). Drug treatment effectiveness and client counselor empathy: Exploring the effects of gender and ethnic congruency. *Journal of Drug Issues, 29,* 59-74.

Fisher, D. G., Reynolds, G. L., Moreno-Branson, C. M., Jaffe, A., Wood, M. M., Klahn, J. A., & Muniz, J. F. (2004). Drug treatment needs of Hispanic drug users in Long Beach, CA. *Journal of Drug Issues, 34,* 879-894.

Gil, A. G., & Vega, W. A. (2001). Latino drug use, scope, risk factors and reduction strategies. In M. Aguirre-Molina, C. W. Molina & R. E. Zambrana (Eds.), *Health issues in the Latino community* (pp. 435-458). San Francisco: Jossey-Bass.

Gilbert, M. J. & Collins, R. L. (1997). Ethnic variation in women's and men's drinking. In R. W. Wilsnack & S. C. Wilsnack (Eds.), *Gender and alcohol* (pp. 357-378). New Brunswick, NJ: Rutgers Center on Alcohol Studies.

Gloria, A. M., & Peregoy, J. J. (1996). Counseling Latino alcohol and other substance users/abusers: Cultural considerations for counselors. *Journal of Substance Abuse Treatment, 13,* 119-126.

Goldberg, E. V. (1997). Hispanic substance abusing men and machismo. In S. L. A. Straussner & E. Zelvin (Eds.), *Gender and addictions: Men and women in treatment* (pp. 451-468). Northvale, N. J.: Jason Aronson.

Golding, J. M., Brurnam, M. A., Benjamin, B., & Wells, K. B. (1990). Alcohol use and depressive symptoms among Mexican Americans and non-Hispanic whites. *Alcohol and Alcoholism, 25,* 421-432.

Golding, J. M., Brurnam, M. A., Benjamin, B., & Wells, K. B. (1992). Reasons for drinking, alcohol use, and alcoholism among Mexican Americans and non-Hispanic whites. *Psychology of Addictive Behaviors, 6,* 155-167.

Grant, B. F., Stinson, F. S., Hasin, D. S., Dawson, D. A., Chou, S. P., & Anderson, K. (2004). Immigration and lifetime prevalence of DSM-IV psychiatric disorders among Mexican Americans and Non-Hispanic Whites in the United States: Results from the National Epidemiologic Survey on Alcohol and Related Conditions. *Archives of General Psychiatry, 61,* 1226-1233.

Grilo, C. M., Anez, L. M., & McGlashan, T. H. (2002). DSM-IV Axis II comorbidity with borderline personality disorder in monolingual Hispanic psychiatric outpatients. *Journal of Nervous and Mental Disease, 190*(5), 324-330.

Guendelman, S., & Abrams, B. (1994). Dietary, alcohol, and tobacco intake among Mexican-American women of childbearing age: Results from HANES data. *American Journal of Public Health, 8*, 363-372.

Hernandez, M. (2000). Puerto Rican families and substance abuse. In J. A. Krestan (Ed.), *Bridges to recovery: Addiction, family therapy, and multicultural treatment* (pp. 253-283). New York: The Free Press.

Hines, A. M., & Caetano, R. (1998). Alcohol and AIDS-related sexual behavior among Hispanics: Acculturation and gender differences. *AIDS Education and Prevention, 10*, 533-547.

Hoffman, F. (1994). Cultural adaptations of alcoholics anonymous to serve Hispanic populations. *The International Journal of the Addictions, 29*, 445-460.

Hohman, M. (1999). Treatment experiences of women in a recovery home for Latinas. *Alcoholism Treatment Quarterly, 17*, 67-78.

Hohman, M. M. & Galt, D. H. (2001). Latinas in treatment: Comparisons of residents in a culturally specific recovery home with residents in non-specific recovery homes. *Journal of Ethnic & Cultural Diversity in Social Work, 9*, 93-109.

Hser, Y. I., Anglin, M. D., & Liu, Y. (1990-1). A survival analysis of gender and ethnic differences in responsiveness to methadone maintenance treatment. *The International Journal of the Addictions, 25*, 1295-131.

Hser, Y. I., Huang, D., Teruya, C., & Anglin, M. D. (2005). Diversity of drug abuse treatment utilization patterns and outcomes. *Evaluation and Program Planning, 27*, 309-319.

Hughes, T. L., Day, L. E., Marcantonio, R. J., & Torpy, E. (1997). Gender differences in alcohol and other drug use among young adults. *Substance Use and Misuse, 32*, 317-342.

Humphreys, K., & Moos, R. H. (1996). Reduced substance abuse-related health care costs among voluntary participants in Alcoholics Anonymous. *Psychiatric Services, 47*, 709-713.

Humphreys, K., Moos, R. H., & Finney, J. W. (1996). Life domains, alcoholics anonymous, and role incumbency in the 3-year course of problem drinking. *Journal of Nervous and Mental Disease, 184*, 475-481.

Institute of Medicine (1990). *Broadening the base of treatment for alcohol problems*. Washington, D.C.: National Academy Press.

Jason, L. A., Davis, M. I., Ferrari, J. R., & Bishop, P. D. (2001). Oxford House: A review of research and implications for substance abuse recovery and community research. *Journal of Drug Education, 31*, 1-27.

Jason, L. A., Davis, M. I., & Ferrari, J. R. (2007). The need for substance abuse aftercare: A longitudinal analysis of Oxford House. *Addictive Behaviors, 32*(4), 803-18.

Jason, L.A., Olson, B.D., Ferrari, J.R., & Lo Sasso, A.T. (2006). Communal housing settings enhance substance abuse recovery. *American Journal of Public Health, 96*, 1727-1729.

Johnson, T. P., VanGeest, J. B., & Cho, Y. I. (2002). Migration and substance use: Evidence from the U.S. National Health Interview Survey. *Substance Use and Misuse, 37*, 941-972.

Kail, B., Zayas, L. H., & Malgady, R. G. (2000). Depression, acculturation and motivations for alcohol use among young Columbian, Dominican and Puerto Rican men. *Hispanic Journal of Behavioral Sciences, 22*, 64-77.

Kaskutas, L. A., Weisner, C., & Caetano, R. (1997). Predictors of help seeking among a longitudinal sample of the general public. 1984-1992. *Journal of Studies on Alcohol, 58*, 155-161.

Kleinman, P. H., Kang, S. Y., Lipton, D. S., Woody, G. E., Kemp, J., & Millman, R. B. (1992). Retention of cocaine abusers in outpatient psychotherapy. *American Journal of Drug and Alcohol Abuse, 18*, 29-43.

Kline, A. (1996). Pathways into drug user treatment: The influence of gender and racial /ethnic identity. *Substance Use and Misuse, 31*, 323-342.

Lee, D. J. & Markides, K. S. (1997). Epidemiology of self-reported heavy drinking in Hispanic adults. *Ethnicity and Health, 2*, 77-89.

Lillie-Blanton, M., Anthony, J. C., & Schuster, C. R. (1993). Probing the meaning of racial/ethnic group comparisons in crack cocaine smoking. *Journal of the American Medical Association, 269*, 993-997.

Longabaugh, R., Beattie, M., Noel, N., Stout, R. L., & Malloy, P. (1993). The effects of social investment on treatment outcome. *Journal of Studies on Alcohol, 54*, 465-478.

Longshore, D., Hsieh, S., Anglin, M. D., & Annon, T. A. (1992). Ethnic patterns in drug abuse treatment utilization. *Journal of Mental Health Administration, 19*, 268-77.

Longshore, D., Hsieh, S., & Anglin, M. D (1993). Ethnic and gender differences in drug user's perceived need for treatment. *The International Journal of the Addictions, 28*, 539-558.

Lown, E. A, & Vega, W. A. (2001). Alcohol abuse or dependence among Mexican American women who report violence. *Alcoholism: Clinical and Experimental Research, 25*, 1479-1486.

Lundgren, L. M., Amaro, H., & Ben-Ami, L. (2005). Factors associated with drug treatment entry patterns among Hispanic women injection drug users seeking treatment. *Journal of Social Work Practice in the Addictions, 5*, 157-174.

Lundgren, L. M., Amodeo, M., Ferguson, F., & Davis, K. (2001). Racial and ethnic differences in drug treatment entry of injection drug users in Massachusetts. *Journal of Substance Abuse Treatment, 21*, 145-153.

Maddux, J. F., & Desmond, D. P. (1996). Ethnic matching of caseworker and patient in methadone maintenance. *Journal of Substance Abuse Treatment, 13*, 233-39.

Majer, J., Jason, L. A., Ferrari, J. R., & North, C. (2002). Co-morbidity among Oxford House residents: A preliminary outcome study. *Addictive Behaviors, 27*, 837-845.

Marin, G. (1993). Influence of acculturation on familialism and self-identification among Hispanics. In M. E. Bernal & G. P. Knight (Eds.), *Ethnic identity formation and transmission among Hispanics and other minorities* (pp. 181-196). Albany, NY: State University of New York Press.

Marin, G., & Posner, S. F. (1995). The role of gender and acculturation on determining the consumption of alcoholic beverages among Mexican-Americans and Central Americans in the United States. *The International Journal of the Addictions, 30*, 770-794.

Markarian, M., & Franklin, J. (1998). Substance abuse in minority populations. In R. J. Frances & S. I. Miller (Eds.), *Clinical textbook of addictive disorders (2nd Edition)* (pp. 397-412). New York: Guilford.

Markides, K. S., Ray, L. A., Stroup-Benham, C. A., & Trevino, F. (1990). Acculturation and alcohol consumption in the Mexican-American population of the Southwest United States: Findings from H-HANES, 1982-1984. *American Journal of Public Health, 80*(Supplement), 43-46.

McCaughrin, W. C., & Howard, D. L. (1995). Variations in outpatient substance abuse treatment units with high concentrations of Latino versus White clients: Client factors, treatment experiences and treatment outcomes. *Hispanic Journal of Behavioral Sciences, 17,* 509-522.

Medina, C. (2001). Toward an understanding of Puerto Rican ethnicity and substance abuse. S. L. A. Straussner (Ed.), *Ethnocultural factors in substance abuse treatment* (pp. 137-164). New York: Guilford.

Montoya, I. D., Covarrubias, L. D., Patek, J. A., & Graves, J. A. (2003). Posttraumatic stress disorder among Hispanic and African-American drug users. *American Journal of Drug and Alcohol Abuse, 29,* 729-741.

Mora, J. (1994). The *chola* life course: Chicana heroin users and the barrio gang. *The International Journal of the Addictions, 29,* 115-1126.

Mora, J. (1998). The treatment of alcohol dependency among Latinas: A feminist, cultural, and community perspective. *Alcoholism Treatment Quarterly, 16,* 163-177.

Mulvaney, F. D. et al. (1999). Methadone maintenance outcomes for Hispanic and African American men and women. *Drug and Alcohol Dependence, 54,* 11-18.

National Institute on Drug Abuse (1987). *Use of selected drugs among Hispanics: Mexican Americans, Puerto Ricans and Cuban Americans: Findings from the Hispanic Health and Nutrition Examination Survey (HHANES).* DHHS Pub. No. (ADM) 87-15-27. Washington, DC: United States Government Printing Office.

National Institute on Drug Abuse (1998). *Drug use among racial/ethnic minorities.* Rockville, MD: Author.

National Institute on Drug Abuse (2003). *Drug use among racial/ethnic minorities, revised.* Rockville, MD: Author.

Neff, J. A. (1993). Life stressors, drinking patterns, and depressive symptomatology: Ethnicity and stress-buffer effects of alcohol. *Addictive Behaviors, 18,* 373-387.

Neff, J. A., Prihoda, T. J., & Hoppe, S. K. (1991). "Machismo," self-esteem, education and high maximum drinking among Anglo, Black, and Mexican-American male drinkers. *Journal of Studies on Alcohol, 52,* 458-486.

Neff, J. A., & Hoppe, S. K. (1992). Acculturation and drinking patterns among U.S. Anglos, Blacks, and Mexican Americans. *Alcohol and Alcoholism, 27,* 293-308.

Nielsen, A. L. (2000). Examining drinking patterns and problems among Hispanic groups: Results from a national survey. *Journal of Studies on Alcohol, 61,* 301-310.

Nielsen, A. L. (2001). Drinking in adulthood: Similarities and differences in effects of adult roles for Hispanic ethnic groups and Anglos. *Journal of Studies on Alcohol, 62,* 745-749.

Ortega, A. N., Rosenheck, R., Alegria, M., & Desai, R. A. (2000). Acculturation and the lifetime risk of psychiatric and substance abuse disorders among Hispanics. *Journal of Nervous and Mental Disease, 188,* 728-735.

Parker, K. D., Weaver, G., & Calhoun, T. (1995). Predictors of alcohol and drug use: A multiethnic comparison. *Journal of Social Psychology, 135*, 581-90.

Pendergast, M. L., Hser, Y. I., & Gil-Rivas, V. (1998). Ethnic differences in longitudinal patterns and consequences of narcotics addiction. *Journal of Drug Issues, 28*, 495-516.

Perez-Arce, P. (1994). Substance use patterns of Latinas: Commentary. *The International Journal of the Addictions, 29*, 1189-99.

Perez-Stable, E. J., Marin, G., & Marin, B. V. (1994). Behavioral risk factors: A comparison of Latinos and non-Latino whites in San Francisco. *American Journal of Public Health, 84*, 971-76.

Porter, J. (1999). The street/treatment barrier: Treatment experiences of Puerto Rican injection drug users. *Substance Use and Misuse, 34*, 1951-1975.

Rebach, H. (1992). Alcohol and drug use among American minorities. In J. E. Trimble, C. S. Bolek, & S. J. Niemcryk (Eds.), *Ethnic and multicultural drug abuse* (pp. 23-57). New York: Haworth Press.

Rebhun, L. A. (1998). Substance abuse among immigrants to the United States. In S. Loue (Ed.), *Handbook of immigrant health* (pp. 493-519). New York: Plenum.

Rios-Bedoya, C. F. & Gallo, J. J. (2003). The association of alcohol use and depression among Puerto Ricans in the United States and in Puerto Rico. *Journal of Ethnicity in Substance Abuse, 2*, 1-13.

Robles, R. R., Matos, T. D., Deren, S., Colon, H. M. Sahai, H., Marrero, C. A., Reyes, J.C., Andia, J., & Shepard, E. W. (2006). Drug treatment disparities among Hispanic drug-using women in Puerto Rico and New York City. *Health Policy, 75*, 159-169.

Rothe, E. M., & Ruiz, P. (2001). Substance abuse among Cuban Americans. S. L. A. Straussner (Ed.), *Ethnocultural factors in substance abuse treatment* (pp. 97-110). New York: Guilford.

Ruiz, P., & Langrod, J. G. (1992). Substance abuse among Hispanic Americans: Current issues and future perspectives. In J. H. Lowinson, P. Ruiz, R. B. Millman & J. G. Langrod (Eds.), *Substance abuse: A comprehensive textbook* (2nd edition) (pp. 868-874). Baltimore: Williams & Wilkins.

Ruiz, P., & Langrod, J. G. (1997). Hispanic-Americans. In J. H. Lowinson, P. Ruiz, R. B. Millman, & J. G. Langrod (Eds.), *Substance abuse: A comprehensive textbook (3rd edition)* (p. 705-711). Baltimore: Williams & Wilkins.

Schweizer, T., Schnegg, M., & Berzbon, S. (1998). Personal networks and social support in a multiethnic community in Southern California. *Social Networks, 20*, 1-21.

Simpson, D. D., Joe, G. W., Rowan-Szal, G., & Greener, J. (1995). Client engagement and change during drug abuse treatment. *Journal of Substance Abuse, 7*, 117-134.

Substance Abuse and Mental Health Services Administration (1998a). *Prevalence of substance use among racial and ethnic subgroups in the United States 1991-1993*. Rockville, MD: Author.

Substance Abuse and Mental Health Services Administration (1998b). *National household survey on drug abuse*. Retrieved on February 6, 2002 from http://www.samhsa.gov/oas.

Substance Abuse and Mental Health Services Administration (1999). *National Household Survey on Drug Abuse*. Retrieved on February 6, 2002 from http://www.samhsa.gov/oas.

Substance Abuse and Mental Health Services Administration (2000). *National household survey on drug abuse.* Retrieved on February 6, 2002 from http://www.samhsa.gov/oas.

Substance Abuse and Mental Health Services Administration (2001). *National household survey on drug abuse.* Retrieved on November 6, 2002 from http://www.samhsa.gov/oas.

Substance Abuse and Mental Health Services Administration (2002a). *National survey on drug use and health.* Retrieved on July 7, 2006 from http://www.samhsa.gov/oas.

Substance Abuse and Mental Health Services Administration (2002b). *Drug and alcohol services information report.* Retrieved on November 6, 2002 from http://www.samhsa.gov/oas.

Substance Abuse and Mental Health Services Administration (2003). *National survey on drug use and health.* Retrieved on July 7, 2006 from http://www.samhsa.gov/oas.

Substance Abuse and Mental Health Services Administration (2004). *National survey on drug use and health.* Retrieved on July 7, 2006 from http://www.samhsa.gov/oas.

Terrell, M. D. (1993). Ethnocultural factors and substance abuse: Toward culturally sensitive treatment models. *Psychology of Addictive Behaviors, 7*, 162-7.

Tonigan, J. S., Connors, G. J., & Miller, W. R. (1998) Special populations in alcoholics anonymous. *Alcohol Health and Research World, 22*, 281-285.

Tonigan, J. S., Miller, W. R.. Juarez, P., & Villanueva, M. (2002). Utilization of AA by Hispanic and non-Hispanic White clients receiving outpatient alcohol treatment. *Journal of Studies on Alcohol, 63*, 215-218.

Trepper, T., Nelson, T. S., McCollum, E. E., & McAvoy, P. (1997). Improving substance abuse service delivery to Hispanic women through increased cultural competencies: A qualitative study. *Journal of Substance Abuse Treatment, 14*, 225-234.

Trimble, J. (1995). Toward an understanding of ethnicity and ethnic identity, and their relationship with drug use research. In G. J. Botvin, S. Schinke, & M. A. Orlandi (Eds.), *Drug abuse prevention with multiethnic youth* (pp.3-27). Thousand Oaks, CA: Sage.

U.S. Bureau of the Census (2000). *Current population survey.* Retrieved on February 5, 2002, from http://www.census.gov.

U.S. Bureau of the Census (2006). *Population Estimates for July, 2005.* Retrieved on June 21, 2006, from http://www.census.gov.

Vega, W. A., Kolody, B., Hwang, J., Noble, A., & Porter, P. A. (1997). Perinatal drug use among immigrant and native-born Latinas. *Substance Use and Misuse, 32*, 43-62.

Vega, W. A., Alderete, E., Kolody, B., & Aguilar-Gaxiola, S. (1998). Illicit drug use among Mexican Americans in California: The effects of gender and acculturation. *Addiction, 93*, 1839-1851.

Vega, W. A. & Sribney, W. M. (2005). Seeking care for alcohol problems: Patterns of need and treatment among Mexican-origin adults in central California. *Alcoholism Treatment Quarterly, 23*, 29-51.

Vega, W. A., Sribney, W. M., & Achara-Abrahams, I. (2003). Co-Occurring Alcohol, Drug, and Other Psychiatric Disorders Among Mexican-Origin People in the United States. *American Journal of Public Health, 93*, 1057-1064.

Vega, W. A., Sribney, W. M., Aguilar-Gaxiola, S., & Kolody, B. (2004). 12-month prevalence of DSM-III-R psychiatric disorders among Mexican Americans: Nativity, social assimilation, and age determinants. *Journal of Nervous and Mental Disease*, 192, 532-541.

Vera, M., Alegria, M., Pattatucci-Aragon, A. M., & Pena, M. (2005). Childhood sexual abuse and drug use among low-income urban Puerto Rican women. *Journal of Social Work Practice in the Addictions, 5*, 45-68.

Wagner-Echeagaray, F., Chilcoat, H. D., & Anthony, J. C. (1994). Degree of acculturation and the risk of crack cocaine smoking among Hispanic Americans. *British Journal of Psychiatry, 168*, 17-30.

Waters, J. A., Fazio, S. L., Hernandez, L., & Segarra, J. (2002). The Story of CURA, a Hispanic/Latino Drug Therapeutic Community. *Journal of Ethnicity in Substance Abuse, 1*, 113-134.

Wells, K., Klap, R., Koike, A., & Sherbourne, C. (2001). Ethnic disparities in unmet need for alcoholism, drug abuse and mental health care. *American Journal of Psychiatry, 158*, 2027-2032.

Welte, J. W., & Barnes, G. M. (1995). Alcohol and other drug use among Hispanics in New York State. *Alcoholism: Clinical and Experimental Research, 19*, 1061-66.

White, J. M., Winn, K. L., & Young, W. (1998). Predictors of attrition from an outpatient chemical dependency program. *Substance Abuse, 19*, 49.

Wilcox, J. A., Briones, D., & Suess, L. (1991). Substance abuse, post-traumatic stress, and ethnicity. *Journal of Psychoactive Drugs, 23*, 83-84.

Zane, N. & Mak, W. (2003). Major approaches to the measurement of acculturation among ethnic minority populations: A content analysis and an alternative empirical strategy. In K. M. Chun, P. B. Organista, & G. Marin (Eds.) *Acculturation: Advances in theory, measurement, and applied research* (pp. 39-60). Washington, D. C.: American Psychological Association.

doi:10.1300/J233v06n02_08

Cruising in Cyber Space: Comparing Internet Chat Room versus Community Venues for Recruiting Hispanic Men Who Have Sex with Men to Participate in Prevention Studies

M. Isabel Fernández, PhD
Jacob C. Warren, PhD
Leah M. Varga, MA
Guillermo Prado, PhD
Nilda Hernandez, AA
G. Stephen Bowen, MD, MPH

M. Isabel Fernández is Professor, Public Health and Preventive Medicine, Nova Southeastern University, College of Osteopathic Medicine, 4th Floor Terry Building, 3200 S University Drive, Fort Lauderdale, FL 33314 (E-mail: mariafer@nova.edu). Jacob C. Warren, Assistant Professor of Public Health and Preventive Medicine, Nova Southeastern University College of Osteopathic Medicine, 3200 S University Drive, Fort Lauderdale, FL 33314 (E-mail: wjacob@nova.edu). Leah M. Varga is Senior Research Associate III, Nova Southeastern University College of Osteopathic Medicine, 3200 S University Drive, Fort Lauderdale, FL 33314 (E-mail: varga@nova.edu). Guillermo Prado is Assistant Professor, Department of Epidemiology and Biostatistics, Stempel School of Public Health, Florida International University, 11200 SW 8th Street, HLS-II 597, Miami, FL 33199 (E-mail: pradog@fiu.edu). Nilda Hernandez is Data Systems Administrator, Nova Southeastern University College of Osteopathic Medicine, 3200 S University Drive, Fort Lauderdale, FL 33314 (E-mail: hnilda@nova.edu). G. Stephen Bowen is Professor of Public Health and Preventive Medicine, Nova Southeastern University College of Osteopathic Medicine, 3200 S University Drive, Fort Lauderdale, FL 33314.

Address correspondence to: M. Isabel Fernández, Public Health and Preventive Medicine, Nova Southeastern University, College of Osteopathic Medicine, 4th Floor Terry Building, 3200 S University Drive, Fort Lauderdale, FL 33314.

This study was supported by R01 DA-16026 from the National Institute on Drug Abuse.

[Haworth co-indexing entry note]: "Cruising in Cyber Space: Comparing Internet Chat Room versus Community Venues for Recruiting Hispanic Men Who Have Sex with Men to Participate in Prevention Studies." Fernández, M. Isabel et al. Co-published simultaneously in *Journal of Ethnicity in Substance Abuse* (The Haworth Press, Inc.) Vol. 6, No. 2, 2007, pp. 143-162; and: *21st Century Research on Drugs and Ethnicity: Studies Supported by the National Institute on Drug Abuse* (ed: Peter L. Myers) The Haworth Press, 2007, pp. 143-162. Single or multiple copies of this article are available for a fee from The Haworth Document Delivery Service [1-800-HAWORTH, 9:00 a.m. - 5:00 p.m. (EST). E-mail address: docdelivery@haworthpress.com].

Available online at http://jesa.haworthpress.com

doi:10.1300/J233v06n02_09

SUMMARY. Difficulties with recruitment of hidden populations, such as Hispanic men who have sex with men (MSM), have hampered HIV prevention research, leading researchers to explore alternative recruitment modalities such as the Internet. In this paper, we compare the efficiency and cost of recruiting HMSM from Internet chat rooms versus community venues and examine the differences between participants recruited from each type of venue. Internet recruitment was more efficient and somewhat less costly than community recruitment. Although the two groups were comparable in most demographic factors and HIV risk behaviors, Internet recruits were more likely to be bisexual, more likely to be HIV seropositive, had a higher level of education, and reported higher levels of psychological distress and lower levels of gay community attachment. Implications of our findings for using Internet chatrooms as recruitment venues are discussed. doi:10.1300/J233v06n02_09

KEYWORDS. Hispanic, MSM, Internet, recruitment

INTRODUCTION

Hispanic men who have sex with men (HMSM) are an underserved, often hidden population at increased risk of acquiring HIV from sexual behavior and/or drug use (Centers for Disease Control and Prevention, 2006). The well documented difficulties faced when recruiting special populations including ethnic minorities and sexual minorities (e.g., Leonard et al., 2003) have hampered development of culturally sensitive risk reduction interventions for those who are most in need. To overcome these challenges, investigators have examined alternative approaches, including respondent-driven sampling, pre-payment of study incentives, and more recently, the Internet (Heckathorn, 2002; Martinez-Ebbers, 1997; Duncan, White, & Nicholson, 2003). The Internet might be particularly effective for reaching hidden populations such as HMSM who use drugs and have risky sex, who might be less willing to respond to more conventional methods (Fernández et al., 2004).

There has been an explosive growth in Internet usage and access in the last decade (Nielsen/NetRatings, 2004; comScore Networks, 2004). Because the Internet provides a virtual environment in which to interact and socialize (Brown, Maycock, & Burns, 2005), it has become a popular place for congregating, communicating, and building communities (Reymers, 2002). The Internet has become a popular venue for many MSM, including HMSM, to exchange information, discuss issues, converse in chat rooms, partake in cybersex fantasies, and find sex partners (Benotsch, Kalichman, & Cage, 2002; McFarlane, Bull, & Rietmeijer, 2000; Tikkanen, & Ross, 2003; Rietmeijer, Bull, McFarlane, Patnaik, & Douglas, 2003; Hospers, Harterink, Van Den Hoek, & Veenstra, 2002). Because personal profiles posted on select Internet sites often describe preferences regarding sexual practices, use of recreational drugs, and contain sexually explicit pictures, Internet users can rapidly and efficiently screen potential sex partners and set up sexual encounters, a practice that is elevating their HIV risk. For instance, there is growing evidence that seeking sex partners through the internet is increasing men's risk for acquiring sexually transmitted infections (STI) including HIV. Significant associations between Internet sex-seeking and high-risk sex have been reported (Elford, Bolding, & Sherr, 2001; Rietmeijer et al., 2003; Halkitis, Parsons, & Wilton, 2003; Bull & McFarlane, 2000; Kim, Kent, McFarland, & Klausner, 2001; Benotsch et al., 2002; Tikkanen & Ross, 2003). In short, the Internet has become the "new erotic oasis" for MSM (Ross, Tikkanen, & Manson, 2000).

Given this, researchers and practitioners are increasingly using the Internet to foster HIV prevention efforts geared towards MSM (Fernández et al., 2004; Fernández, Perrino, Collazo et al., 2005; Rietmeijer et al., 2003; Hospers et al., 2002; Ross et al., 2000; Rhodes, 2004). Studies have demonstrated the feasibility and acceptability of using the Internet to provide prevention messages, collect data, or offer automated interventions through static websites (Benotsch et al., 2002; Tikkanen & Ross, 2003; Rietmeijer et al., 2003; Hospers et al., 2002; Ross et al., 2000; Strom, Pettersson, & Andersson, 2004; Christensen, Griffiths, & Jorm, 2004; Strom, Pettersson, & Andersson, 2000; Devinini & Blanchard, 2004; Rhodes, 2004; Brown, Winzelberg, Abascal, & Taylor, 2004; Linke, Brown, & Wallace, 2004; Escoffery, McCormick, & Bateman, 2004). Rosser et al. (2006) are currently examining highly interactive web-based HIV risk-reduction interventions for men who use the Internet to seek sex with other men.

Because of its intermediary position between a mass medium and an interpersonal source of communication, the Internet could also be a powerful recruitment tool since it provides an efficient venue for explaining a study, piquing interest, and even screening a large number of potential participants. Although on-line recruitment of employees has been discussed since the mid-1980s (Galanaki, 2002), initiation of its use as a recruitment tool in scientific research has only recently begun. For example, a recent study employed "banner ads" to recruit men who have sex with men to participate in an internet-based survey study (Bowen, 2005). We previously reported utility of the internet in recruiting Hispanic MSM to participate in community-based trials (Fernández et al., 2004; Fernández, Perrino, Collazo et al., 2005); however, studies have not yet directly compared Internet chat room versus community recruitment.

In this paper we report on a large sample of Hispanic MSM living in Miami-Dade County, Florida. The study objectives were to: (1) compare the efficiency and cost of using Internet chatroom versus community venues for recruiting Hispanic MSM to participate in community-based prevention studies; and (2) examine the differences in behavioral, psychosocial, and sociocultural factors between participants recruited from the two types of venues.

METHOD

Design

We used a quasi-experimental design to compare "Internet" and "community" recruitment. To minimize the potential for cross contamination from men being approached through both methods within a short time frame, the recruitment approaches were implemented sequentially in 4 month cycles, alternating between methods. Each cycle consisted of 2 months of "active" recruitment (when recruitment was conducted) followed by 2 months of "passive" recruitment (when no recruitment was done but the offices remained opened for screening and enrollment). We implemented 2 cycles per method controlling for time of year to equalize seasonal variations (e.g., inclement weather) and external events (e.g., scheduled circuit parties–multi-day gatherings of gay/bisexual men where rates of risky sex and drug use are high) that could impact recruitment.

Following the principles of participatory research (Fairweather & Tornatzky, 1977; Fairweather & Davidson, 1986) we formed a Program Advisory Committee (PAC) composed of respected members of the Hispanic MSM community and a representative from the local health department to guide protocol development, implementation, and dissemination of study findings. In addition, the majority of our research team are members of the Hispanic MSM community; many have worked in our program since the late 1990s. The protocol was approved July of 2003 by the Institutional Review Board at University of Miami (data collection phase) and January of 2005 at Nova Southeastern University (data analysis phase).

Participants

From October 15, 2003 to December 19, 2004, we recruited 566 Hispanic MSM from Internet chat rooms and community venues frequented by or that cater to Hispanic MSM in Miami-Dade. Participants met the following eligibility criteria: (1) self-identified as being Hispanic or Latino; (2) had sex with a man in the last 5 years; (3) were 18 years of age or older; (4) resided in South Florida; (5) were directly approached by research staff; and (6) visited one of two community assessment sites for screening and enrollment. Approximately 97% of men who presented to our community sites met the eligibility criteria; 100% of eligible men enrolled.

Summary of Procedures

We used time and space sampling procedures (Stueve, O'Donnell, Duran, San Doval, & Blome, 2001; Valleroy et al., 2000; Fernández et al., 2003) for community recruitment and our adapted version of these procedures for Internet recruitment (Fernández et al., 2004; Fernández, Perrino, Collazo et al., 2005). Formal screening and data collection were conducted at our two community offices that were strategically situated in two demographically distinct neighborhoods, South Beach and South Miami. Our South Beach office was located in the zip code with the highest density of gay men in the county. The South Miami office, situated in an area with high Hispanic density, has easy freeway access and plenty of free parking.

Community Venues: Selection, Sampling, and Recruitment. In consultation with our Program Advisory Committee, we developed a list of community venues (e.g., beaches, parks, gyms, bars, dance clubs, coffee houses) frequented by Hispanic MSM and randomly selected 15 venues from the list. Next, following the procedures used in our previous research (Fernández, Perrino, Royal, Ghany, & Bowen, 2002; Fernández et al., 2003) we enumerated the number of men at each venue during different times of the day/night to determine periods of "peak" and "off-peak" activity. For each venue, we drafted a list of "*recruitment periods*" (systematically selected days and 3 hour blocks of time corresponding to high activity for that venue). Each month, we randomly selected venues and recruitment periods, developed a calendar of "*sampling events*" (days and blocks of time for each venue during which data were collected), and assigned staff in teams to each event. At each venue, we defined a specific geographic area and used systematic sampling to approach men who entered the defined area. At low traffic areas, we used a sampling interval of 1 and at high traffic areas the interval was 3. Staff used a 5 step, IRB approved introductory script in English or Spanish to determine whether or not each man approached met the age, ethnicity and residency requirements. The steps were: (1) introduction; (2) preliminary screen; (3) consent to proceed; (4) study description; and (5) procedures for enrollment. If preliminary eligibility requirements were met, staff described the study and invited the man to participate. Men who wished to participate were given a business card with the addresses and telephone numbers of our community offices (English on one side; Spanish on the other) and instructed to present the card at one of the sites for screening and enrollment. For each man approached, the staff logged whether or not he was: (1) eligible; (2) interested; and (3) referred for screening and enrollment.

Internet Venues: Selection, Sampling, and Recruitment. We used parallel procedures to select Internet venues (non-fee based regional chat rooms that were not specifically sex or dating focused) frequented by Hispanic MSM (Fernández et al., 2004; Fernández, Perrino, Collazo et al., 2005). For each venue, we specified "peak" and "off-peak" periods by logging the number of chat room users during different times of the day/night and days of the week. Each month, we randomly selected venues and "*recruitment periods*," developed a calendar of "*sampling events*," and assigned staff teams to each event. Following this monthly schedule of sampling events, experienced male researchers entered the selected Internet venue using IRB approved screen names, profiles, and three-dimensional non-human images. Using systematic sampling methods, staff approached every fifth screen name posted and initiated a dialogue following a 5 step script in English or Spanish that paralleled the one used in community recruitment. To enhance credibility and describe the eligibility criteria, staff invited interested chat room users to visit to the project website during the chat. If the chat room user met the preliminary eligibility requirements, staff described the study including the need to remember the screen name used during the chat, and invited him to visit one of our 2 field offices for screening and enrollment.

For each chat room user engaged in an active dialogue, we recorded the screen name; chat room; screen name used by researcher; who initiated the approach (investigator or chat room user); whether the chat room user visited the project website while chatting; and general comments (e.g., "not Hispanic," or "not interested"). As a protocol adherence and quality assurance check, every 20th interaction was copied as an MS Word document, stored in a locked, password protected electronic folder, and reviewed for protocol adherence by the project director.

Assessment Procedures. When potential participants presented themselves at the field offices, staff confirmed referral by asking community recruits to present their referral card and Internet recruits to provide the screen name used during the chat. Once referral was confirmed, men were screened for eligibility, and if eligible, invited to participate after a full explanation of the study procedures. To minimize duplication, as part of the eligibility screen we asked men if they had previously participated in the study and cross-referenced his birthday and zip code with the list of study participants prior to enrollment. After giving informed consent, participants completed an audio-computer assisted self-interview (ACASI) which lasted 60 to 90 minutes and were given $50 as compensation.

Measures

Demographics. Participants self-reported their age, education level, monthly income, employment status, sexual identification (gay, bisexual, or straight), and place of birth. Participants born in other countries reported the number of years they had lived in the United States and their age at migration.

HIV status. Participants stated whether or not they had been tested for HIV. Those who had been tested were asked to report their test results.

Sexual behavior in the last 6 months. Participants reported their number of male sex partners, whether or not they engaged in insertive anal sex and/or receptive anal sex, and the frequency with which they had used a condom for each type of sex act. In addition, participants were asked whether or not they had a primary partner, and if so, a series of questions about their sexual behavior with their primary partners (e.g., use of condoms in and outside the relationship, satisfaction with relationship, partner serostatus, etc.).

Recreational drug use in the last 6 months. Participants reported their use of each of the following drugs within the preceding 6 months: marijuana, cocaine, crystal methamphetamine (crystal), amphetamines, amylnitrites (poppers), ecstasy (N-methyl-3,4-methylenedioxyamphetamine), gamma-hydroxybutyrate (GHB), ketamine (Special K), and Viagra. We operationally defined recreational drugs to include these 8 drugs based on our previous work (Fernández et al., 2004; Fernández, Bowen, Varga, Collazo & Perrino, 2005; Fernández, Perrino, Bowen et al., 2005; Fernández, Perrino, Collazo et al., 2005). Drug use during specific sexual encounters was not assessed.

Cultural Orientation. We measured cultural orientation with the "*Americanism*" and "*Hispanicism*" subscales from *The Behavioral Acculturation* Scale (Szapocznik et al., 1980). This instrument assesses identification with mainstream English-speaking American culture (21 items scored on a 5 point Likert scale, $\alpha = .93$) and Hispanic (21 items scored on a 5 point Likert scale, $\alpha = .93$) culture separately, as well as level of bicultural identification. Developed and validated in Miami, it has good reliability with Hispanics from diverse subgroups. For this and subsequent measures, we calculated Cronbach alpha coefficients using study data.

Homophobia. We used Díaz, Carrillo, Williams, and Bein's (2001) 11-item scale ($\alpha = .78$) that uses 4 points ("never" to "many times") to assess how often a respondent had been the subject of discrimination as a child and/or an adult based on his sexual orientation. For instance, participants reported the number of times they have been made fun of, beaten up, called names, or had to move away because of their homosexuality (e.g., "As you were growing up, how often did you feel that your homosexuality hurt and embarrassed your family?"; "As an adult, how often have you had to pretend that you are straight to be accepted?"). The scale has three factors: Shame, Consequences, and Harassment.

Racism. We used Díaz et al.'s (2001) 10-item scale ($\alpha = .79$) that uses 4 points ("never" to "always") to assess how often a respondent had been the subject of racial discrimination. For example, the participant was asked whether or not he had ever been made fun of, beaten up, called names, or harassed by the police because of his race/ethnicity (e.g., "How often have you been turned down for a job because of your race or ethnicity?").

Self-Esteem. We used Díaz et al.'s (2001) 5-item scale ($\alpha = 0.837$) that uses 3 points ("yes," "somewhat yes," and "no") to assess the respondent's level of self-esteem (e.g., "Do you feel that you respect yourself?").

Impulsivity. We used Díaz et al.'s (2001) 6-item scale ($\alpha = 0.716$) that uses 5 points ("never" to "always") to assess the respondent's level of impulsivity (e.g., "How often do you act on the spur of the moment?").

Gay Community Attachment. We used McKirnan, Vanable, and Stokes's (2005) 8-item *Identification and Involvement with the Gay Community Scale* to measure men's level of involvement in and perceptions of closeness to the gay community ($\alpha = .67$). Using a 5-point scale ranging from "do not agree at all" to "strongly agree," participants rated how strongly they agreed with statements such as the following: (1) it is important to have some of my friends be gay or bisexual; (2) being gay makes one feel part of a community; and (3) being attracted to men is important to one's sense of self.

Social Connections. We used 4 items (e.g., "Do you feel you matter to people around you?"; "Are you satisfied with your friendships?"; "Are you satisfied with your romantic relationships?"; and "Are you satisfied with the relationship to your family?") to assess connections to family and friends. Responses were either yes, somewhat yes, or no ($\alpha = .70$).

Psychological Distress. We used the 10 item scale developed by Díaz et al. (2002). Using 7 points ranging from daily to never, participants rate how frequently in the past 6 months they had experienced such things as: "feeling everything is an effort" and "feelings of worthlessness" ($\alpha = .90$).

Loneliness. We used an abridged version (4 items) of Díaz et al.,'s (2001) Loneliness Scale (e.g., "How often do you feel you lack companionship?"). Response categories ranged from never (1) to many times (4) ($\alpha = .88$).

History of Suicide Attempts. Participants reported whether or not they had ever attempted to take their own life and how many times they had attempted.

History of Childhood Sexual Abuse. Participants reported whether or not they experienced sexual abuse while under the age of 18.

Recruitment Variables. To examine the relative efficiency of Internet and community recruitment, we used the research logs to calculate the: (1) number of person hours spent recruiting; (2) number of men approached; (3) number of men invited to visit our community offices; and (4) number of men who enrolled and completed the ACASI. To examine whether or not we were reaching distinct groups with each method, we asked participants to report if they had been approached by study staff during previous recruitment cycles. Participants in the first recruitment cycle were not asked this item because it was not relevant.

Analysis Plan

We first compared the efficiency of Internet versus community recruitment. Using the number of person hours spent recruiting and the number of participants recruited by method, we calculated the mean person-hour per participant recruited for each method. To estimate recruitment costs by method, we multiplied this mean value by $15, the average hourly rate of research staff. In the next set of analyses, we compared characteristics of participants recruited at Internet (n = 294) and community (n = 272) venues using chi-square tests (for categorical variables) and t-tests (for continuous variables) to examine potential differences. Continuous variables that were not normally distributed were tested using Mann-Whitney U-tests.

RESULTS

Comparison of Recruitment Venues

As shown in Table 1, we approached 1,726 men through Internet venues and 1,618 at community venues. Almost 30% (509/1,726) of those approached through the Internet and 46% (745/1,618) of those approached at community venues met the preliminary eligibility screen and were invited to visit our field offices for formal screening and enrollment. Of the 509 men from Internet venues invited to visit our community offices, 294 (57.8%) enrolled. Of the 745 men from community venues invited to visit our community offices, 272 (36.5%) enrolled. Overall, 45.1% of men invited to visit our offices enrolled in the study. Internet recruiting was significantly more efficient than community recruitment (57.8% vs 36.5%, $Z = 7.43$, $p < 0.000$). It took a mean of 1.51 hours of staff time per participant to recruit 294 study participants on the Internet and 1.73 hours of staff time per participant to recruit 272 participants at community venues. On average, it cost $3.37 less to recruit a participant through the Internet than at community venues. Ninety-seven percent of participants recruited through community venues reported that they had

TABLE 1. Comparison of Efficiency and Cost of Recruiting Hispanic MSM Through Internet and Community Venues

	Internet	Community
Hours Spent Recruiting	443	471
Number of Men Approached	1726	1618
Number of Men Eligible and Invited	509	745
Number of Participants Enrolled	294	272
Average Hours per Participant Recruited	1.51	1.73
Estimated Average Cost of Recruitment per Participant (Recruitment Staff Time)	$22.60	$25.97
Average Cost Savings per Participant for Internet	$3.37	

not been approached by study staff on the Internet and 96% of participants recruited during the second Internet cycle had not been approached at community venues.

Demographic Comparisons

As shown in Table 2, we found no significant differences between Internet and community recruits in age, being foreign born, choosing to be interviewed in English, level of Hispanicism, level of Americanism, employment status, or income. Participants born outside the United States did not differ in age at immigration or number of years having

TABLE 2. Comparisons of the Personal Characteristics of Internet and Community Recruits

	Internet (n = 294)	Community (n = 272)	p-value
Age	31.54	30.89	0.263†
Ever Approached on Street	4.1%	–	–
Ever Approached on Internet	–	3.3%	–
Foreign Born	88.4%	86.8%	0.546‡
Interviewed in English	28.9%	29.8%	0.821‡
Years in US[1]	8.30	8.30	0.999†
Age at Immigration[1]	22.13	22.26	0.866†
Hispanicism	80.33	82.45	0.090†
Americanism	77.60	78.85	0.309†
Level of Education*			0.050‡
Less than High School	6.5%	5.5%	
High School	18.5%	27.9%	
Some College	26.4%	29.8%	
Vocational Graduate	7.5%	5.1%	
College Graduate	29.8%	23.5%	
Post-College Schooling	11.3%	8.1%	
> HS Education*	75.0%	66.5%	0.027‡
Employed	77.7%	80.5%	0.407‡
Gay (vs bisexual)*	89.7%	95.2%	0.015‡
Income < $1500/month	42.2%	39.3%	0.497‡
Income < $2500/month	72.8%	72.8%	0.994‡

[1] Internet: n = 259; Community: n = 236

† Student's t-test; mean values reported

‡ Chi-square test; percentages reported

* $p \leq 0.05$

lived in the United States. Significant differences were found in level of education and likelihood of being bisexual. Seventy-five percent of Internet recruits had higher than a high school education compared with only 67% of community recruits ($p = 0.027$). Ten percent of Internet recruits self-identified as bisexual, compared to less than 5% of community recruits ($p = 0.015$).

Psychosocial Comparisons

Comparisons of the two groups on psychosocial variables are found in Table 3. Internet recruits did not differ from community recruits on levels of loneliness, social connections, racism, self-esteem, impulsivity, homophobia, history of suicide attempts, or history of childhood sexual abuse. Internet recruits had significantly higher levels of psychological distress ($p = 0.032$) and lower levels of gay community attachment ($p = 0.006$) than community recruits.

TABLE 3. Comparisons of Internet and Community Recruits on Psychosocial Variables

	Internet ($n = 294$)	Community ($n = 272$)	p-value
Psychological Distress*	2.41	2.20	0.032†
Loneliness	2.27	2.20	0.288†
Social Connections	2.50	2.52	0.477†
Gay Community Attachment**	3.03	3.19	0.006†
Racism	1.27	1.28	0.784†
Self-Esteem	1.37	1.32	0.234†
Impulsivity	2.36	2.40	0.359†
Homophobia Total Scale	1.96	1.96	0.981†
Factor 1 (Shame)	2.78	2.73	0.493†
Factor 2 (Consequences)	1.24	1.27	0.366†
Factor 3 (Harassment)	1.82	1.85	0.600†
History of Suicide Attempt	14.0%	12.9%	0.695‡
History of Childhood Sexual Abuse	19.1%	19.9%	0.808‡

† Student's t-test; mean values reported

‡ Chi-square test; percentages reported

* $p \leq 0.05$

** $p \leq 0.01$

Sexual Behavior Comparisons

As shown in Table 4, Internet and community recruits did not differ significantly in number of partners, likelihood of having anal sex (protected or unprotected), history of HIV testing, or having a primary partner.

TABLE 4. Comparisons of Internet and Community Recruits on Sexual Behavior Variables, Previous Six Months

	Internet (*n* = 294)	Community (*n* = 272)	*p*-value
Number of Partners	5 (IQR = 2, 12)	4 (IQR = 2, 10)	0.132
Unprotected Receptive Anal Sex	34.1%	30.3%	0.338‡
Unprotected Insertive Anal Sex	32.8%	33.3%	0.885‡
Either Type of Unprotected Anal Sex	47.2%	43.4%	0.369‡
HIV+ *	19.4%	12.0%	0.017‡
Ever Tested for HIV	86.1%	86.8%	0.805‡
Tested for HIV in Past 12 Months	56.5%	61.4%	0.233‡
Satisfied with Romantic Relationships			0.455‡
Yes	44.1%	44.4%	
Somewhat Yes	25.5%	21.5%	
No	30.3%	34.1%	
Satisfied with Sex Life			0.876‡
Yes	58.8%	60.7%	
Somewhat Yes	28.6%	27.9%	
No	12.6%	11.4%	
Currently Have a Primary Partner	42.5%	42.4%	0.984‡
Live with Partner[1]			0.290‡
Yes	55.6%	46.1%	
No	35.5%	45.2%	
Sometimes	8.9%	8.7%	
Sex Outside Primary Relationship[1]	35.2%	30.7%	0.460‡
Financially Dependent on Partner[1]			0.725‡
Yes	5.6%	7.0%	
No	80.0%	81.7%	
Sometimes	14.4%	11.3%	
Partner Serostatus[1]			0.188‡
Positive	15.4%	8.8%	
Negative	78.0%	80.7%	
Unknown	6.5%	10.5%	

[1] Internet: $n = 124$; Community: $n = 115$

‡ Chi-square test; percentages reported

Mann-Whitney U Test; median and interquartile range reported

* $p \leq 0.05$

Internet recruits were more likely to report being HIV seropositive (19.4% vs. 12.0%; $p = 0.017$) than community recruits. For participants with a primary partner, no differences were demonstrated in likelihood of living with the primary partner, having sex outside the relationship, being financially dependent upon the partner, or having a seropositive partner.

Drug Use

Comparisons of drug use behaviors are found in Table 5. Internet recruits did not differ from community recruits in drug use in the past 6 months, number of drugs used, and use of: marijuana, crystal methamphetamine, other amphetamines, cocaine, ecstasy, Viagra, or ketamine. A higher proportion of internet recruits used poppers than did community recruits (31.6% vs. 23.2%; $p = 0.024$), while a lower proportion of Internet recruits used GHB than did community recruits (3.1% vs. 6.6%; $p = 0.047$).

TABLE 5. Comparisons of Internet and Community Recruits on Recreational Drug Use, Previous Six Months

	Internet ($n = 294$)	Community ($n = 272$)	p-value
Recreational Drug Use			0.905‡
None	54.1%	61.0%	
Single	23.5%	20.2%	
Multiple	22.4%	18.8%	
Number Recreational Drugs Used	0 (IQR = 0, 1)	0 (IQR = 0, 1)	0.137
Marijuana Use	35.0%	33.1%	0.626‡
Crystal Methamphetamine Use	9.9%	10.3%	0.865‡
Other Amphetamine Use	2.7%	2.2%	0.693‡
Cocaine Use	13.6%	10.7%	0.285‡
Poppers Use*	31.6%	23.2%	0.024‡
Ecstasy Use	12.2%	12.5%	0.927‡
GHB Use*	3.1%	6.6%	0.047‡
Viagra Use	17.0%	16.9%	0.976‡
Ketamine Use	3.7%	4.4%	0.687‡

Mann-Whitney U Test; median and interquartile range reported

‡ Chi-square test; percentages reported

* $p \leq 0.05$

DISCUSSION

To our knowledge, this is the first study that compares the efficiency and cost of recruiting Hispanic MSM from Internet and community venues to participate in community-based research focusing on drug use and risky sex. Our previous work demonstrated the viability of using Internet chat rooms to recruit Hispanic MSM (Fernández et al., 2004; Fernández, Perrino, Collazo et al., 2005). By directly comparing chat room recruitment to community recruitment, this study extends our previous work. Internet recruitment was more efficient and required less staff time than community recruitment. It was also more effective than community recruitment in accessing men who are HIV positive and men who have sex with both men and women. The lack of overlap among men approached via each method suggests that we reached relatively distinct groups of HMSM. These data point to the importance of using both types of recruitment venues in studies that call for broader and more representative samples of HMSM. Alternatively, studies targeting select subgroups (i.e., HIV positive men) or more hidden groups (i.e., bisexual men) might benefit from Internet recruitment.

One of the more significant aspects of this study is that all participants had to present themselves for screening, enrollment, and data collection at our field offices. While the effectiveness of recruiting MSM research participants at community venues has been well documented (Fernández et al., 2002; Fernández et al., 2003; Valleroy et al., 2000; Stueve et al., 2001), we were among the first to explore use of the Internet to recruit Hispanic MSM for community research (Fernández et al., 2004; Fernández, Perrino, Collazo et al., 2005). The willingness of men to come to our community offices for screening and data collection points to the success of our engagement procedures. It also eliminates some of the problems inherent in many Internet studies that collect data on-line including determining true eligibility, obtaining informed consent (Ross, Rosser, Stanton, & Konstan, 2004), minimizing duplication of participants, and others.

Furthermore, the majority of chat room users that we engaged in private dialogues readily answered the screening questions. Many visited the study website while chatting, prompting further discussions with our recruiters. Not only did a large number of chat room users come to the community sites, but the majority who did also met the eligibility criteria. These findings suggest that private chat room dialogues can be effective forums for describing research studies, generating interest, and conducting initial screening of potential participants. However, the importance of engaging chat room users to the success of Internet recruitment must be stressed. Participants in qualitative interviews conducted to further understand the motivating factors that contributed to men's willingness to present themselves at our community sites consistently reminded us of the importance of those initial few minutes when they were approached by our team (Fernández et al., 2004). In the fast-paced environment of the typical chat room where chatters pop in and out and have multiple screens open simultaneously, recruiters have only seconds in which to "hook" potential participants. Researchers and prevention providers are strongly encouraged to dedicate careful attention to the engagement process and to maintain on-going participation from community representatives in the development of these procedures.

The comparability of Internet and community recruits on most demographic factors, psychosocial variables as well as on sexual and drug use behaviors was surprising. Given the relatively large size of our sample, it could be that our sample reflects the overall characteristics of HMSM from Miami-Dade County. A more cautious extrapolation is that it reflects the characteristics of HMSM who are willing to enroll in community-based prevention trials.

The high rates of unprotected sexual intercourse and drug use reported by our participants points to the importance of developing tailored, culturally appropriate interventions to reduce risk of HIV in this population. Given the relatively few differences between the two groups, multivariate analyses were not indicated for the present study. This study provides support for combining the two groups in future studies to more fully examine the predictors of HIV related sexual and drug use behaviors.

CONCLUSIONS

This study highlights the utility of the Internet for recruiting Hispanic MSM to participate in community based studies. In addition, our ability to recruit MSM who use recreational drugs indicates that the internet could be an important new recruitment venue for drug use and prevention studies. Our findings suggest that the Internet should not supplant existing recruitment approaches; rather, it should be added to our current armamentarium of recruitment tools. Given the Internet's success at accessing special populations (e.g., HIV positive men and bisexual men), researchers and practitioners are encouraged to consider the characteristics of their target population and the goals of their work when selecting the most appropriate recruitment modality.

ACKNOWLEDGMENT

We thank the dedicated staff of the Behavioral Health Promotion Program (Cesar de Fuentes, Luis Alzamora, and Alfredo Rehbein) for their contributions. We appreciate the support and advice of our Program Advisory Committee, our other community partners, and our NIDA Project Officer, Dr. Dionne Jones. We are particularly grateful to Dr. Bill Grace for his thoughtful and thorough review of the manuscript. Finally, of course, this study would not have been completed if not for the men who willingly shared their experiences as study participants. We are grateful to all of them.

REFERENCES

Benotsch, E. G., Kalichman, S., & Cage, M. (2002). Men who have met sex partners via the Internet: Prevalence, Predictors, and Implications for HIV Prevention. *Archives of Sexual Behavior, 31*, 177-183.

Bowen, A. (2005). Internet sexuality research with rural men who have sex with men: Can we recruit and retain them? *The Journal of Sex Research, 42*, 317-323.

Brown, G., Maycock, B., & Burns, S. (2005). Your picture is your bait: Use and meaning of cyberspace among gay men. *Journal of Sex Research, 42*, 63-73.

Brown, J. B., Winzelberg, A. J., Abascal, L. B., & Taylor, B. (2004). An evaluation of an Internet-delivered eating disorder prevention program for adolescents and their parents. *Journal of Adolescent Health, 35*, 290-296.

Bull, S. S. & McFarlane, M. (2000). Soliciting sex on the internet: What are the risks for sexually transmitted diseases and HIV? *Sexually Transmitted Diseases, 27*, 545-550.

Centers for Disease Control and Prevention (2006). Racial/ethnic disparities in diagnoses of HIV/AIDS–33 states, 2001-2004. *MMWR Weekly, 55*, 121-125.

Christensen, H., Griffiths, K. M., & Jorm, A. F. (2004). Delivering interventions for depression by using the internet: Randomised controlled trial. *British Medical Journal, 328*, 265-268.

comScore Networks. (2004). Hispanic internet users in U.S. now exceed the total online population of many major Spanish-speaking nations, comScore reports. Retrieved December 3, 2004 from http://www.comscore.com/press/release.asp?press+306.

Devinini, T. & Blanchard, E. B. (2004). A randomized controlled trial of an internet-based treatment for chronic headache. *Behavioral Research Therapy, 43*, 277-292.

Díaz, R. M., Carrillo, H., Williams, A., & Bein, E. (2002). Drug use and HIV risk among Latino gay men. Unpublished survey.

Duncan, D. F., White, J. B., & Nicholson, T. (2003). Using internet-based surveys to reach hidden populations: Case of nonabusive illicit drug users. *American Journal of Health Behavior, 27*, 208-218.

Elford, J., Bolding, G., & Sherr, L. (2001). Seeking sex on the internet and sexual risk behavior among gay men using London gyms. *AIDS, 77,* 224-225.

Escoffrey, C., McCormick, L., & Bateman, K. (2004). Development and process evaluation of a web-based smoking cessation program for college smokers: Innovative tool for education. *Patient Education and Counseling, 53,* 217-225.

Fairweather, G. W. & Tornatzky, L. G. (1977). Experimental methods for social policy research. Elmsford, NY: Pergamon Press.

Fairweather, G. W., & Davidson, W. S. (1986). An introduction to community experimentation: Theory, methods and practice. New York: Mc Graw Hill.

Fernández, M. I., Bowen, G. S., Varga, L. M., Collazo, J. B., & Perrino, T. (2005). High rates of club drug use and risky sexual practices among Hispanic men who have sex with men in Miami, Florida. *Substance Use & Misuse, 40,* 1347-1362.

Fernández, M. I., Perrino, T., Bowen, G. S., Royal, S., & Varga, L. (2003) Repeat HIV testing among Hispanic men who have sex with men–A sign of risk, prevention, or reassurance? *AIDS Education & Prevention, 15*(Supplement A), 105-116.

Fernández, M. I., Perrino, T., Bowen, G. S., Hernandez, N., Cardenas, S. Y., Marsh, D. et al. (2005). Club drug use, sexual behavior, and HIV risk among community and internet samples of Hispanic MSM: Implications for clinicians. *Journal of Social Work Practice in the Addictions, 5,* 81-100.

Fernández, M. I., Perrino, T., Collazo, J. B., Varga, L. M., Marsh, D., Hernandez, N. et al. (2005). Surfing new territory: Club drug use and risky sex among Hispanic MSM recruited on the Internet. *Journal of Urban Health, 82,* i79-i88.

Fernández, M. I., Perrino, T., Royal, S., Ghany, D., & Bowen, G. S. (2002). To test or not to test: Are Hispanic men at highest risk for HIV getting tested? *AIDS Care, 14,* 375-384.

Fernández, M. I., Varga, L. M., Perrino, T., Collazo, J. B., Subiaul, F., Torres, H. et al. (2004). The Internet as recruitment tool for HIV studies: Viable strategy for reaching at-risk Hispanic MSM in Miami. *AIDS Care, 16,* 1-11.

Galanaki, E. (2002). The decision to recruit online: A descriptive study. *Career Development International, 7,* 243-251.

Halkitis, P. N., Parsons, J. T., & Wilton, L. (2003). An exploratory study of contextual and situational factors related to methamphetamine use among gay and bisexual men in New York City. *Journal of Drug Issues, 33,* 413-432.

Heckathorn, D. D. (2002). Respondent-driven sampling II: Deriving valid population estimates from chain-referral samples of hidden populations. *Social Problems, 49,* 11-34.

Hospers, H. J., Harterink, P., Van Den Hoek, K., & Veenstra, J. (2002). Chatters on the Internet: A special target group for HIV prevention. *AIDS Care, 14,* 539-544.

Kim, A. A., Kent, C., McFarland, W., & Klausner, J. D. (2001). Cruising on the internet highway. *Journal of Acquired Immune Deficiency Syndromes, 28,* 89-93.

Leonard, N. R., Lester, P., Rotheram-Borus, M. J., Mattes, K., Gwadz, M., & Ferns, B. (2003). Successful recruitment and retention of participants in longitudinal behavioral research. *AIDS Education and Prevention, 15,* 269-281.

Linke, S., Brown, A., & Wallace, P. (2004). Down Your Drink: A web-based intervention for people with excessive alcohol consumption. *Alcohol & Alcoholism, 39,* 29-32.

Martinez-Ebers, V. (1997). Using monetary incentives with hard-to-reach populations in panel surveys. *International Journal of Public Opinion Research, 9,* 77-86.

McFarlane, M., Bull, S. S., & Rietmeijer, C. A. (2000). The Internet as a newly emerging risk environment for sexually transmitted diseases. *Journal of the American Medical Association, 284,* 443-446.

McKirnan, D. J., Vanable, P. A., & Stokes, J. P. (2005). HIV risk sexual behavior among bisexually active men: The role of gay identification and social norms. Manuscript submitted for publication.

Nielsen/NetRatings. (2004). Three out of four Americans have access to the internet, according to Nielsen/Ratings. Retrieved December 3, 2004 from http://www.nielsen-netratings.com/news.jsp?section = new_pr

Reymers, K. (2002). Identity and the internet: A symbolic interactionist perspective on computer-mediated social networks. Paper presented at the Association of Internet Researchers Annual Conference, Maastricht, The Netherlands.

Rhodes, S. D. (2004). Hookups or Health Promotion? An exploratory study of a chat room-based HIV prevention intervention for men who have sex with men. *AIDS Education and Prevention, 16,* 315-327.

Rietmeijer, C. A., Bull, S. S., McFarlane, M., Patnaik, J. L., & Douglas, J. M. (2003). Risks and benefits of the Internet for populations at risk for sexually transmitted infections (STIs): Results of an STI Clinic Survey. *Sexually Transmitted Diseases, 30,* 15-19.

Ross, M. W., Tikkanen, R., & Manson, S. (2000). Differences between Internet samples of men who have sex with men: Implications for research and HIV interventions. *Social Science and Medicine, 51,* 749-758.

Ross, M. W., Rosser, B. R. S., Stanton, J., & Konstan, J. (2004). Characteristics of Latino men who have sex with men on the Internet who complete and drop out of an Internet-based sexual behavior survey. *Journal of HIV Prevention and Education,* in press.

Rosser, B. R. S., Hooper, S., Naumann, C., Konstan, J., Manning, T., Bratland, D. et al. (2006). Next generation HIV prevention: Building highly interactive web-based HIV interventions for men who use the internet to seek sex with other men. Poster presented at the XVI International AIDS Conference, Toronto, August 13-18, 2006.

Strom, L., Pettersson, R., & Andersson, G. (2000). A controlled trial of self-help treatment of recurrent headache conducted via the internet. *Journal of Consulting and Clinical Psychology, 68,* 722-727.

Strom, L., Pettersson, R., & Andersson, G. (2004). Internet-based treatment for insomnia: A controlled evaluation. *Journal of Consulting and Clinical Psychology, 72,* 113-120.

Stueve, A., O'Donnell, L. N., Duran, R., San Doval, A., & Blome, J. (2001). Time-space sampling in minority communities: Results with young Latino men who have sex with men. *American Journal of Public Health, 91*(6), 922-926.

Szapocznik, J., Kurtines, W. M., & Fernández, T. (1980). Bicultural involvement and adjustment in Hispanic-American youth. *International Journal of Intercultural Relations, 4,* 353-365.

Tikkanen, R. & Ross, M. W. (2003). Technological Tearoom Trade: Characteristics of Swedish men visiting gay internet chat rooms. *AIDS Education and Prevention, 15,* 122-132.

Valleroy, L. A., MacKellar, D. A., Karon, J. M., Rosen, D. H., McFarland, W., & Shehan, D. A. (2000). HIV prevalence and associated risks in young men who have sex with men: Young Men's Survey Study Group. *Journal of the American Medical Association, 284,* 198-204.

doi:10.1300/J233v06n02_09

Cultural Adaptations in Data Collection: Field Experiences

Mario De La Rosa, PhD
Guitele J. Rahill, LCSW, CTS
Patria Rojas, MSW, MPH
Elsa Pinto, MS, RD

SUMMARY. We assessed the data collection phase of a study that examines the substance using and other health behaviors of a cohort of 160 dyads of Latino mothers and daughters living in South Florida (N = 320), by conducting a focus group with the study's interviewers. The objective of the focus group was to assess the appropriateness of the questionnaire utilized in the Latino Women's Study, and identify potential barriers and challenges that may be encountered when conducting research with Latino women in the United States. The results from this focus provide useful

---

Mario De La Rosa is Professor in the School of Social Work and the Director of the Center for Research on US Latinos HIV/AIDS and Drug Abuse (CRUSADA) at FIU funded by NIDA.

Guitele J. Rahill is a PhD candidate at the School of Social Work at Florida International University, Miami, FL (E-mail: guitele.rahill@fiu.edu).

Patria Rojas, MSW, MPH is a PhD candidate at the School of Social Work at Florida International University, Miami, FL.

Elsa Pinto is a PhD candidate at the School of Public Health at Florida International University.

Address correspondence to: Mario De La Rosa, School of Social Work, Florida International University, 11200 SW 8th St. PCA 356, Miami, FL 33199 (E-mail: delarosa@fiu.edu).

This study was funded by NIH grant # R24 DA 14260-01A1.

[Haworth co-indexing entry note]: "Cultural Adaptations in Data Collection: Field Experiences." De La Rosa, Mario et al. Co-published simultaneously in *Journal of Ethnicity in Substance Abuse* (The Haworth Press, Inc.) Vol. 6, No. 2, 2007, pp. 163-180; and: *21st Century Research on Drugs and Ethnicity: Studies Supported by the National Institute on Drug Abuse* (ed: Peter L. Myers) The Haworth Press, 2007, pp. 163-180. Single or multiple copies of this article are available for a fee from The Haworth Document Delivery Service [1-800-HAWORTH, 9:00 a.m. - 5:00 p.m. (EST). E-mail address: docdelivery@haworthpress.com].

Available online at http://jesa.haworthpress.com

doi:10.1300/J233v06n02_10

insight into the practice of cultural adaptations in research studies, and illustrate the need for employing culturally-informed interviewers and for devising well-adapted questionnaires in studies with Latino women.
doi:10.1300/J233v06n02_10 *[Article copies available for a fee from The Haworth Document Delivery Service: 1-800- HAWORTH. E-mail address: <docdelivery@haworthpress.com> Website: <http://www.HaworthPress.com>*

KEYWORDS. Latino women, focus group, substance use, questionnaire

INTRODUCTION

Latinos are the fastest growing and largest ethnic minority group in the United States (Ramírez & De La Cruz, 2002). Accordingly, there has been significant progress made in the past two decades in understanding the etiology of drug use among US Latinos, as well as research which has linked the role of acculturation, acculturation related stress, parental drug use, and peer drug use to substance use behaviors of Latino adolescents (Warner et al., 2006; Canino et al., 2003; De La Rosa, Holleran & Straussner, 2005). Despite this scientific progress, there continues to be a lack of information regarding the development of data collection strategies and the validity of questionnaires utilized to collect sensitive information such as drug use and health behaviors in Latino communities and in the context of what are normative health behaviors for Latinas.

The Center for Research on US Latinos HIV/AIDS and Drug Abuse (CRUSADA) conducted a study to address some of the gaps in the literature on substance use behaviors among Latino women. Latino women over the age of 18 were chosen to participate in the Latino Women Study since studies on the etiology of substance abuse frequently target Latina adolescents and few of these studies have followed their samples into early adulthood and adulthood (Alegría, Vera, Shrout, Canino, Lai et al., 2004). Moreover, few community-based substance abuse studies have targeted Latino women over the age of 18 because the prevalence of drug use and related health problems among this population was relatively low until recently (Sloboda, 2002). Particularly needed is research that documents the influence that daughters' relationships with their mothers have on their substance using and other health behaviors, given the primacy of these relationships for Latino women (Newcomb, Romero,

Wayment, Wyatt et al., 1998; Suarez-Al-Adam, Raffeaelli & O'Leary, 2000).

Interviewers in the Latino Women's Study collected information on the drug using and other health behaviors of a cohort of 160 dyads of Latino mothers and daughters living in South Florida (N = 320). All interviewers were female since previous studies have indicated that Latino women have difficulty answering questions on sexuality if interviewed by a male (Marin-VanOss, Gomez, & Tschann, 1993). Interviewers were also bilingual, with one exception, to accommodate the participants' preference of the language in which they wanted to be interviewed.

Latino women were defined as women who self-identified as Latina regardless of their place of birth, and women from any Spanish-speaking country, including South America, Central America and the Caribbean. The primary objective of the Latino Women's Study was to investigate the influence of the mother-daughter relationship on the intergenerational transmission of substance use between Latino mothers and daughters. Specifically, the Latino Women's Study focused on exploring the quality of relationships between Latino mothers and their daughters and its influence on the daughters' substance use and other health behaviors. Also, participants' acculturation level, sexual behavior, nutrition, and other health behaviors were measured using scales developed for specific Latino groups (e.g., Mexicans, Puerto Ricans) or for white non-Latino women such as the Inventory of Parent and Peer Attachment (Armsden & Greenberg, 1987), and the Addiction Cognitive Orientation Scale, also known as the Understanding Alcoholism Scale (Humphreys, Greenbaum, Noke & Finney, 1996).

As drug abuse researchers have shown, many of the scales utilized to measure drug using behaviors and the community, peer, and familial risk factors associated with Latino drug using behaviors were originally created in English and administered primarily to White, non-Hispanic samples (Bravo, Ribera, Rubio-Stipec, Canino et al., 2001). When these scales were utilized to collect similar information on Latino individuals, with few exceptions, the only modifications made to the scales were to translate them into Spanish and back translate them into English to ensure the integrity of the questions and their meaning (Canino et al., 1999; Vega, Kolody, Aguilar-Gaxiola, Alderete, Catalano et al., 1998). However, the translation of the scales does not necessarily make the scales culturally appropriate in measuring key variables (e.g., parent-child bonding relationship, attitudes toward illicit drug use and non-medical use of prescription drugs).

The lack of culturally congruent data collection measurements is significant because it challenges the validity of the data collected (De La Rosa & Adrados, 1993; Lugo-Steidel & Contreras, 2003) and because efforts have not been made to assess the cultural relevancy of such scales when collecting data among Latino populations. Equally important is the concern of researchers who conduct substance abuse research with Latino population regarding issues associated with collecting accurate information on the drug using behaviors of Latino populations, particularly among Latino women, given the high level of stigma ascribed to the use of drugs and alcohol among women in the Latino culture (Flaskerud & Nyamathi, 2000; Trepper, Nelson, McCollum & McAvoy, 1997; Vega, Kolody, Porter & Noble, 1997).

Relevant to conducting research on sensitive issues such as substance use and other health behaviors with Latino women are matters related to trust and confidentiality. Unfortunately few studies have been conducted that assess how interviewer skills and personal biases may affect the building of trusting relationships while interviewing Latino participants and the environment where such interviews take place–all factors of utmost importance, impact the collection of valid information from Latino participants (Sormanti, Pereira, El-Bassel, Witte & Gilbert, 2001). Moreover, while human protection assurance of anonymity backed by certificates of confidentiality are always emphasized to participants in substance abuse research studies, the interviewers' ability to establish a trusting relationship during the face-to-face interview with the participants is essential. The availability of an environment that is favorable to conducting such interviews is also crucial for accurate and reliable collection of data on such hard-to-reach populations as drug using Latino women.

Accordingly, the purpose of this paper is to report on the results from data gathered from the interviewers of the Latino Women's Study. The Latino Women's Study collected information on the drug using behaviors and the underlying individual, familial, peer, and cultural factors associated with the drug use behaviors of Latino women. The data gathered from the interviewers assessed the relevance and appropriateness of the questionnaire utilized in the Latino Women's Study, and other challenges that could be encountered when conducting research with Latino women in the United States. These included: (1) exploring the level of consensus and dissent among interviewers on the face validity, relevance and appropriateness of the questionnaire as a research tool for use with Latino women; (2) assessing interviewer attitudes and beliefs about their role in the research, and their knowledge about what the study was trying to accomplish; (3) identifying the challenges and limitations perceived by the interviewers in collecting information and, (4) identifying feelings evoked in the interviewers as a result of their conducting interviews with the Latino Women Study participants.

METHODS

When trying to obtain the perceptions and challenges of individuals in their own words, qualitative inquiry is the most viable option (Miles & Huberman, 1994; Saunders, 2006). This paper is the result of a focus group conducted with seven of the interviewers who collected data for the Latino Women's Study. Focus groups allow for the collection of a large amount of data at one time, with little expense (Simon, 1999). In utilizing focus groups, researchers also acknowledge the value of participants as experts, involving them in the research process, and benefiting from their contribution and expertise (Goss & Leinbach, 1996). An important outcome of the interaction among focus group participants is that they are able to better understand and express their own experiences as they contribute and listen to the experience of other participants (Kitzinger, 1994). Research underscores the value of focus groups for obtaining organized discussions and consensus, and for fostering collaboration between group participants and the researchers.

The focus group was held at 6:30 pm at the Florida International University Park Campus in Miami, Florida. The focus group lasted a total of two hours and 19 minutes. Data collection was completed by the authors with the use of a digital audio recorder, and a timer. The focus group was conducted in English by a moderator and one of the participants served as translator for a Spanish speaking participant when necessary. The moderator read the oral consent form to all participants that thoroughly explained the purpose of the focus group and assured their confidentiality. Otherwise, the only time the moderator intruded in the conversation was to ask additional questions that were part of the data collection protocol. All participants provided oral informed consent.

The moderator used a structured guide to lead the discussion and explained the purpose of the study based on a model used by Krueger and Casey (2000). Table 1 illustrates the list of questions used for the focus group, the research objective each question addressed, and the type of data being solicited. These questions and prompts were designed to explore facts, opinions, sensory experiences and feelings of the group participants,

TABLE 1. Demographic and Other Characteristics of Focus Group Participants

ID	Place of Birth	Age	Nationality	Yrs. living in US	Last grade completed
1	Nicaragua	53	Nicaraguan	8	Bachelors
2	Dominican Republic	34	Dominican	19	Masters
3	Cuba	53	Cuban	30	Masters
4	Puerto Rico	30	Puerto Rican	3	Masters
5	Cuba	35	Cuban	24	Bachelors
6	Haiti	46	Haitian-American	37	Masters
7	US	21	Colombian-American	n/a	Bachelors

according to Krueger and Casey's recommendations (2000). The facilitator prompted participants that did not readily respond to questions, and involved them in the discussion.

Characteristics of Focus Group Participants

The average age of focus group participants was 39 years old and the average number of years that they had resided in the U.S. was 20 years for those that were foreign born. The average educational level was a Bachelors degree (~17.1 years in school). See Table 2 for specific demographic information of focus group participants.

ANALYTIC APPROACH

The session was audio taped and the tapes were transcribed by two Masters level researchers. Data transcribed from the audio-recording of the focus group was coded by two independent investigators who noted the frequency of various responses and the intensity of the discussions. Codes were then compared and emergent and variant themes were identified. Three research team members and an outside expert were engaged in reviewing the codes in the final analysis, to insure accuracy and to obtain consensus on the interpretation of the results. The results obtained were evaluated as to how well they addressed the study's central objectives. Finally, to increase the study's validity, obtained results were shown to selected participants, who confirmed that we had recorded what they actually meant to say.

TABLE 2. Questions / Prompts used in Focus Group Facilitation

Questions/ Prompts	Research Objective	Type of Data
1. Let's discuss what you know about the objectives of the Latino Women Study	Identify interviewer attitudes and beliefs about their role in the research, and assess their knowledge about what the study is trying to accomplish	Fact
2. Discuss the greatest challenge/s that presented itself for you when doing the interviews	- Obtain and describe the personal experiences of the interviewers - Identify feelings evoked in the interviewers as a result of their interaction with study participants	Sensory, experiences feelings
3. Let's discuss the questionnaire as a tool for gathering the data that the Latino Women's Study is seeking to collect	- Explore the degree of consensus and dissent on the face validity of the research instrument	Fact, Opinion
4. Let's discuss the questionnaire as a tool for use with Latino women	Assess the face validity, relevance and appropriateness of the questionnaire as a research tool for use with Latinas	Fact, Opinion
5. Let's discuss some recommendations for improving the questionnaire as a research tool; As a tool that is user-friendly	- Explore the degree of consensus and dissent on the face validity of the research instrument	Opinion
6. Let's discuss how the director and staff of the Women's Study can optimize your own confidence and efficacy as an interviewer in the study ▪ Training and support needs identified by the interviewers	- Describe the personal experiences of the interviewers - Identify feelings evoked in the interviewers as a result of their interaction with participants	Fact, Opinion Feelings
7. Tell us about what you have learned doing the interviews: ▪ About Latino women ▪ About yourself as an individual ▪ About the community	-Obtain and describe the personal experiences of the interviewers as a consequence of interacting with study participants	Opinion, Feelings
8. Complete the following sentences: ▪ When I do the interviews, the easiest part for me is _______ ▪ When I do the interviews, the hardest part for me is_______ ▪ In doing the interviews, the greatest challenge for me has been__________	- Describe the personal experiences of the interviewers - Identify feelings evoked in the interviewers as a result of their interaction with the participants - Identify interviewer attitudes and beliefs about their role in the research	Fact, Opinion, Feelings

RESULTS

The results of the focus group with interviewers of the Latino Women Study highlight several challenges that can be encountered in conducting face-to-face structured interviews with Latino women in relation to substance use and health behaviors. Described below are the findings for each of the study's objectives.

1. Face validity and appropriateness of the questionnaire for use with Latino women

Regarding the face validity and the appropriateness of the questionnaire as a research tool for use with Latinas, the responses were varied, and ranged from the comprehensiveness of the instrument used to issues regarding the actual vocabulary level in subscales used. Some participants stated:

> Definitions of some words in the questionnaire were not clear
>
> We tap into almost everything
>
> I knew we were asking the right questions when sometimes the women would answer the next three questions in one.

Interviewers also indicated how some of the words used in the instrument were not easy to understand by study participants. This required them to explain the meaning in simpler words in order for participants to respond to the question. Not only were some of the words at a high educational level for some of the participants but many were also not necessarily the words used to describe the same concept in their Latino contexts and in the regional Spanish idiom. For example, when asked about partners, an interviewer related how the participant indicated she did not have a partner and later indicated she had a boyfriend because she had not understood what the question meant by the term partner.

2. Interviewer's attitudes and beliefs about their role in the research

The consensus from the focus group participants included the belief that their outside occupations contributed to their ability to effectively collect the data:

> Because I am therapist, I found it easy to establish rapport.

However, these same occupational strengths sometimes served as challenges to interviewers who reported difficulty with remaining in interviewer mode versus the familiar intervention roles that their jobs entailed:

> Establishing rapport with participants is one thing; making sure not to offer advice or counseling is another
>
> I just wanted to help sometimes and we gave them referrals to community agencies, but I wanted to get personally involved in helping, and that was frustrating.

Data from our focus group also revealed that interviewers experienced feelings of pride and community in being involved in the study as a project that addressed the important issue of relationships and substance use among Latino mothers and daughters:

> I felt like I was part of something very big and very important
>
> I am excited to see the study's completion and what the data tells us, knowing that I was personally involved in the data collection.

Cultural similarities of the interviewers to the Latino mothers and daughters were reported as facilitating the establishment of rapport and of general interaction for the interviewers:

> Participants were so friendly and accommodating, offering food, coffee, making me feel at home
>
> The women would say, 'You know how it is in Latino families'
>
> Some of them would be so grateful to pour their hearts out in their own language, it was touching.

The interviewers also recognized that they were a critical part of the research process. This critical role resulted from one of the challenges of conducting the interviews which was the need to rephrase questions to participants due to lower educational level of participants or cultural differences in the vocabulary used.

"It was a matter of us as . . . the interviewers understanding what the question really meant and then being really able to explain or . . . to say it differently to them but that definitely came with experience with doing it and doing it."

3. Challenges or limitations experienced during the interviews

While cultural similarities between interviewer and interviewee were reported as necessary, they were not sufficient for conducting research with the study participants and comprised some of the challenges reported by focus group participants:

> I found out there was more than one culture involved, the ethnic background of the participant was different from mine, but so was the drug culture to which they belonged.

Maintaining neutrality during the interviews was a common challenge for interviewers when participants reported certain substance using behaviors and other behaviors assessed during the interview. For example, one interviewer related how she was surprised to listen to the responses related to sexual activity. The multiplicity of partners of some participants was startling to her and made it difficult to maintain neutrality.

> I sometimes had a hard time keeping a poker face when women would divulge a behavior very alien to me

> Sometimes I found myself amazed or in shock at some responses and then would remember this was her journey and she has done what she could.

The sexual activity questions were particularly uncomfortable for some interviewers but the interviewers also perceived these were very uncomfortable for the participants as well–particularly for the mothers and less for the daughters that participated.

"Only problem was sexual content, which is a natural thing, because imagine that they are now living in two cultures. There was a difference between the mothers and the daughters, therefore in how they responded to the sexual questions . . . . those who were born here seemed completely comfortable with the questions. . . ."

Figure 1 illustrates the number of interviewers identifying a particular challenge with the interview instrument and the interview process.

Participants in the Latino Women's Study are given the choice of being interviewed at their homes or at the university. The majority of them chose their home as the place for the interview since many did not have reliable transportation, worked until late at night and preferred

FIGURE 1. Challenges Identified by Interviewers During the Interview Process with Latino Women

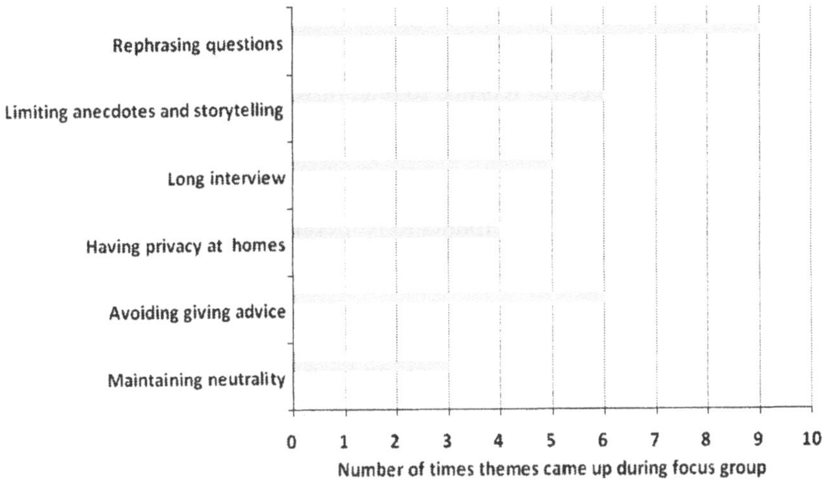

interviewers to come to them. Thus, on many occasions family members would be present at the participant's home during the interview, making it difficult to have complete privacy and avoiding interruptions while answering the questions.

4. Feelings evoked in the interviewers as a result of their interaction with participants

Concerning the personal experiences of the interviewers, and the feelings evoked in them because of their interaction with study participants, we found a variety of themes ranging from feelings of sympathy, personal and professional satisfaction. Interviewers were also concerned for the safety of study participants and to a lesser extent for their own safety. It is important to note, that during the interviewer's training and in their training protocol, they were instructed on how to leave an uncomfortable situation if they felt their personal safety was compromised. During the data collection phase of the study none of the interviewers had to leave a home or interview setting. Some of the interviewers' statements included:

> Sometimes when I was in a home and the woman was discussing an abusive spouse and the spouse was in the next room, I was concerned for her safety as well as mine

> I thought, 'There . . . but for the goodness of God!'
>
> We have a lot to be grateful for
>
> It was hard to accept that some of these women grew up in the US, and many had never learned to read or write, and somehow slipped through the cracks.

The consensus was that by the end of the session, interviewers moved from feeling sorry for participants to respecting them, and to achieving cognitive gains about themselves as individuals and as professionals:

> These women seem very strong to have endured so much
>
> I learned so much about myself and my own process, just from the questions themselves
>
> I stopped thinking about 'those women and their habits,' and began to put myself in their place
>
> If you started out judging them for using, then you realized, they are trying to cope, and can use some help with healthier coping skills

The personal experiences of interviewers included aspects requiring improvement as well, including the need for additional training in areas related to the research objectives and the need for regular debriefing by trained professionals.

> Sometimes I felt that I might have benefited from additional training or that training should cover all the domains addressed in the questionnaire
>
> I felt I needed more information to elicit data about the drug use
>
> I would be exhausted after particularly sad or long interviews and just needed someone to bring my mind back to what is normal, whatever that is

The results reported in this manuscript underscore the methodological challenges experienced in the process of collecting research data on drug using behaviors of Latino women. These results could be used to develop protocols for addressing such barriers and problems in future community based research with Latina women.

DISCUSSION

During the focus group, several questions led to the discussion related to the participants' choice to be interviewed at their homes. The location of the interview seemed to be a critical element in the course of the interview, eliciting concerns for the safety of study participants as well as of the interviewers. Of particular importance were the issues of privacy and interruptions by family members at their homes during the interview that can impact the participant's responses. This highlights the importance of emphasizing to participants the need for them to be alone. Perhaps the ideal setting for the interviews should be in a centrally located field office to avoid these issues of interruptions and privacy instead of providing participants the option to go to their homes. In this case, it may be also necessary to determine whether it is feasible to offer transportation or reimbursement of fees to all participants to attend the interview. Nevertheless, offering the option to conduct the interviews at the Latino women's homes facilitated recruitment and scheduling of interviews.

In addition to the challenge of privacy and avoiding interruptions, the interviewers indicated other barriers that could be addressed in future research. Many Latino women interviewed shared stories and anecdotes that often gave additional information which clarified some of their responses, but were at times discursive and unnecessarily lengthened the interview. Thus, part of the interviewers training may include strategies and skills to guard the dignity and worth of the Latino women interviewed, while keeping the interview focused. The frequent anecdotes and verbose answers of participants may have also been partly due to the difficulty some of them expressed in choosing the answers for the questions that used a Likert scale-type of response.

Although there was not a high level of consensus, language and bilingual skills were recurrent themes during the focus group. A majority of the interviewers spoke Spanish fluently and were also familiar with the cultural background of participants. These seemed to be essential skills for requesting explanation of responses, since interviewers had to interpret specific words and phrases that were not frequently used in their own native language and regionalisms. Still, the different nationalities included in our sample of Latino women was a challenge for some interviewers that were not familiar with the different words and phrases commonly used in other Spanish speaking countries. Other researchers have also highlighted the difficulties of the vocabulary used in scales used for collecting data among minority women (Mastronianni, 1999).

When conducting research with bilingual and/or bicultural teams, researchers may consider the acculturation variability among the interviewers, since the level of acculturation among the interviewers may be an important factor influencing participants' comprehension of questions.

Additional training was also a recurrent theme in the focus group and in relation to different questions. While experienced interviewers in the focus group possessed a significant advantage over newcomers, most interviewers agreed that they would benefit from additional training in the different areas investigated in this study. Specifically, interviewers expressed interest in the Latino Women's Study's objectives and in increasing their knowledge on the constructs being measured by each scale in order to feel more effective in their attempts to collect the necessary data. Therefore, in order to avoid interviewers shifting from the structure of the interview and misrepresenting questions and definitions that compromise the quality of the data, training of interviewers in similar research should be an ongoing part of the data collection process. A more extensive knowledge base on the psychosocial issues and on the measures incorporated in research studies will increase the interviewers' ability to probe and to evaluate meaningful answers in future studies with comparable populations.

Being able to achieve rapport and engage participants during an interview is considered to be an important aspect of every interviewer training and a necessary skill. The interviewers in the Latino Women's Study did not express any difficulty to achieve this rapport with the participants. This may be partly due to a combination of the interviewers being familiar with their cultural background and traditional cultural norms among Latino women. Some interviewers reported how participants even offered food and drinks while they were at their homes during the interview. Furthermore, several of the interviewers were majoring in social work, public health or had positions in which they routinely did assessments to clients and had received previous training in counseling and assessment procedures.

Some factors that remained challenging to focus group participants during the data collection phase of the Latino Women's Study were participants' tardiness, and frequent re-scheduling due to last minute cancellations by participants. Each of these challenges was addressed in meetings of the research team and suggestions were provided for minimizing their occurrence and mitigating their impact in future research with Latino women. When asked about their recommendations and critical aspects for conducting the interviews, the interviewers once again mentioned the importance of a favorable physical environment for the interview, which refers in part to the challenge of lack of privacy.

The authors believe it is essential to assess the interviewer's feelings and challenges as an ongoing process during data collection among similar populations. Substance using individuals can disclose information about their lives that can also influence the interviewers' mood and fatigue. In fact, some of the interviewers suggested talking about their interviews with the Latino Women's Study staff as a way of debriefing from data collection experiences.

LIMITATIONS

One limitation of the present study is that only one focus group was conducted, in part due to the number of the interviewers; there were only ten interviewers and seven of them agreed to participate in the focus group. However, a high level of convergence was reached among the participants' comments. Furthermore, as suggested by Krueger (1994) some of the analysis procedures were performed while the group was still gathered and this process helped address some of the inconsistencies during the group's session. This study also has the typical limitation of focus group methods in which a participant's response can elicit and influence another participant's views and responses to questions and discussions. The moderator has limited control over this issue since he or she must allow participants to interact and express their opinions freely. The small sample size of our study also limits the generalizability of our findings to all studies of similar design and populations. However, for the purposes of data collection objectives, this sample size was adequate enough to generate information which led to the development of consistent themes/issues among the study participants that will probably have persisted even with larger samples than the sample size in our study (Kruger, p. 144, 1994).

Compared to individual interviews and other study designs, there is little control of the data collected during a focus group. However, focus groups may generate unexpected information that may not be captured in a more structured and controlled study design. The results from this focus group of interviewers from the Latino Women's Study yielded valuable data over a short span of time, providing several important contributions to consider when doing research with Latino women.

CONCLUSION

The findings of our focus group provide valuable knowledge regarding the potential barriers and challenges encountered when conducting research with Latino women in the United States. Essential strengths and training needs were identified by the interviewers which should be considered in projects with similar targeted populations and comparable designs. The experiences of the interviewers during the data collection of the Latino Women's Study highlight the importance of integrating culturally relevant measures with the understanding of important group norms in research involving health beliefs and health practices.

REFERENCES

Alegría, M., Vera, M., Shrout, P., Canino, G., Lai, S. H. & Albizu, C. (2004). Understanding hard-core drug use among urban Puerto Rican women in high-risk neighborhoods. *Addictive Behaviors, 29*(4), 643-664.

Armsden, G. C., & Greenberg, M. T. (1987). The Inventory of Parent and Peer Attachment: Relationships to well-being in adolescence. *Journal of Youth and Adolescence, 16*(5), 427-454.

Bravo, M., Ribera, J., Rubio-Stipec, M., Canino, G., Shrout, P. et al. (2001). Test-retest reliability of the Spanish version of the Diagnostic Interview Schedule for Children (DISC-IV). *Journal of Abnormal Child Psychology, 29*, 433-444.

Canino, G., Bravo, M., Ramírez, R., Febo, V. E., Rubio-Stipec, M., Fernández, R. L., & Hasin, D. (1999). The Spanish Alcohol Use Disorder and Associated Disabilities Interview Schedule (AUDADIS): Reliability and concordance with clinical diagnoses in a Hispanic population. *Journal of Studies on Alcohol, 60*, 790-799.

Canino, G., De La Rosa, M., Turner, J., Valdez, A., Vega, W., & Warner, L. (2003). Epidemiology of drug abuse among Hispanics in the United States. In H. Amaro & D. Cortez (Eds.), *National Strategic Plan on Hispanic Drug Abuse Research: From the Molecule to the Community.* Northeastern University Press, Boston, Mass.

De La Rosa, M. R., & Adrados, J. L. R. (Eds.). (1993). Drug abuse among minority youth: Methodological issues and recent research advances (NIDA Research Monograph Number130). Rockville, MD: National Institute on Drug Abuse.

De La Rosa, M. R., Holleran, L., & Straussner, S. L. A. (2005). *Substance Abusing Latinos: Current research on epidemiology, prevention and treatment.* New York, New York: Haworth Press, Inc.

Flaskerud, J. H., & Nyamathi, A. M. (2000). Collaborative inquiry with low-income Latina women. *Journal of Health Care for the Poor and Underserved, 11*, 326-342.

Goss, J. D., & Leinbach, T. R. (1996). Focus groups as alternative research practice. *Area, 28*, 115-23.

Humphreys, K., Greenbaum, M. A., Noke, J. M., & Finney, J. W. (1996). Reliability, validity, and normative data for a short version of the Understanding of Alcoholism Scale. *Psychology of Addictive Behaviors, 10*(1), 38-44.

Kitzinger. J. (1994). The methodology of focus groups: The importance of interaction between research participants. *Sociology of Health,16*, 103-21.

Krueger, R. A., & Casey, M. A. (2000). *Focus groups: A practical guide for applied research.* (3rd edition). London, England: Sage Publications, Inc.

Krueger. R. A. (1994). Focus groups: A practical guide for applied research. (2nd edition). London, England: Sage Publications, Inc.

Lugo-Steidel. A., & Contreras, J. M. (2003). A new familism scale for use with populations. *Hispanic Journal of Behavioral Sciences. 25*, 312-330.

Marin-VanOss, B., Gómez, C., & Tschann, J. M. (1993). *Condom use among Hispanic men with secondary female sexual partners* (No. 6). San Francisco: Department of health and human services.

Mastronianni, A. C., Faden, R., Federman, D., Grodin, M. A., & Glantz, L. H. (1994). Women and Health Research: Ethical and Legal Issues of Including Women in Clinical Studies (2 vols): Children as Research Subjects: Science, Ethics and Law. *British Medical Journal, 309*, 1095.

Miles, M. B., & Huberman, A. M. (1994). *Qualitative data analysis: An expanded source book* (2nd ed.). Thousand Oaks: Sage Publications.

Newcomb, M., Romero, G., Wayment, H. A., Wyatt, G. E., Tucker. B. M., Carmona, J., Solis. B., & Mitchell-Kernan, C. (1998). Acculturation, sexual risk training, and HIV health promotion among Latinas. *Journal of Counseling Psychology, 45*(4), 454-467.

Ramírez, R.. & De La Cruz. P. (2002). The Hispanic Population in the United States: March 2002 (No. P20-545). Washington DC: US Census Bureau.

Saunders. C. M. (2006). Insuring the uninsured: Reducing the barriers to public insurance. *The Qualitative Report*, 499-515.

Segal. B., & López, R. (Eds.). *Conducting Drug Abuse Research with Minority Populations.* Haworth Press, pps.1998.

Simon, J. S. (1999). How to conduct a Focus Group. *The Grantsmanship Center Magazine.* Retrieved online, June 12, 2005 from http://www.tgci.com/magazine/99fall/focus3.asp

Sloboda, Z. (2002). Changing patterns of "drug abuse" in the United States: Connecting findings from macro- and microepidemiologic studies. *Substance Use & Misuse, 37*(8-10), 1229-1251.

Sormanti, M., Pereira, L., El-Bassel, N., Witte. S., & Gilbert, L. (2001). The role of community consultants in designing an HIV prevention intervention. *AIDS Education and Prevention. 13*, 311-328.

Suarez-Al-Adam, M., Raffeaelli, M., & O'Leary, A. (2000). Influence of Abuse and Partner Hypermasculinity on the Sexual Behavior of Latinas. *AIDS Education and Prevention, 12*(3), 263-274.

Trepper, T. S., Nelson. T. S., McCollum, E. E., & McAvoy, P. (1997). Improving Substance abuse service delivery to Hispanic women through increased cultural competencies: A qualitative study. *Journal of Substance Abuse Treatment, 14*, 225-234.

Vega, W. A., Kolody, B., Porter, P., & Noble, A. (1997). Perinatal drug use among immigrant and native born Latinas. *Substance Use and Misuse, 32*, 43-62.

Vega, W. A., Kolody, B., Aguilar-Gaxiola, S., Alderete. E., Catalano, R., & Caraveo-Anduaga, J. (1998). Lifetime prevalence of DSM-III-R psychiatric disorders among urban and rural Mexican Americans in California. *Archives of General Psychiatry, 55*(9), 771-778.

Warner, L. A., Valdez, A., Vega, W. A., De La Rosa, M., Turner, J., & Canino, G. (2006). Hispanic drug abuse in an evolving cultural context: An agenda for research. *Journal Drug and Alcohol Dependence, 84*, S8-16.

doi:10.1300/J233v06n02_10

The Effect of Neighborhood Context on the Drug Use of American Indian Youth of the Southwest

Scott T. Yabiku, PhD
Andrea Dixon Rayle, PhD
Scott K. Okamoto, PhD
Flavio F. Marsiglia, PhD
Stephen Kulis, PhD

Scott T. Yabiku is Assistant Professor, School of Social and Family Dynamics, Arizona State University, PO Box 873701 Tempe, AZ 85287-3701 (E-mail: syabiku@asu.edu).

Andrea Dixon Rayle is Assistant Professor, Department of Counselor Education, University of Florida, 1207 Norman Hall, PO Box 117046, Gainesville, FL 32611 (E-mail: rayle@ufl.edu).

Scott K. Okamoto is Assistant Professor, Social Work Program, Hawaii Pacific University, FS 302, 1188 Fort Street Mall, Honolulu, HI 96813 (E-mail: sokamoto@hpu.edu).

Flavio F. Marsiglia is Professor, Arizona State University, School of Social Work, 411 N. Central Avenue, Phoenix, AZ 85004-0689 (E-mail: marsiglia@asu.edu).

Stephen Kulis is Professor, School of Social and Family Dynamics, Arizona State University, PO Box 873701, Tempe, AZ 85287-3701 (E-mail: kulis@asu.edu).

This study was supported by National Institutes of Health/National Institute on Drug Abuse funding for the Southwest Interdisciplinary Research Center at Arizona State University (R-24 DA 13937-01), and the Drug Resistance Strategies-3 project (R01 DA05629).

[Haworth co-indexing entry note]: "The Effect of Neighborhood Context on the Drug Use of American Indian Youth of the Southwest." Yabiku, Scott. T. et al. Co-published simultaneously in *Journal of Ethnicity in Substance Abuse* (The Haworth Press, Inc.) Vol. 6, No. 2, 2007, pp. 181-204; and: *21st Century Research on Drugs and Ethnicity: Studies Supported by the National Institute on Drug Abuse* (ed: Peter L. Myers) The Haworth Press. 2007. pp. 181-204. Single or multiple copies of this article are available for a fee from The Haworth Document Delivery Service [1-800-HAWORTH, 9:00 a.m. - 5:00 p.m. (EST). E-mail address: docdelivery@haworthpress.com].

Available online at http://jesa.haworthpress.com

doi:10.1300/J233v06n02_11

SUMMARY. This study examined neighborhood effects on the drug use of American Indian youth of the Southwest. We compared these effects with American Indian and non-American Indian youth in order to examine the universality of neighborhood disorganization as a risk factor for drug use. Neighborhood level variables included unemployment, poverty, education, and violent crime rate. Results indicated that American Indian youth were not as adversely affected by these neighborhood factors. American Indian youth may possess cultural characteristics that protect them from the adverse effects of neighborhood disorganization, including close familial relationships and ethnic pride. Culturally competent practice with American Indian youth may best be implemented through the enhancement of relational and cultural strengths as described in the literature. doi:10.1300/J233v06n02_11 *[Article copies available for a fee from The Haworth Document Delivery Service: 1-800- HAWORTH. E-mail address: <docdelivery@haworthpress.com> Website: <http://www.HaworthPress.com>*

KEYWORDS. American Indians, drugs, substance abuse, neighborhoods

INTRODUCTION

Drug use is one of the major issues facing American Indian populations, including American Indian youth. Research indicates that by 11 years of age, nearly one third of all American Indians have tried alcohol (Mail, 1995; NIAAA), and that 78% of American Indians have tried alcohol, compared with 53% of the general population (Cabape & Howley, 1992; Spicer et al., 2003). Much of the literature has examined the reasons that account for these alarming statistics, such as peer group and family offerers (Kulis, Okamoto, Dixon Rayle, & Nyakoe, 2006) and forced assimilation, colonization, and acculturation (Beauvais, 1998; Frank, Moore, & Ames, 2000; OTA, 1990). In general, these studies have examined the various contexts of drug use for American Indian youth, including the historical and relational contexts that may contribute to its development. However, to date, no studies have examined the possible effects of the neighborhood context on the drug-using behaviors of American Indian youth. While prior studies have examined the neighborhood influence on youth substance use in general (Boardman, Finch, Ellison, Williams, & Jackson, 2001; Dembo, Schmeidler, Burgos, & Taylor, 1985; Schier, Botvin, &. Miller, 1999), American Indian youth may respond differently to these neighborhood contexts due to their unique experiences and position within American society.

Using data from a large-scale drug prevention efficacy trial, this study examined the neighborhood effects on the drug use of American Indian youth of the Southwest. In this study, we compared these effects with non-American Indian youth, in order to examine the universality of neighborhood disorganization as a risk factor for youth drug use. Finally, we explored the role that cultural resiliency might play in protecting youth from adverse outcomes associated with neighborhood disorganization. The implications of this study for understanding the culturally specific etiology of drug use of American Indian youth are discussed.

LITERATURE REVIEW

Social Disorganization and Control

Social disorganization theory suggests that when neighborhoods have higher levels of social and ecological disorder, adolescents who live within them have poorer outcomes on a variety of domains (Sampson & Groves, 1989). For example, Brooks-Gunn et al. (1993) found that neighborhood socioeconomic status was positively related to adolescent intellectual development, even after controlling for the socioeconomic status of the adolescents' families. In addition, young African American female adolescents were found to have higher rates of sexual initiation when they lived in neighborhoods with less professional employment (Brewster, 1994), and disadvantaged neighborhoods had higher levels of teen high school dropouts and delinquency (Chow, 1998) and drug use (Crum, Lillie-Blanton, & Anthony, 1996). Specifically for adolescents, three mechanisms that link social and ecological disorganization to substance use are a lack of social control, a lack of positive role models, and psychological stress.

Social control of young people is challenging in neighborhoods with high social and ecological disorganization, such as those with a high proportion of single parent families, and those with high levels of poverty and crime (Sampson & Groves, 1989). Neighborhoods with a high concentration of single parent families are commonly characterized by increased adolescent risk, even controlling for the fact that these parents (overwhelmingly mothers) are disproportionately likely to be poor (Coulton & Pandey, 1992). The single parents' burden of the sole responsibility for supporting and raising children may lessen the capacity for monitoring adolescent behavior compared to two-parent households, resulting in increased peer influence toward the acceptance of deviant behaviors such as alcohol and drug use (Oetting, Donnermeyer, & Deffenbacher, 1998; Sampson, 2001). Research suggests that after marital disruption, parents are less effective at monitoring their children. Reasons may include the reduced number of parents in single-parent households, the loss of parental respect by children, and the increased influence of peers (Thornton, 1991).

Additionally, high poverty neighborhoods often lack funding and support for local institutions that may provide societal stability such as clubs, after-school centers, and community groups (Boardman et al., 2001; Pattillo, 1998; Peterson, Krivo, & Harris, 2000). Instead of these prosocial institutions, high poverty neighborhoods typically have a surplus of liquor stores, empty lots, and abandoned buildings (Freisthler, Needell, & Gruenewald, 2005; Peterson, Krivo, & Harris, 2000). These features can increase the availability of substances and provide neighborhood sites for youth to congregate without ready supervision. In addition to poverty, social and ecological disorganization in the form of crime also reduces the monitoring of youth within neighborhoods. Sampson and Raudenbush (1999) found that violent crime in neighborhoods reduced "collective efficacy" in neighborhoods, defined as residents' feelings of cohesion and their willingness to monitor neighborhood children and intervene in their delinquent behaviors.

Another mechanism that links neighborhood social and ecological disorganization to youth substance use is a lack of positive role models. The lack of role models has been often used to describe a wide-ranging set of problems among inner city youth, often focusing on the issues of disadvantage of young African Americans (Wilson, 1987). These problems include single-parent families, early teen sexual activity, and teen childbearing (Brewster, 1994; South & Baumer, 2000; South & Crowder, 2000). With regard to crime and deviance, youth living in disorganized neighborhoods may mimic the behaviors of those who appear the most successful in these communities, which may be violent, gang-affiliated individuals (Massey, 1995; Pattillo, 1998). Selling drugs is often viewed as a way to make money in communities where there are limited opportunities for formal employment. Participating in the drug trade is also one way adolescents can support their own drug habits (Joseph & Pearson, 2002). The high availability and use of drugs and alcohol also promotes harmful role models. In these neighborhoods, youths encounter more pro-drugs norms and they are more likely to see adults drinking and "getting high" in public (Kadushin et al., 1998; Raudenbush & Sampson, 1999).

Research also suggests that social disorganization can lead to substance use via stress and strain (Boardman et al., 2001). Strain theory predicts that individuals faced with stress and strain will be more likely to be deviant (Agnew, 1985). For example, clinical studies of stress and drug abuse have shown a relationship between these phenomena (Fox et al., 2005; Sinha, 2001). Further, in youth, stress has been found to be correlated with substance use (Hoffman & Su, 1997). Recent research has broadened the notions of stress and strain and expanded them to examine the neighborhood as a root cause of strain. Boardman et al. (2001) proposed that living in highly disorganized neighborhoods stricken with crime and poverty leads to psychological stress and subsequent drug use. A proposed reason for this relationship is that neighborhood disadvantage presents numerous stressors in coping with everyday life in these neighborhoods, and drug use is one strategy of "stress reduction" (Boardman et al., 2001). Thus the stress caused by life in crime and violence-ridden neighborhoods may be an important predictor of adolescent alcohol and other drug use (Dembo et al., 1985; Schier et al., 1999) and may weaken youth resilience.

Another mechanism of stress may be the minority or majority status of a young person within a neighborhood. For example, prior research found that when American Indian youth perceive discrimination, they have higher substance use (Whitbeck, Hoyt, McMorris, Chen, & Stubben, 2001). Other research found that an ethnic group's size within a school influences the substance use of students from that ethnic group (Kulis, Marsiglia, Nieri, Sicotte, & Hohmann-Marriott, 2004). Being a member of a minority group, relative to the majority ethnic composition of the neighborhood or school, may cause stress and possibly subsequent substance use.

Resiliency Theory

Resilience has been defined as "positive adaptation in response to adversity" (Waller, 2001, p. 292). Related to the concept of resilience are the concepts of risk and protective factors. Matsen and Coatsworth (1998) identify two categories of risk factors: (1) challenging life circumstances (e.g., parental drug use, financial stress in the family), and (2) trauma (e.g., death of a parent, family or community violence). Conversely, protective factors are individual or environmental characteristics that enhance youths' ability to resist stressful life events and promote adaptation and competence (Bogenschneider, 1996). Individual protective factors include problem-solving skills, high intelligence, and a strong positive ethnic identity, while environmental protective factors include a sense of community and supportive friends or neighbors (Waller, 2001). Resiliency theory suggests that these factors operate when risks are present to prevent adverse life outcomes (Rutter, 1987).

Recent drug prevention research indicates that risk and protective factors are discrete and separate, and are moderated by gender and ethnicity (Moon, Jackson, & Hecht, 2000). However, the relationship between risk and protection factors and drug use has also been shown to be complex, such that similar circumstances might constitute risk in one situation and protection in another, or might simultaneously present both risk and protection (Waller, Okamoto, Miles, & Hurdle, 2003). This phenomenon is particularly true for American Indian populations, as various environmental contexts (e.g., family, school, neighborhood, and community) tend to be more fluid and may overlap with each other (Waller et al., 2003).

Early conceptualizations of resiliency suggested that protective factors reflected individual attributes. For example, Garmezy, Mastgen, and Tellegen (1984) suggested that resilience consisted of the influence of adaptive personal attributes and stress on the manifested competence of youth. Adaptive personal attributes were thought to function as a kind of "immunity" against life stress. However, contemporary resiliency theorists have challenged this notion in two ways. First, they have argued that resiliency is best conceptualized as a process, rather than an attribute (Bogenschneider, 1996; Rutter, 1987). The term *protective processes* suggests that resiliency is dynamic and reflects a bi-directional relationship between the person and the environment (Waller, 2001). Second, contemporary resiliency theorists emphasize that the concept exists within an ecosystemic context (Bogenschneider; 1996; Waller, 2001). Risk and protective processes occur at several levels of the human ecology, such as the individual, family, and community levels. The ecological risk and protective process model is reflected in research focused in the etiologies of disease (Link & Phelan, 1995) and mental illness and violence (Hiday, 1995), which argue that individually based risk factors must be contextualized in order to understand the development of adverse health outcomes. Finally, contemporary resiliency theorists also emphasize the importance of a strong, positive cultural/ethnic identity (ethnic pride) as a protective factor, which has been supported in recent research on drug use and American Indian youth (Kulis, Napoli, & Marsiglia, 2002).

In addition to the protective effect of ethnic pride (Kulis et al., 2002), a developing body of literature has emphasized the protective effect of immediate and extended family members on drug use and American Indian youth. For example, two focus group studies examined the protective impact of siblings and cousins on the drug use of Southwestern American Indian middle school students (Hurdle, Okamoto, & Miles, 2003; Waller et al., 2003). Because these family members attended schools and lived in the same communities as these youth, Waller et al. suggested that protection is intensified for these youth compared to their non-American Indian counterparts because same-generation family members were present in multiple environmental contexts. These findings were consistent with recent quantitative studies that have illustrated the importance of the relational context on substance use of American Indian youth (Kulis et al., 2006; Okamoto, LeCroy, Dustman, Hohmann-Marriott, & Kulis, 2004). While many minority cultures are collectivist in nature, the research on American Indian youth and drug use is unique, in that it illustrates the influence of interrelationships among same generation peers across multiple environmental contexts (e.g., school, home, reservation and non-reservation communities). This unique impact might protect these youth against factors that typically predispose other youth to risk, such as neighborhood disorganization.

This study examined the impact of one ecosystemic context–the neighborhood–on the drug use of both American Indian youth and non-American Indian youth, and the potential role that resiliency or protective factors may play in their drug use behaviors. This study has implications for understanding the unique social and environmental contributors related to the etiology of drug use of American Indian youth. We hypothesized that, while neighborhood social disorganization will have a harmful impact on substance use for all youth, these effects will differ between American Indian and non-American Indian youth. Due to their strong and unique patterns of ethnic pride and familial bonds, we hypothesized that American Indian youth would exhibit resiliency to their neighborhood social context.

METHOD

Participants

The data for our analyses were from the *keepin' it REAL* substance use prevention study. The *keepin' it REAL* curriculum is a SAMSHA model program that has been shown to be effective in reducing substance use among adolescents (Hecht et al., 2003). In 1998, researchers recruited 35 Phoenix middle schools to participate in the program. These 35 schools represented more than 75% of all the middle schools in the city of Phoenix. Of the 35 schools, 25 were randomly chosen as treatment schools that received the *keepin' it REAL* program, and 10 were designated as control schools and received the standard substance prevention program already in place. Before the *keepin' it REAL* program was implemented, baseline assessments were conducted on students in all 35 schools. This pretreatment survey measured 7th grade students' past experience with substance use, their norms towards substance use, and ethnic and demographic background information. The pretreatment surveys were self-administered by students, and were available in both English and Spanish translations. Survey administrators from the research team conducted the survey during regular class periods and responded to student questions regarding completion of the survey. Although some students were not present to take the survey due to absences, 87% of enrolled students in the 7th grade completed the pretreatment survey instrument. After the initial survey interviews in fall, 1998, the *keepin' it REAL* program was implemented in the treatment schools, and a post-treatment interview was conducted in all schools in the spring of 1999. Two additional post-treatment interviews were conducted once the students had progressed to the 8th grade. Because our aim was to examine how patterns of American Indian substance use differed from non-American Indian adolescents before intervention, our analysis utilized the data only from the pre-treatment interview.

We also use data from the neighborhoods in which the adolescents' schools were located. The source of the data is a combination of United States Census data and data from the city of Phoenix. Students in a school were assigned the neighborhood measures from the census tract or tracts of the school's official enrollment boundaries. These boundaries, carved through 10 separate school districts, yielded 35 school enrollment areas using data obtained from the Arizona Department of Education. It is possible that the areas in which the students actually lived may not have been the same area in which their school was located. Parents could enroll children in schools that were outside the boundaries of their home school's district, but such transfers are uncommon, and nearly all children within each area lived nearby. Even for the relatively few cases where the school's census tract did not match the home of the student, the characteristics of the neighborhood surrounding the school should most likely be an important influence. The school is a location that students frequent on a regular basis, and thus exposure to the school's surrounding neighborhood is likely to be high, forming another context in which young people receive socialization (Bronfenbrenner, 1989).

Substance Use Measures

The three main substances assessed in the pre-treatment survey were the use of alcohol, cigarettes, and marijuana. Other substances were also examined, but for this age group in 1998, their use was too rare to be effectively analyzed. Less than 5% of respondents said they had any lifetime experience with cocaine, crack, LSD, PCP, heroin, downers, speed or crystal methamphetamine. Use of alcohol was measured by a question that asked, "How many drinks of alcohol have you had in the past 30 days?" The response categories were a nine point ordinal scale, that varied from "none" and "only sips" on the low end to "8-15 drinks," "16-30 drinks," and "more than 30 drinks" on the high end. Using similar ordinal scales, cigarette use was measured with a question that asked, "How many cigarettes have you smoked in the past 30 days?" and marijuana use was measured by asking, "How many hits of marijuana have you had in the last thirty days?" Because substance use measures tended to be skewed, they were transformed with a logarithmic function.

Neighborhood Measures

Using ArcView (GIS) software, neighborhood level variables were constructed by mapping census tracts on to each school's official enrollment boundaries. Enrollment boundaries, however, did not consistently correspond to census tracts in our study. When an enrollment boundary was completely contained within a single census tract, that tract's characteristics were assigned to the school. When an enrollment boundary spanned multiple census tracts, data was proportionately assigned, by geographic area, from each spanned census tract to the school. For example, if 50% of a census tract fell into an area, ArcView designated 50% of the population within that tract to that area.

Neighborhood level variables constructed from the 2000 U.S. Census Summary File 1 or Summary File 3 were used in this study, and included the percent of individuals in the school enrollment area who (a) were unemployed, (b) lived in poverty, and (c) possessed less than a high school education. A fourth neighborhood level variable the violent crime rate per 1,000 people was constructed from Phoenix Police Department reports that provided the geographic location of crimes.

These four neighborhood variables were chosen to match important dimensions identified by the social disorganization literature (Sampson & Groves, 1989; South & Baumer, 2000; Wilson, 1987). Unemployment captures economic hardship, distressed neighborhoods, and a lack of role models in steady jobs. Low levels of education also represent economic disadvantage and a dearth of role models for higher educational aspirations. Neighborhoods with high levels of poverty lack community institutions that provide social control, such as clubs and community groups. Crime in neighborhoods may be a source of stress, and may be linked to negative role models for violent and drug behaviors.

Student Characteristics

Ethnicity was assessed through student responses to the question "What is your race/culture?" American Indian status was coded 1 if the student marked American Indian affiliation, and 0 otherwise. Students were allowed to choose as many ethnic and racial identities as desired. Students without any American Indian heritage were the reference group. Although this group contains all other students, they are mostly students of Latino origin. Several basic sociodemographic controls were also included: gender, grades, and free or reduced lunch status. Grades were self-reported and measured on a scale from 1 (mostly F's) to 9 (mostly A's). Socioeconomic status was captured with a dummy variable that indicated if the students received free or reduced lunches through the Federal school lunch program. Because students may not accurately know their household income, free or reduced lunch status is a frequent way of collecting socioeconomic measures from school-based surveys of students (Bankston & Caldas, 1996; Gerard & Buehler, 1999).

Analysis

We use linear regression to predict the level of alcohol, cigarette, and marijuana use in the last 30 days. Because we examined American Indian youths' resiliency within neighborhood social disorganization, we estimated models in which we interacted the American Indian measure with the neighborhood measures. A significant interaction coefficient for this term indicates the effect of neighborhoods is significantly different for American Indian compared to other youth.

Multilevel modeling techniques addressed the issue of clustered data. Because students were sampled in 35 schools, there is non-independence between students in the same school. This violation of regression assumptions biases the estimates, most likely in the form of deflated standard errors. Multilevel or hierarchical modeling procedures incorporated the clustered data and protected against Type I error (i.e., wrongly rejecting the null hypothesis). We used PROC MIXED in SAS 9.1 to estimate multilevel models with random intercepts, which allowed for different schools to have different base levels of drug use (Raudenbush & Bryk, 2002).

RESULTS

Table 1 presents descriptive statistics for the sample. In terms of substance use in the last 30 days, the average level of use among 7th grade adolescents tended to be low. Alcohol use averaged 1.8 on the 9 point scale, which was between the categories of "none" and "only sips." Cigarette use averaged 1.3, which was between "none" and "only one puff." Marijuana use averaged 1.5, which was between "none" and "one small hit." Behind these low averages, however, there was substantial variation in use. Although not shown in Table 1, in the last 30 days, about 5% of students had more than 4 drinks, about 6% of students had more than 2 cigarettes, and about 7% of students had more than 4 hits of

TABLE 1. Descriptive Statistics

	Mean	Std.Dev	Minimum	Maximum
Substance Use in Last 30 Days (Ordinal Scales)				
Alcoholic Drinks	1.84	1.65	1.00	9.00
Cigarettes	1.32	1.03	1.00	8.00
Marijuana	1.51	1.46	1.00	8.00
Neighborhoods				
% Unemployed	0.09	0.04	0.03	0.30
% In Poverty	0.23	0.09	0.05	0.54
% Less than HS Education	0.46	0.18	0.07	0.70
Total Crime Rate	206.74	97.98	6.45	543.63
American Indian (1 = Yes, 0 = No)	0.10	0.30	0.00	1.00
Male (1 = Yes, 0 = No)	0.51	0.50	0.00	1.00
Grades (1-9 scale)	6.60	1.83	1.00	9.00
Free/Reduced Lunch (1 = Yes, 0 = No)	0.83	0.38	0.00	1.00

marijuana. Thus, some students in this population are regular monthly users of these substances.

The demographics of the sample indicated that 10% of the students claimed at least partial American Indian heritage. Of the American Indian students, 28% claimed exclusive American Indian heritage, suggesting that most of the American Indian students were multiracial. The sample was equally divided by gender (51% male), and students' self-reported grades averaged 6.6 on the 1 to 9 scale, which was between categories "B's and C's" and "mostly B's." A very large portion of the sample (83%) was receiving free or reduced cost lunches, which indicates a high level of economic disadvantage in this population of students. The school context was particularly relevant for our sample, as almost all of the American Indian youth in the study attended schools outside of their reservation communities. In this way, they were considered "urban" or "semi-urban" in nature.

The neighborhood measures suggested substantial variation in the social disorganization present near the students' schools. Unemployment averaged 9% (range = 3% to 30%), the average poverty level was 23% (range = 5% to 54%), and the percent of adults over age 25 without a high school diploma was 46% (range = 7% to 70% across neighborhoods). Lastly, crime data from the city of Phoenix showed that the total crime rate averaged about 207 incidents per 1000 people. From these neighborhood statistics, it is clear that the students in the population came from a wide variety of neighborhoods. When we compared differences in neighborhood social disorganization across American Indian and non-American Indian youth (table not shown), American Indian youth went to school in neighborhoods with slightly less unemployment (8% versus 9%), poverty (21% versus 24%), and adults without high school diplomas (42% versus 47%). The crime rate, however, was modestly higher in the American Indian neighborhoods (217 versus 206). T-tests comparing neighborhood conditions indicated that these differences across the two groups of students were significant at the .05 level.

In the multivariate tables, we examined if the effects of these neighborhood conditions varied by whether or not the student has claimed American Indian affiliation. Table 2 examines alcohol use in the last 30 days. In model 1, higher grades are significantly protective against alcohol use. Free or reduced lunch receipt, as a proxy of socioeconomic status, is also negatively correlated with use. Being male as opposed to female, however, was not a significant predictor of alcohol usage.

A significant test statistic for the interaction between a neighborhood measure and the American Indian indicator is evidence that neighborhood

TABLE 2. Neighborhoods, American Indian Status, and Logged Alcohol Consumption

	1	2	3	4
Neighborhoods				
% Unemployed	0.23			
	(0.51)			
% Unemployed * American Indian	–2.13*			
	(0.96)			
% In Poverty		0.00		
		(0.22)		
% In Poverty * American Indian		–0.91**		
		(0.33)		
% Less than HS Education			0.14	
			(0.13)	
% Less than HS Education * American Indian			–0.40*	
			(0.17)	
Total Crime Rate				0.05*
				(0.02)
Total Crime Rate * American Indian				–0.01
				(0.03)
American Indian	0.18*	0.20*	0.17*	0.03
	(0.08)	(0.08)	(0.08)	(0.07)
Male	0.01	0.01	0.01	0.01
	(0.02)	(0.02)	(0.02)	(0.02)
Grades	–0.05***	–0.05***	–0.05***	–0.05***
	(0.01)	(0.01)	(0.01)	(0.01)
Free/Reduced Lunch	–0.10***	–0.10**	–0.11***	–0.10***
	(0.03)	(0.03)	(0.03)	(0.03)
Intercept	0.74***	0.76***	0.70***	0.67***
	(0.07)	(0.07)	(0.08)	(0.06)
N	4137	4137	4137	4137

Coefficients are estimates from multilevel linear regression
Standard errors are in parentheses
*p <. 05
**p <. 01
***p <. 001

effects vary by American Indian status. In model 1, the interaction between neighborhood unemployment and American Indian affiliation was significant and negative. For non-American Indian students, each 1 percent increase in neighborhood unemployment increased logged alcohol consumption by .0023 units (.01 * .23 = .0023). Conversely, for American Indian students, a one percent increase in unemployment decreased alcohol consumption by .019 units (.01 *.23 – .01 * 2.13 = –.019). The test statistic for the interaction indicated that the difference in these two slopes (.0023 and –.019) was significant. In model 2, similar results were found for neighborhood poverty the significant interaction suggests that American Indian students showed resiliency to neighborhood poverty that was not seen for non-American Indian students. In model 3, the percent of residents in the neighborhood with less than a high school diploma tended to increase the rate of alcohol consumption for non-American Indian students, whereas for American Indian students, alcohol consumption decreased. As with the previous models, the significant interaction term is evidence that the slopes between American Indian and non-American Indian students are different. In model 4, however, there was no evidence that the total crime rate affected alcohol consumption differently across either of the student groups.

The main effects of neighborhood variables in models 1 through 3 were not significant. This means that for the reference group (non-American Indian students), neighborhood unemployment, poverty, and education were not significantly related to substance use. This finding is similar to previous studies of this population, which found weak neighborhood effects on substance use (Kulis, Marsiglia, & Nieri, 2004). However, the significant interaction coefficients in models 1 to 3 showed that these neighborhood effects differed significantly for American Indian and non-American Indian students–even if the main effects were not significant. The main effect in model 4 was significant, which indicated that the total crime rate had a positive effect on alcohol consumption for non-American Indian youth. In addition to models 1 through 4, we also estimated a combined model that included all four neighborhood variables (results not presented). In this combined model, however, none of the interactions were significant. This suggests that the neighborhood variables are related, and they represent an underlying dimension of neighborhood disadvantage.

Table 3 repeats these same models, but for cigarette consumption. The overall pattern of results for cigarettes was similar to the results for alcohol, although the effect of free or reduced price lunch was no longer

TABLE 3. Neighborhoods, American Indian Status, and Logged Cigarette Consumption

	1	2	3	4
Neighborhoods				
% Unemployed	0.15			
	(0.24)			
% Unemployed * American Indian	−1.95*			
	(0.64)			
% In Poverty		0.14		
		(0.10)		
% In Poverty * American Indian		−0.79***		
		(0.22)		
% Less than HS Education			0.06	
			(0.05)	
% Less than HS Education * American Indian			−0.35**	
			(0.12)	
Total Crime Rate				0.01
				(0.01)
Total Crime Rate * American Indian				0.03
				(0.02)
American Indian	0.23***	0.25***	0.22***	0.01
	(0.06)	(0.05)	(0.05)	(0.04)
Male	0.01	0.01	0.01	0.01
	(0.01)	(0.01)	(0.01)	(0.01)
Grades	−0.03***	−0.03***	−0.03***	−0.03***
	(0.00)	(0.00)	(0.00)	(0.00)
Free/Reduced Lunch	−0.03	−0.04	−0.04	−0.03
	(0.02)	(0.02)	(0.02)	(0.02)
Intercept	0.37***	0.35***	0.36***	0.37***
	(0.04)	(0.04)	(0.04)	(0.04)
N	4145	4145	4145	4145

Coefficients are estimates from multilevel linear regression
Standard errors are in parentheses
*p <. 05
**p <. 01
***p <. 001

significant. Neighborhood unemployment, poverty, and low educational attainment appeared to decrease cigarette use for American Indians, while for non-American Indian students these slopes were positive. The main effects were not significant, but the interaction coefficients were, indicating significant differences in effects across the two groups of students. As before, the effects of the total neighborhood crime rate did not significantly differ for the two groups.

Lastly, Table 4 examined marijuana use in the last 30 days. The results in Table 4 differed from the prior substances in that the interaction results were not as robust. The signs of the interactions in models 1 to 3 were identical to the coefficients in Table 2 and Table 3 (negative), but only one interaction–American Indian * neighborhood poverty was significant. The main effects of neighborhood variables were significant in models 1 to 3, which suggested that these neighborhood conditions increased marijuana use for non-American Indian students.

DISCUSSION

This study examined the effects of neighborhood contexts on the drug use of an ethnically diverse sample of youth living in the Southwest. Drawing upon social disorganization and resiliency theories, we hypothesized that different neighborhood contexts might affect the drug use among American Indian youth differently compared to non-American Indian youth. Specifically, we compared the resulting effects with non-American Indian youth in order to examine the universality of neighborhood disorganization as a potential risk factor for youth drug use. We also explored the role that cultural resiliency might play in protecting American Indian youth from adverse outcomes associated with neighborhood disorganization.

Initial results revealed that a large proportion of the youth in our sample were from economically disadvantaged families/neighborhoods based on the percentage of students receiving free or reduced cost lunch and local crime statistics. In addition, it was evident that varying levels of social disorganization existed around the youths' school settings. Demographic results of drug use behavior suggested that varying percentages of the total sample of 7th grade students, which typically range in age from 11-13 years, had participated in regular monthly drug usage. For alcohol and cigarettes, the differences in the slopes of neighborhood effects between American Indian and non-American Indian youth were significant for neighborhood unemployment, poverty, and education. For marijuana, the

TABLE 4. Neighborhoods, American Indian Status, and Logged Marijuana Consumption

	1	2	3	4
Neighborhoods				
% Unemployed	1.21***			
	(0.35)			
% Unemployed * American Indian	–0.69			
	(0.8)			
% In Poverty		0.37*		
		(0.15)		
% In Poverty * American Indian		–0.60*		
		(0.28)		
% Less than HS Education			0.24**	
			(0.09)	
% Less than HS Education * American Indian			–0.25	
			(0.14)	
Total Crime Rate				0.02
				(0.01)
Total Crime Rate * American Indian				0.03
				(0.02)
American Indian	0.16*	0.23***	0.21**	0.04
	(0.07)	(0.07)	(0.07)	(0.05)
Male	0.07***	0.07***	0.07***	0.07***
	(0.02)	(0.02)	(0.02)	(0.02)
Grades	–.05***	0.05***	0.05***	0.05***
	(0.00)	(0.00)	(0.00)	(0.00)
Free/Reduced Lunch	–.09***	–.09***	–.09***	–.07**
	(0.02)	(0.03)	(0.03)	(0.02)
Intercept	0.45***	0.47***	0.45***	0.52***
	(0.05)	(0.05)	(0.06)	(0.05)
N	4130	4130	4130	4130

*p <. 05
**p <. 01
***p <. 001
Standard errors are in parentheses

differences in neighborhood effects were less robust, with only poverty showing a different effect according to American Indian status.

Thus, when exploring possible differences between non-American Indian youth and American Indian youth, we found significant differences in the effects of neighborhood contexts on the alcohol, cigarette, and marijuana use behaviors. The current findings reveal somewhat unexpected trends among the American Indian youth participants. Our findings might suggest that the American Indian youth in our sample were "super-resilient" to socially disorganized neighborhoods and factors that traditionally have been found to negatively influence drug use behaviors among adolescents (Brooks-Gunn et al., 1993; Sampson & Groves, 1989; Sampson & Raudenbush, 1999). Instead, it was the non-American Indian youth that appeared to be using drugs more frequently when living within in these neighborhoods, despite past studies that reveal that American Indian youth actually report significantly greater drug usage (Cabape & Howley, 1992; Spicer et al., 2003). This "super resiliency" might have been the result of supportive immediate and extended family members in their ecosystem, which has been found to be a protective factor for American Indian youth in prior studies (Hurdle et al., 2003; Waller et al., 2003). Future research should examine the relative contributions of multiple environmental systems in which American Indian youth are exposed and embedded, in order to further delineate the separate and combined effects of family members, friends/peers, and neighborhood contexts on drug use decisions for American Indian youth.

Another interpretation of the findings might be that the American Indian youth in our sample were in the ethnic, social, and economic minority in neighborhoods with higher socioeconomic status, prompting them to use drugs to cope with the ecological stress associated with this status in their communities. In other words, these youth may have been considered relatively poor or from disadvantaged families in their communities, and therefore experienced greater stress and discrimination from living in these neighborhoods in which their peers and neighbors were better off socioeconomically. American Indians were only 2.0% of the Phoenix population in 2000 (U.S. Bureau of the Census, 2000), and thus American Indian youth were likely to be a small minority in most social settings within Phoenix. As mentioned earlier, compared to non-American Indian youth, the American Indian youth in the sample also went to schools in neighborhoods that had lower levels of unemployment and poverty, and higher education levels. Because these youth may have not felt as if they fit in within their neighborhoods, the stress of believing that others were watching them more often may have led to their drug usage. This interpretation of our findings is consistent with prior research, which has shown that perceived discrimination can be a pathway to substance use in American Indian youth (Whitbeck et al., 2001). Future research should focus on American Indian youths' perceptions of their neighborhoods, how they view themselves fitting in within these contexts, and whether they feel comfortable in the neighborhoods within which they live.

Another explanation for our findings may be considered within the context of social desirable responding. Social desirable responding is the tendency of individuals to cast themselves in a positive light according to current cultural norms when answering questions in a research study (Messick, 1960; Paulhus, 1984). The adolescents in this study were asked to reflect upon their actual drug usage behaviors within the last 30 days and they were sure to know that their responses would be examined and reported. They may have reported less drug usage in order to "better" themselves and their current life situations, which in turn may have helped them feel better and view themselves more positively (Paulhus).

Interestingly, there were no significant differences in alcohol, cigarette, and marijuana use between American Indian and non-American Indian youth based on neighborhood crime rates. Community level poverty and crime have been found to reduce the monitoring of youth within neighborhoods (Sampson & Raudenbush, 1999) and have led to youth crime and deviance (Massey, 1995; Pattillo, 1998) such as the selling and trafficking of drugs as well as drug usage. Contrary to these research findings, our results also indicated no direct link between American Indian youth drug use and neighborhood crime rates. This suggests that these youth in our sample may have experienced neighborhood crime and drug use as separate events within their ecosystem, which did not have an influence on each other. As such, neighborhood crime did not appear to directly affect American Indian youths' decisions to use drugs in our study.

Finally, with regard to the reported drug use behaviors of American Indian youth in our study, it is important to note the distinct differences between cultural/ceremonial and neighborhood recreational drug use for American Indian youth. Hallucinogens and other drugs play critical roles at valued tribal and familial cultural activities; however, this practice represents religious and spiritually sanctioned use of substances and is believed to reinforce cultural cohesion and commitment (Grob, 1994; Grob & Dobkin de Rios, 1996). Most likely, based on the framing of the survey questions, the American Indian youth in this study were not reporting drug use that occurred in culturally appropriate situations.

LIMITATIONS OF THE STUDY

The generalizability of this study's findings are limited because our sample included American Indian youth in public middle schools which include a majority of non-American Indian students in a large southwestern metropolitan area, and nearly all the American Indian youth lived off tribal reservations. Further, the American Indian sample consisted of youth with complex multi-ethnic identities, as more than two thirds of the sample claimed American Indian ethnicity with another ethnic affiliation (e.g., Mexican). This may limit the generalizability of the findings to American Indian youth in primarily reservation communities or those of "pure" descent. Additionally, there are 562 federally recognized tribes across the U.S. (Bureau of Indian Affairs, 2002) and numerous non-recognized tribes, with significant cultural and regional differences such as living situations, degree of Indian ancestry or blood quantum, and cultural affiliation, identity, and participation (Hawkins, Cummins, & Marlatt, 2004). The findings from the current study may not reflect these differences, and thus may not be generalizable to American Indian youth across the U.S.

Another limitation from our study reflected the lack of precision in the measurement of neighborhood variables. Specifically, the four measures of neighborhood social disorganization were correlated with each other, suggesting an underlying dimension of neighborhood disadvantage. Therefore, it was not possible to identify which specific features of neighborhoods were related to American Indian resiliency. Further, the data lacked the ability to control for parental-level variables (e.g., unemployment, education). Thus neighborhood measures of unemployment or education could partially reflect individual-level phenomena.

CONCLUSIONS

Despite these limitations, findings from this study have implications for furthering our understanding of the possible effects of social disorganization and neighborhood contexts on the reported drug use among American Indian and non-American Indian youth. The results contribute to our knowledge of resiliency and protective factors that exist among American Indian youth in the Southwest in regard to neighborhood drug use behaviors. The differences in American Indian and non-American Indian drug use patterns based on neighborhood factors from this study contribute to a larger body of future research related to the ecological risk and protective factors for American Indian youth and Indigenous youth populations. Further, the findings from this study may also inform drug prevention programs for these youth, particularly in their incorporation of neighborhood and school contexts that place these youth at risk for drug use. Future research might explore these phenomena, as well as examine other culture-specific aspects of drug use risk and resiliency with American Indian youth in a variety of regional contexts across the U.S.

REFERENCES

Agnew, R. (1985). A longitudinal test of the revised strain theory. *Journal of Quantitative Criminology, 5,* 373-387.

Boardman, J. D., Finch, B. K., Ellison, C. G., Williams, D. R., & Jackson, J. S. (2001). Neighborhood disadvantage, stress, and drug use among adults. *Journal of Health and Social Behavior, 42,* 151-165.

Bogenschneider, K. (1996). An ecological risk protective theory for building prevention programs, policies, and community capacity to support youth. *Family Relations, 45,* 127-138.

Brewster, K. L. (1994). Neighborhood context and the transition to sexual activity among young Black women. *Demography, 31,* 603-614.

Bronfenbrenner, U. (1989). Ecological systems theory. In R. Vasta (Ed.), *Annals of child development. Six theories of child development: Revised formulations and current issues* (pp. 187-249). London: JAI.

Brooks-Gunn, J., Duncan, G. J., Klebanov, P. K., & Sealand, N. (1993). Do neighborhoods influence child and adolescent development? *American Journal of Sociology* 99(2), 353-395.

Bureau of Indian Affairs. (2002). Indian entities recognized and eligible to receive services from the United States Bureau of Indian affairs. *Federal Register, 67.*

Chow, J. (1998). Differentiating urban neighborhoods: A multivariate structural model analysis. *Social Work Research, 22,* 131-142.

Coulton, C., & Pandey, S. (1992). Geographic concentration of poverty and risk to children in urban neighborhoods. *American Behavioral Scientist, 35,* 238-257.

Crum, R. M., Lillie-Blanton, M., & Anthony, J. C. (1996). Neighborhood environment and opportunity to use cocaine and other drugs in late childhood and early adolescence. *Drug and Alcohol Dependence, 43,* 155-161.

Dembo, R., Schmeidler, J., Burgos, W., & Taylor, R. (1985). Environmental setting and early drug involvement among inner-city junior high school youths. *The International Journal of the Addictions, 20,* 1239-1255.

Fox, H. C., Talih, M., Malison, R., Anderson, G. M., Kreek, M. J., Sinha, R. (2005). Frequency of recent cocaine and alcohol use affects drug *craving* and associated responses to stress and drug-related cues. *Psychoneuroendocrinology, 30,* 880-891.

Freisthler, B., Needell, B., & Gruenewald, P. J. (2005). Is the physical availability of alcohol and illicit drugs related to neighborhood rates of child maltreatment? *Child Abuse & Neglect, 29,* 1049-1060.

Garmezy, N., Masten, A. S., & Tellegen, A. (1984). The study of stress and competence in children: A building block for developmental psychopathology. *Child Development, 55,* 97-111.

Garrett, M. T., & Herring, R. D. (2001). Honoring the power of relation: Counseling Native adults. *Journal for Humanistic Counseling, Education, and Development, 40,* 139-151.

Grob, C. S. (1994). Psychiatric research with hallucinogens: What have we learned? In C. Ratsch & J. Bakers (Eds.), *Yearbook of Ethnomedicine* (pp. 91-112). Berlin: Verlagfýr Wissenschaft und Bildung.

Grob, C. S., & Dobkin de Rios, M. (1996). Hallucinogens, suggestibility and adolescence in cross-cultural perspective. *Journal of Drug Issues, 22,* 121-138.

Hawkins, E. H., Cummins, L. H., & Marlatt, G. A. (2004). Preventing substance abuse in American Indian and Alaska Native youth: Promising strategies for healthier communities. *Psychological Bulletin, 130,* 304-323.

Hecht, M. L., Marsiglia, F. F., Elek, E., Wagstaff, D. A., Kulis, S., Dustman, P., & Miller-Day, M. (2003). Culturally grounded substance use prevention: An evaluation of the *keepin' it REAL* curriculum. *Prevention Science, 4,* 233-248.

Herring, R. D. (1997). Counseling indigenous American youth. In C. C. Lee (Ed.), *Multicultural issues in counseling: New approaches to diversity* (2nd ed., pp. 53-70). Alexandria, VA: American Counseling Association.

Hiday, V. A. (1995). The social context of mental illness and violence. *Journal of Health and Social Behavior, 36,* 122-137.

Hoffman, J. P., & Su, S. S. (1998). Stressful life events and adolescent substance use and depression: Conditional and gender differentiated effects. *Substance Use & Misuse, 33,* 2219-2262.

Hurdle, D. E., Okamoto, S. K., & Miles, B. (2003). Family influences on alcohol and drug use by American Indian youth: Implications for prevention. *Journal of Family Social Work, 7,* 53-68.

Joseph, J., & Pearson, P. G. (2002). Black youths and illegal drugs. *Journal of Black Studies, 32,* 422-438.

Kadushin, C., Reber, E., Saxe, L., & Livert, D. (1998). The substance use system: Social and neighborhood environments associated with substance use and misuse. *Substance Use & Misuse, 33,* 1681-1710.

Kulis, S., Okamoto, S. K., Dixon Rayle, A., & Hawkins, S. (2006). Social contexts of drug offers among American Indian youth and their relationship to drug use: An exploratory study. *Cultural Diversity and Ethnic Minority Psychology, 12*(1), 30-44.

Kulis, S., Marsiglia, F. F., Nieri, T., Sicotte, D., & Hofmann-Marriott, B. (2004). Majority rules: The effects of school ethnic composition on substance use by Mexican heritage adolescents. *Sociological Focus, 37,* 373-393.

Kulis, S., Marsiglia, F. F., & Nieri, T. (2004, May). Neighborhood effects on youth alcohol use in the borderlands. Paper presentation at the Society for Prevention Research annual meeting, Quebec City, Canada.

Kulis, S., Napoli, M., & Marsiglia, F. F. (2002). Ethnic pride, biculturalism, and drug use norms of urban American Indian adolescents. *Social Work Research, 26*, 101-112.

Link, B. G., & Phelan, J. (1995). Social conditions as fundamental causes of disease. *Journal of Health and Social Behavior, 35*(Extra Issue), 80-94.

Massey, D. (1995). Getting away with murder: Segregation and violent crime in urban America. *University of Pennsylvania Law Review, 143*, 1203-1232.

Matsen, A. S., & Coatsworth, J. D. (1998). The development of competence in favorable and unfavorable environments: Lessons from research on successful children. *American Psychologist, 53*, 205-220.

Messick, S. (1960). Dimensions of social desirability. *Journal of Consulting Psychology, 24*, 279-287.

Moon, D. G., Jackson, K. M., & Hecht, M. L. (2000). Family risk and resiliency factors, substance use, and the drug resistance process in adolescence. *Journal of Drug Education*, 30, 373-398.

Oetting, E. R., Donnermeyer, J. F., & Deffenbacher, J. L. (1998). Primary socialization theory: The influence of the community on drug use and deviance, III. *Substance Use & Misuse, 33*, 1629-1665.

Okamoto, S. K., LeCroy, C. W., Dustman, P., Hohmann-Marriott, B., & Kulis, S. (2004). An ecological assessment of drug related problem situations for American Indian adolescents of the Southwest. *Journal of Social Work Practice in the Addictions, 4*, 47-63.

Pattillo, M. E. (1998). Sweet mothers and gangbangers: Managing crime in a Black middle-class neighborhood. *Social Forces, 76*, 747-774.

Paulhus, D. L. (1984). Two-component models of socially desirable responding. *Journal of Personality and Social Psychology, 46*, 598-609.

Peterson, R. D., Krivo, L. J., & Harris, M. A. (2000). Disadvantage and neighborhood violent crime: Do local institutions matter? *Journal of Research in Crime and Delinquency, 37*, 31-63.

Raudenbush, S. W., & Sampson, R. J. (1999). Econmetrics: Toward a science of assessing ecological settings, with application to the systematic social observation of neighborhoods. *Sociological Methodology, 29*, 1-41.

Rutter, M. E. (1987). Psychosocial resilience and protective mechanisms. *American Journal of Orthopsychiatry, 57*, 316-331.

Sampson, R. J. (2001). How do communities undergird or undermine human development? Relevant contexts and social mechanisms, pp. 3-30 in A. Booth and A. C. Crouter (Eds.), *Does it take a village? Community effects on children, adolescents, and families*. Mahwah, New Jersey: Lawrence Erlbaum Associates.

Sampson, R. J., & Groves, W. B. (1989). Community structure and crime: Testing social-disorganization theory. *American Journal of Sociology, 94*, 774–802.

Sampson, R. J., & Raudenbush, S. W. (1999). Systematic social observation of public spaces: A new look at disorder in urban neighborhoods. *American Journal of Sociology, 105*, 603-651.

Schier, L. M., Botvin, G. J., &. Miller, N. L. (1999). Life events, neighborhood stress, psychosocial functioning, and alcohol use among urban minority youth. *Journal of Child & Adolescent Substance Abuse, 9*, 19-50.

Sinha, R. (2001). How does stress increase risk of drug abuse and relapse? *Psychopharmacology, 158*, 343-359.

South, S. J., & Baumer, E. P. (2000). Deciphering community and race effects on adolescent premarital childbearing. *Social Forces, 78*, 1379-1407.

South, S. J., & Crowder, K. D. (2000). The declining significance of neighborhoods? Marital transitions in community context. *Social Forces, 78*, 1067-1099.

Thornton, A. (1991). Influence of the marital history of parents on the marital and cohabitational experiences of children. *American Journal of Sociology, 96*, 868-894.

U.S. Bureau of the Census (2000). Census, 2000. Retrieved on August, 19, 2006, from http://factfinder.census.gov.

Waller, M. A. (2001). Resilience in ecosystemic context: Evolution of the concept. *American Journal of Orthopsychiatry, 71*, 290-297.

Waller, M. A., Okamoto, S. K., Miles, B. W., & Hurdle, D. E. (2003). Resiliency factors related to substance use/resistance: Perceptions of Native adolescents of the Southwest. *Journal of Sociology & Social Welfare, 30*, 79-94.

Whitbeck, L., Hoyt, D., McMorris, B., Xiaojin, C., & Stubben, J. (2001). Perceived discrimination and early substance abuse among American Indian children. *Journal of Health and Social Behavior, 42*, 405-424.

Wilson, W. (1987). *The truly disadvantaged: The inner city, the underclass, and public policy*. Chicago: University of Chicago Press.

doi:10.1300/J233v06n02_11

Index